CONSTRUCTING THE
CRIOLLO ARCHIVE

Purdue Studies in Romance Literatures

Editorial Board

CONSTRUCTING THE *CRIOLLO* ARCHIVE

Subjects of Knowledge in

the *Bibliotheca Mexicana* and the

Rusticatio Mexicana

Antony Higgins

Purdue University Press
West Lafayette, Indiana

04   03   02   01   00   5   4   3   2   1

∞The paper used in this book meets the minimum requirements of
American National Standard for Information Sciences—Permanence of
Paper for Printed Library Materials, ANSI Z39.48-1992.

Printed in the United States of America
Design by Anita Noble

Library of Congress Cataloging-in-Publication Data
Higgins, Antony, 1964–
    Constructing the criollo archive : subjects of knowledge in the
Bibliotheca mexicana and the Rusticatio mexicana / Antony Higgins.
        p.   cm. — (Purdue studies in Romance literatures ; v. 21)
    Includes bibliographical references (p. -) and index.
    ISBN 1-55753-198-6 (cloth : alk. paper)
    1. Mexico—History—Spanish colony, 1540-1810. 2. Creoles—
Mexico—Politics and government—18th century. 3. Creoles—Mexico—
Intellectual life—18th century. 4. Subjectivity. 5. Eguiara y Eguren,
Juan José de, 1696-1763. Biblioteca mexicana. 6. Landívar, Rafael,
1731-1793. Rusticatio mexicana. I. Title. II. Series.

F1231 .H54 2000
972'.02—dc21
                                                    99-057971

For Winifred

Contents

Preface

The central project of this book is to carry out an investigation into the emergence of theoretical discourses of *criollo* subjectivity in the viceroyalty of New Spain and the kingdom of Guatemala during the eighteenth century. I track this process in terms of two interrelated problematics. First, I have sought to test the hypothesis that shifts in *criollo* thought are tied up with a complex negotiation of a conjunctural intellectual moment in which moves between traditional structures and a form of modernity are in the process of being conceptualized and realized, a process that is rendered all the more complex by the particular dynamics of a colonial cultural and historical situation. Second, my reflections on the trajectory of *criollo* subjectivity constitute an attempt to address the question of how to discuss the development of forms of selfhood and association within and against the system of norms established by a colonial regime.

Within this framework, I am concerned, first, to track the contradictory movements of *criollo* subjectivity as it weaves between identifications with Western paradigms of culture and subjectivity, on the one hand, and with the available models of indigenous civilizations, on the other. In particular, I am interested in how such a subjectivity becomes bound up with the assumption of an ambivalent stance toward indigenous peoples. At one level, it manifests itself in the unfolding of a discourse of interested knowledge about the cultures of those societies, a process that I regard to be similar to that which Edward Said traces in his study of European and North American knowledge about the Near and Far East (1–28). At another level, it shows up in the form of a tension that underpins the articulation of *criollo* selfhood even as it assumes a façade of homogeneity, to the extent that within the complex racial matrix of colonial society, the act of identifying oneself as *criollo* was often predicated on the suppression of one's mixed racial background. The second focus of my study is a dynamic through which *criollos* deploy the new modes of scientific investigation of nature and natural phenomena that emerge in the eighteenth century with a view to developing a body of knowledge about the specificities of the natural environment of their homeland. Most importantly, I posit that *criollo* intellectuals seek to constitute such a body of knowledge as a theoretical ground for *criollo* claims to authority and power.

Over the course of my study I analyze how these two problematics unfold in two eighteenth-century neo-Latin texts. These texts are the *Bibliotheca Mexicana* (1755), by Juan José de Eguiara y Eguren (1696–1763), and the *Rusticatio Mexicana* (1781; 1782), by Rafael Landívar (1731–93). I bring these two works together, in spite of their apparent differences, out of a desire to investigate how they both play a part in the construction of visions of *criollo* subjectivity and association. Specifically, their involvement in such a practice is endlessly marked by contradiction, largely as a function of their positioning within some of the very institutions where Spanish rule was simultaneously maintained and contested. In addition to being *criollos* and educators, both were clerics with serious involvements in religious institutions. While Eguiara y Eguren served in various capacities in the Cathedral of Mexico City, Landívar was educated and came to work within the colleges of the Society of Jesus in Guatemala and New Spain, eventually writing his poem from a position of exile and estrangement, in the aftermath of the expulsion of the Jesuits from America in 1767. Landívar's positioning is further complicated by his having been born and raised in the region of Guatemala, which maintained a substantial degree of autonomy with respect to the northern viceroyalty from the moment of its earliest settlement by the Spanish in the sixteenth century (Jones xii–xiii; 36–41).

At first sight, it might appear that the fact of having been written in Latin is the only thing the *Bibliotheca Mexicana* and the *Rusticatio Mexicana* have in common. It would have been as natural for Eguiara y Eguren and Landívar, as clerics and educators, to write in Latin as in Spanish. Moreover, the prestige that Latin enjoyed as the appropriate medium for the representation of the most exalted topics made it the logical choice as the language in which to compose their works. In this respect, it serves to lend authority to the American topics Eguiara y Eguren and Landívar treat in their works, helping to consolidate the discourses of *criollo* association and subjectivity they seek to articulate. At the same time, nevertheless, Eguiara y Eguren and Landívar's positioning within this regime of writing underlines the contradictions embedded in those discourses. The very fact that they wrote in Latin serves to illustrate the specifics of a sociocultural formation that does not conform to the model of a nation-state whose hegemony is predicated, in part, on the emergence of a literature written in vernacular language (Anderson).

It is my contention that Eguiara y Eguren and Landívar are key figures in a genealogy that comprises a significant portion of the literary production of the so-called period of colonial stabilization, the phrase used by Hernán Vidal and others to designate the stage of Latin American history during which the viceregal system was established and consolidated (Vidal 89; González Stephan, "Narrativa" 7–8). Specifically, I choose to focus on these texts in order to critique the conventional scholarly wisdom that regards them as successive steps in the history of period concepts established by Latin American literary historiography. While the *Bibliotheca Mexicana* is usually read as the product and synthesis of a scholastic regime of textual authority and highly stylized poetics, the *Rusticatio Mexicana* is represented as an articulation of an Enlightenment epistemology and aesthetics. In accordance with the precepts of an inherited European historical narrative, scholars tend to place these texts within a story of ruptures and paradigm shifts, marking the transition from Baroque (Eguiara y Eguren) to Enlightenment (Landívar).

In place of that superimposed model, this study attempts to re-create a narrative that pays closer attention to the particular, heterogeneous dynamics of intellectual culture in the Spanish colonies. An important feature of these dynamics is the manner in which colonial history is not composed of a series of clean breaks from one discrete historical moment to another. Rather, it is characterized more by the overlapping of intellectual frameworks and practices drawn from periods that tend to be regarded as organic and successive within the scheme of European history. This reality is, in part, the result of the particular racially and culturally heterogeneous regime that distinguishes viceregal society from the ostensibly more homogeneous formations of the Western European nation-states. It is also, in part, a function of the dynamics of the colony's relationship to the metropolis, according to which the activities of peripheral socioeconomic elites tend to gravitate toward the practice of importing from the center ideas that are always already anachronisms, and applying them awkwardly to contexts very different from those in which they evolved.

Therefore, this study does not conserve the practice of using the concept of the Baroque as a homogenizing master sign by means of which colonial culture can be read, a tendency that can be found in the work of a long line of scholars including Mariano Picón Salas, Pedro Henríquez Ureña, Irving Leonard, Emilio Carilla, Alfredo Roggiano, and Roberto González Echevarría. This does not mean that I have abandoned the concept of the Baroque, but rather that I envisage it as a "cultural dominant," as a mode of representation that exists in a relationship of hegemony to other kinds of discourse, both in colonial Mesoamerica and in twentieth-century interpretations of that earlier period (Jameson 4; Williams 121–27). Nevertheless, instead of maintaining the privilege generally accorded to the Baroque, I do seek, in this study, to investigate the viability of a different reading that privileges the notion of a genealogy through which *criollos* seek to articulate a body of practical and theoretical knowledge of their environment and the history of its inhabitants, with a view to constructing for themselves a position and space of authority within colonial society. It is my contention that such a body of information and expertise is characterized less by any ruptures between paradigms than by a continuing process in which multiple, often conflicting, forms of knowledge are synthesized and reconciled in accordance with the necessities of *criollo* intellectuals at different historical moments in the dynamics of their constitution as a social group. Within this dynamic, I argue, both Eguiara y Eguren and Landívar compose their works primarily, although not exclusively, for the *criollo* component of their readership, which, in part through the absorption of the knowledge presented in the texts, will come to occupy a position of subjectivity that will subvent a future social and economic order.

In the first part of the book, I consider the treatment given in Eguiara y Eguren's *Bibliotheca Mexicana* to questions of cultural and literary historiography, in an explicitly textual matrix. Through my analysis, I scrutinize the process through which the coordinates of an emergent discourse of local identification and association become fixed and are rendered meaningful within an inherited and universalist intellectual framework. In particular, I argue that in this work one discerns the combination of humanist philology (in the concern to establish primary texts) and scholasticism (in the collation and summarizing of theological treatises, sermons, and information pertaining to religious history in New Spain). At the same time, I discuss how the text also expresses the contradictory character of an emergent Mexican subjectivity and modernity. Specifically, Eguiara y Eguren does not neatly conform to the model of the bourgeois "man of letters" engaged in educated debate in an informal setting, outside the realm of established institutions. Rather, in large part he is able to articulate the form of intellectual agency produced in the project of the *Bibliotheca Mexicana* as a result of the position of authority he had acquired by 1755, as rector of the Real y Pontificia Universidad de México and canon of the Metropolitan Cathedral of Mexico City. With this in mind, I seek to demonstrate that his case illustrates that it is from an ambivalent position within existing power structures that a critique and reformulation of notions of what constitutes legitimate knowledge is realized. Only within this framework can the *Bibliotheca Mexicana* project a shift in such notions, establishing the value of a mode of knowledge based on the particular historical trajectory of the cultures specific to Mexico, from pre-Hispanic times up to the mid-eighteenth century, and calling into question the substantive values on which Spanish authority was founded. This discourse of knowledge is not, therefore, the product of a disinterested labor but, rather, serves to sketch the outline of a *criollo* subjectivity differentiated from that of the bureaucratic representatives of the Spanish state, one whose coordinates can no longer be situated solely within the matrix of Spanish cultural authority.

In chapters 1, 2, and 3, through my reading of the *Bibliotheca Mexicana* I seek to demonstrate that the articulation of a differentiated position of *criollo* subjectivity is not so much based on actual ethnic or linguistic divergence, but is realized through the work of cataloguing and interpreting information pertaining to the cultural history of Mexico. In chapter 1, I study the *Aprilis Dialogus,* a text written as a kind of preface to Eguiara y Eguren's text by his friend Vicente López. Through my discussion of this text, I analyze how a transformative program is framed within the hegemonic codes of the colonial regime of knowledge, based on the philological practices and conception of the value of the literary text fostered by humanism. In the second chapter, I focus on the processes through which, in Eguiara y Eguren's own prologues to the catalogue itself, a discourse of differentiation comes to be predicated, in part, on the recuperation of the cultures and values of pre-Hispanic societies. In this fashion, I endeavor to track how a theorization of the divergence of *criollo* subjectivity and interests with respect to Spanish norms is inextricably bound up with, and predicated upon, the development of a mode of knowledge in which the *criollo* assumes the metonymic role of representing, textually and politically, the more heterogeneous range of subjects inhabiting New Spain, in particular, the indigenous subject, and strives to set up an organic sphere, operating according to its own system of rules within a self-sufficient institutional space. In chapter 3, I conclude my analysis of the *Bibliotheca Mexicana* with a discussion of some of the information presented in the catalogue itself.

In the second part of the book, I attempt to trace how the *criollo* archive metamorphoses and unfolds in Rafael Landívar's *Rusticatio Mexicana.* I investigate how Landívar's text transposes the focus of knowledge onto realms more readily identifiable as material. This gesture forms part of a project of gathering information pertaining to the particularities of colonial space and elevates that space's prestige in the process. My concern is to study how a thesis of the differentiation of *criollo* subjectivity and interests from those of the Spanish state shifts, in this work, and becomes predicated on the task of detailing the particularities and transcendent features that distinguish New Spain's natural environment from that of Europe and representing the scientific norms derived by eighteenth-century natural historians from the observation of the flora and fauna of the Old World.

In the first chapter of part 2, I investigate the particular turn that Landívar gives to the dialectic of intellectual rationalism and affect that unfolds over the course of the eighteenth century. By analyzing his depictions of lakes, volcanoes, and waterfalls in the first three cantos of the poem, I develop the thesis that one of the ways in which *criollo* subjectivity emerges is out of the concern to represent sublime images of nature that elude and dwarf human capacities. It is my contention that this dynamic is based on an ideology that envisages the sublime not as something unattainable or apocalyptic, but as a utopian sign that conveys some sense of the infinite and, thereby, drives the desire of individuals and groups to constitute themselves as agents by undertaking projects through which they seek to achieve mastery of their surroundings and selves. At the same time, the sublime emerges as a cipher for the protean movement of *criollo* ideology. In Landívar's negotiations with large-scale images, one discerns the workings of a mechanism through which the sublime is represented and the subject comes to be articulated before and in the sublime. Specifically, in Landívar's representations of landscapes there is an attempt to reconstitute the grounds for intellectual subjectivity through the dynamic of the sublime at a time when the relation of the *criollo* to regimes of power—the imperial state and the Jesuit order— is in flux. Amid the crisis of these sources of authority, and the uncertainty thus produced in those who had lived under them, the drama of the sublime serves as a means through which to attempt to overcome that uncertainty and, thereby, stabilize a new, ordering form of *criollo* subjectivity.

In the second chapter of part 2, I trace the regime of mastery over self and nature that is projected in cantos 4 through 11 of Landívar's poem in the aftermath of the drama of the sublime. My reading of this section focuses on the importance accorded in it to human action within Mexican nature, ranging from the manufacturing of purple dye, made from insect larvae, to the production of gold and silver. In these cantos, I argue, one discerns the thought of a *criollo* subject of knowledge now cast in the role of overseer of the exploitation of natural resources and the subjection of human bodies as sources of labor.

The focus of the last chapter of part 2 is the section comprising cantos 12 to 15 and an appendix, in which Landívar plots a form of mastery over the fields of nature and culture through classificatory descriptions of birds, wild animals, leisure pastimes, and a natural icon. Following the representation of the dynamics of the sublime and of rationalized economy, in this final section Landívar portrays a selection of the natural species and cultural practices of New Spain in terms of the discourses of natural history and of the aesthetics of the beautiful. These two modes of representation complete the work of the construction of the basis for the binding of individuals into the structure of a reconfigured social order.

This book is the product of an attempt to reconceptualize the manner in which late colonial writing is classified by literary historiography. By placing the *Bibliotheca Mexicana* and the *Rusticatio Mexicana* together, I seek to subsume two texts within the complex process of the emergence of an ideology of *criollo* subjectivity and association in New Spain. In this fashion, I seek to trace how Eguiara y Eguren and Landívar project that the first stage in this process is the imagining of a discursive space of knowledge production about the natural and cultural history of New Spain and Guatemala, articulated by and for *criollos,* who seek to establish a position of autonomous subjectivity with respect to Spanish institutions and norms.

Acknowledgments

I would like to express my deepest gratitude to all those people without whose criticisms, guidance, help, and observations this book would have been impossible. I would like to thank, in particular, John Beverley, Paul Bové, Antonio and Cristina Cornejo Polar, Gerald Martin, Mabel Moraña, and Juan Zevallos Aguilar. I would also like to thank Andrea Junguito for her assistance in preparing the index.

I would like to express my thanks to the editors and staff at Purdue University Press for the interest they have shown in this study and the excellent work they have done in helping see it through to publication.

Chapter 1 appeared in a much earlier form as "Sobre la construcción del archivo criollo: el *Aprilis Dialogus* y el proyecto de la *Bibliotheca Mexicana*," *Revista iberoamericana* 172–73 (1995): 573–89. Parts of chapter 2 appeared as "La *Bibliotheca Mexicana*: hacia una poética de la legitimidad criolla," *Revista de crítica literaria latinoamericana* 43–44 (1996): 77–87. I thank the editors of *Revista iberoamericana* and *Revista de crítica literaria latinoamericana* for permission to reproduce my revised versions of those essays.

Introduction

The Question of the Subject

One of the key issues raised by contemporary criticism and theory has concerned the philosophical category of the subject. This line of investigation has focused upon the figure that grounds the epistemology and value system of modernity, as it has been articulated in Western Europe, sometimes producing consideration of its trajectory with respect to non-European geographical-cultural spaces within the dynamics of imperialism.[1] Significant moments in the interrogation of the category of the subject are Martin Heidegger's critique of phenomenological thought, and the more recent critical projects of Jacques Lacan, Jacques Derrida, and Michel Foucault, which, in the Anglo-American world, have tended to become grouped, albeit problematically, under the banner of poststructuralism.[2] Following differing paths and with often divergent motives and outcomes, these three thinkers have sought to destabilize or fragment the imputed coherence of the transcendent, autonomous subject of Western philosophy and reason as established in the work of a series of thinkers, among whom René Descartes and Immanuel Kant stand out as the principal architects.

In Lacan's account the philosophical subject of consciousness and reason is trapped in a structure of *méconnaissance,* or misrecognition, its self-image as the autonomous purveyor of knowledge being nothing more than a manifestation of the mechanisms underpinning the instantiation of the ego.[3] This appearance of coherence and self-sufficiency is irrevocably undermined by the division of the subject between the realms of the imaginary and the symbolic, and by the destabilizing effects of the dynamics of desire.[4] In Derrida it is the logic of the figurative aspect of language, or *différence,* that is mobilized with a view to exposing the rationale of the "metaphysics of presence." Through the unfolding of Derrida's writings, this subject is shown to be dispersed, and the semantic coherence of the thought and knowledge it expresses is endlessly undermined.[5] The significance and transformational potential of the Derridean critique is still the question of much debate, but its influence and implications have had wide-ranging effects.[6]

The work of Foucault tends to relativize and render visible the contradictions immanent to the position of the subject— understood again as the guarantor of modern Western epistemology and philosophy—as it is brought into tension with its mirror reflection: the subject, in the sense of the individual who is subjected to the complex mechanisms of power that are characteristic of modernity.[7] Somewhat problematically, the trajectory of Foucault's research is often divided into two stages by his interpreters. In the first, he is seen to deploy the concepts of archaeology and the archive in order to track the process of the subject's emergence within modernity and then project its subsequent immersion and dispersal within discourses. This line of thought is articulated most forcefully in *The Order of Things,* culminating in the pronouncement of the disappearance of the subject (386–87), and in *The Archaeology of Knowledge.*[8] Later, Foucault moves on to develop the mechanism of genealogical investigation in order to argue that the subject's imputed location at the center of the paradigm of Enlightenment is overdetermined by its coetaneous envelopment within a penal economy of darkness and shadow.[9] This picture is drawn most strikingly in *Discipline and Punish,* in which the subject is displaced from its position of autonomy and transcendence, and fragmented into a multiplicity of gazes, a network of subjects who are all continuously surveilling and policing each other, caught in the structure of the panopticon (195–228).

Subjects of Hispanism

The investigation of the category of the subject in Spanish and Spanish American literary studies is rendered complex and problematic by a series of divergences in the trajectories of modernity in the Hispanic world with respect to the classic paradigm of the history of Western metaphysics and modernity. The course of Spain's history, along with that of its colonies over the period loosely classified as early modern (c.1500– 1800), tends to be marked by a more sustained resistance on the part of traditional, or substantive, matrixes of authority and reason than in paradigmatic cases of modernity such as those of England, France, and Germany.[10] The issues bound up with this problematic have been cogently explored by Anthony Cascardi (*The Subject of Modernity;* "The Subject of Control") and George Mariscal (*Contradictory Subjects*) in the context of Spanish thought and literature. Foremost among the features that differentiate the Spanish situation is a less mystified notion of the subject as product of a dynamic of subjection than is to be found in regions where liberal ideals achieved a certain hegemony at an earlier stage.[11]

In the sphere of Latin American colonial studies, the topic has been explored most notably by Ángel Rama (*La ciudad letrada*), and by subsequent critics who have attempted to explore the lines of investigation proposed by the Uruguayan scholar.[12] Quite logically, the focus on subjects as products of mechanisms of subjection has been made more explicitly a key aspect of such investigations in this field. Beginning with the work of Rama, Rolena Adorno (*Guaman Poma;* "El sujeto colonial"), and Walter Mignolo ("El metatexto"; "La lengua") in the 1980s, Latin American colonial studies has carefully scrutinized the dynamics of the construction and destruction of subjected peoples and individuals by the interwoven technologies of economic imperialism, military violence, and writing. Nevertheless, although the contradictory positionings of subjects as both effects and agents—often simultaneously—constitute part of the thematics of such research, their complexities tend to be flattened out in explanatory narratives of pure subjection, or humanistic recuperations of subaltern authorship.[13] Such contradictions have been acknowledged and foregrounded more in recent work on the "Barroco de Indias," where *criollo* and *mestizo* subjects are more ambiguously situated in positions between different discourses and investments, at times identifying themselves closely with the Spanish cultural heritage and power structure, at other times distancing themselves from colonial institutions.[14]

Some of this more recent scholarship reflects a concern to articulate visions of more ambiguous, less coherent Hispanic colonial subjects, the configurations of which are overdetermined by relations of exclusion and oppression, particularly along lines of race and gender.[15] The trajectories of this criticism are emerging, in part, as a result of encounters with postcolonial theory, and the interrogations of the positions and strategies available to, or assumed by, subjects within and/or against different modes of imperialism.[16]

Within postcolonial theory a concept of resistance based on a poststructuralist vision of semiotic indeterminacy appears to be displacing more orthodox Marxist narratives of subaltern consciousness and national-popular revolution.[17] Such work assumes contradiction, hybridity, and fluidity as the necessary logic of (post)colonial subjectivity. This turn marks the beginnings of a shift of emphasis away from colonial discourse analysis and toward the theorization of postcoloniality, a shift the implications of which are still unclear for Latin American cultural and literary analysis.[18]

The focus of my own investigation differs somewhat from the two dominant modes of reading colonial and postcolonial texts and situations. Nevertheless, I believe that it can offer certain insights that will complement, or supplement, the workings and discoveries of those analyses. My concern is to look back to a particular moment in Mexican colonial history, with a view to interrogating attempts to theorize, in two key texts, the position of a philosophical subject within and against the framework of empire. Such a position of subjectivity would be conceived with a view to its grounding a knowledge and regime of cultural authority that would seek to differentiate itself from the established imperial symbolic order. This figure is caught in an ambiguous positioning that reproduces some of the features of the subject of modernity but lives a series of contradictions in addition to those of its European counterpart. In the colonial context, the task of the theorization of a system of secularizing norms and values in place of a regime based on religious and seigneurial authority is overdetermined by the problem of projecting a cultural and political order that might coexist with, or displace, forms of rule and authority imposed from an external source. Specifically, the problem of the establishment of this philosophical subject-position is rendered more complicated in a situation where the problematics of a partial shift from traditional, or substantive, to modern, or formal, modes of reason and authority are supplemented by the complex negotiation of a form of intellectual and economic autonomy from an existing structure of political and cultural subordination to Spanish rule.[19]

As Cascardi has argued, the peculiar problem with which the philosophical subject of Western modernity is faced centers on the labor of establishing an ethical and epistemological ground for knowledge and action in a moment when substantive modes of order and authority are being eroded or dissolved (*The Subject of Modernity* 1–15). The situation in the Spanish colonies is rather different, although, as I will argue below, such tensions do begin to appear there in the latter part of the eighteenth century. In New Spain and the other viceroyalties, the structure of an imperial and, at least nominally, theocratic regime remains largely in place, albeit marked by a potentially destabilizing contingency and heterogeneity vis-à-vis subsisting indigenous and African belief systems.[20] Instead, the salient features of a conjunctural tension are located in the domains of authority and knowledge: first, in the spheres of literature and culture; and, second, in the modes of scientific knowledge that can be articulated within the traditional regime, so long as they do not threaten its own authority and order.[21]

It is my contention that within this context one can glimpse not so much a unified subject, but the unfolding of a subject-in-process, [22] moving between different discourses, assuming diverse and contradictory positions. The central focus of my study is the trajectory of this subject-in-process, about which I will make two prefatory observations. First, it finds itself divided between the state—specifically, institutions closely linked to it, such as universities and colleges—with its regime of Spanish political and cultural authority, on the one hand, and a nascent form of *criollo*-dominated civil society, composed of various spheres of economic production that, by the mid-eighteenth century, had come to function in a position of relative autonomy with respect to the state, on the other.[23] This split is exacerbated over the course of the eighteenth century by an intensified policy of exclusion of *criollos* from important political offices within viceregal government.[24] Second, and in close relation to the first aspect, the division of this subject functions also at a more explicitly discursive level, in its positioning between different sources of cultural authority, mainly between Spanish inflections of literary and religious discourse, on the one hand, and kinds of texts produced by pre-Hispanic indigenous peoples or by individuals born in the colony, on the other.

I argue that during a moment in which the officials of the Bourbon monarchy are seeking to consolidate Spanish absolutist power in the political realm, the form of a *criollo* subject-in-process unfolds in, and between, the spaces of educational institutions and civil society, in both written culture and economic production. Over the course of this study, I trace the articulation of this subjectivity in and through the processes of the accumulation and presentation of knowledge about the cultures, geography, and economy of the region of New Spain during the eighteenth century.

Given my proposition that the movements and mutations of a *criollo* subject are inextricably bound up with practices of knowledge accumulation and production, I seek to deploy certain concepts developed by Foucault over the course of his revisionary querying of the trajectory of the modern Western philosophical subject and the concomitant production of Western rationality. Most importantly, I adapt the notion of the "archive," understood as a matrix of practices and discursive arrangements, in order to theorize the dynamics of a *criollo* subject. In addition to this key concept, this study also shares with Foucault a concern for the sociohistorical construction of epistemology, a conception of power as something relatively dispersed, rather than concentrated in a sovereign center, and an interest in exploring the complex relationships between knowledge and power.[25]

At the same time, it is important to note that there are some marked differences between the tenets of this investigation and the principles that underpin Foucault's work. First, I maintain a concern to analyze certain specific texts that I take to constitute signal points in the story of this *criollo* subject. There is no radical attempt here to dislodge the humanist privilege accorded to certain texts, although the texts I am considering do belong to a relatively neglected corpus, and I seek to situate them within material historical contexts and processes.[26]

In the second place, my concern for the discursive shifts registered between the two texts I analyze derives from my reflections on the notion of the epistemological break—central to Foucault's thought, following Bachelard in the French tradition of the conceptualization of the history of science—as a means to make sense of changes in systems of thought and modes of representation. In a reading that is partially informed by Cascardi's genealogy of the subject of modernity, I interrogate how the very idea of a rupture, or foundational moment, is a necessary fiction within the process of the *criollo* subject's unfolding.[27] I argue that embedded in such a fiction is another story, one in which the shift or mutation is never abrupt or complete, but that the new formation conserves elements of the old even as it appears to suppress them.

That is not to claim that I see a continuous unfolding of the subject toward a horizon of plenitude, but rather a complex dynamic of accretion and mutation.[28] Rather than attempt to reconstruct the image of a coherent (post)colonial subject, always pitted against a dominant order and prefiguring a story of progressive national liberation, I mean to portray a subject who moves between identifications with the Hispanic and the native, enacting the contradictions that come to mark Mexican cultural and political thinking of the postindependence era. This thinking must endlessly invoke, then suppress, the indigenous components of its symbolic economy.[29] In my analysis of this thought, therefore, I seek to track how the trajectory of the subject cannot be viewed in isolation from the dynamics of European imperialism and colonial societies.

Reconstructing the Intellectual History of Colonial Mexico and Guatemala

In order to foreground my discussion, I will first provide a brief account of the development of Spanish intellectual culture in Mesoamerica from 1553, the year in which classes began at the Real y Pontificia Universidad de México, to the middle of the eighteenth century.[30] The first important element in this dynamic is the trajectory and role of literary humanism in the region. Although there is a tendency to regard the colonial Latin American intellectual realm as a space dominated by scholasticism, where all manifestations of humanism faded away within the overall context of the Counter-Reformation, I will sketch here an alternative picture, one of a more complex and fluid conjuncture. In effect, literary humanism—specifically the pedagogic principles bound up with the development of skills in writing, public speaking, and the philological arts of reading and translating secular texts—did come to form a key component of the basis of power relations in the colonial world.[31] While most of the ideological program of humanism, such as the promotion of the worth of the individual and the impulse to return Christianity to a simpler form, was for the most part suppressed, the formal practices it developed and disseminated were absorbed and exploited by the Spanish Crown and the educational infrastructure of the viceroyalty, insofar as they could be adapted as tools for the work of bureaucratic administration, and for the study of Scripture and the modes of representation used in indigenous artifacts and monuments.[32] What arose, therefore, was a hybrid matrix in which scholasticism functioned as the ideological ground, or *doctrina,* of the viceregal regime, while humanism, understood as the practical application of a variety of formal exercises and techniques, served a more dynamic role within a sociocultural praxis. First, in the sphere of law, it facilitated the administration of material spaces and social structures.[33] Second, in the realm of rhetoric and imaginative writing, it granted authority to certain groups and institutions, to the extent that it provided a framework in which sublime artifacts, particularly works of poetry, could be composed. Such was the role the cult of eloquence and writing came to play within the regime Rama called "la ciudad letrada."

It was, therefore, within the domain of this matrix of scholasticism and humanism that discourses of *criollo* power and ideology began to assume a certain shape. This produced a second key element, or step, in the dynamics of colonial intellectual culture. Using the collection of practices and theoretical devices established in the aforementioned regime of writing and philology, in the eighteenth century *criollo* intellectuals sought to fashion a discourse of knowledge oriented toward the specificities of Mexican nature and indigenous cultures.

In my narrative, therefore, I seek to track how the mechanisms of *criollo* knowledge and subjectivity unfold in relation to the process of the emergence of sociocultural spaces and practices that articulate a markedly contradictory form of modernity. First, in keeping with the heterogeneous order of colonial culture, this intellectual discourse does not "progress" from a scholastic regime of textual authority to one based on an "enlightened" ideology of empiricism and experimentation, but rather moves endlessly between these two epistemes along a series of conjunctural points.[34] *Criollo* intellectual culture absorbs the tools proffered by those modes of knowledge, using them to elaborate practices and data that come to provide a legitimating basis for the actions of American-born whites within viceregal society.

In particular, I am concerned to analyze attempts to construct a source of intellectual authority for *criollos,* a basis for association, an autonomous, transcendent position of subjectivity, through my deployment of the theoretical concept of the "*criollo* archive." My understanding of this concept derives, in part, from Foucault's research into the problematic of the "archive," a term that he uses to designate a broad framework of texts, institutions, and practices in his investigations into the emergence of Western European modernity.[35] In using the framing device of the "*criollo* archive," I attempt to probe how certain forms of *criollo* subjectivity become predicated first on the cult of textual erudition and then on the gathering and presentation of scientific knowledge. Specifically, I contend that this dynamic arises out of the disjunction between *criollos'* access to extensive learning and their simultaneous exclusion from positions of administrative power during the eighteenth century. In my analysis of this situation, the concept of the *criollo* archive serves as a means to theorize the process of the constitution of a network of intellectuals and institutional formations articulating authoritative texts and statements about Mexico's history and natural environment. In this respect, I adapt and utilize this notion in a modality that diverges from that of Foucault. In contrast with Foucault's own understanding of the concept, which is situated within a sustained polemic against dialectical thinking, I conceive of it as a protean formation that mutates and changes through time in relation to shifting economic and political contingencies.

At the same time, I do not seek to pursue a line of investigation identical to that developed by Roberto González Echevarría in applying the problematic of the archive to the study of Latin American literature (*Myth and Archive*). Paying particular attention to the Inca Garcilaso de la Vega, he utilizes the concept of the archive to account for the power that writing assumes in the colonial context as a result of the Spanish preoccupation with law and the greater significance acquired by the factor of orality in dealings between whites and indigenous peoples (*Myth and Archive* 45–55; 83–87). González Echevarría uses the concept to designate the manner in which certain Spanish American authors adopt and master European discourses of knowledge, with a view to constituting their own body of learning. By means of this technique of appropriation, González Echevarría argues, literature begins to be constituted as an autonomous realm in the viceroyalties. My divergence with respect to this thesis stems from a conviction that in seeking to produce a teleological narrative of the emergence of Spanish American intellectual subjectivity that culminates in the twentieth-century novel, González Echevarría tends to restrict the concept of the archive to the level of a timeless discursivity, giving it a sense very different from that which it assumes in the work of Foucault.

While in González Echevarría's work the sense of the word *archive* tends to designate the authority of writing and law, my concern is to expand its semantic range, a gesture that I judge to be more appropriate for the study of a later historical moment, where colonial intellectual culture had undergone a certain mutation.[36] Specifically, the eighteenth-century context in which Eguiara y Eguren and Landívar write is one in which the regime of textual authority that González Echevarría privileges is being reformulated in the face of interrelated factors of economic, social, and intellectual change. In studying these two *letrados,* I am concerned to investigate how the emergence of forms of knowledge needs to be viewed within a more complex dynamic, where the discursive is seen to be inextricably bound up with material factors, particularly, institutional matrixes, class, and race. Taking such elements into account, I seek to tell a story of discontinuities, appropriations, and suppressions.

By the middle of the eighteenth century, *criollos* had come to constitute a social formation with interests increasingly differentiated from those of the Spanish state. Seeing their role in the system of viceregal government diminished by the Bourbon reforms, *criollos* concentrated their activities more in the realms of economy and education.[37] Although the running of haciendas was an uncertain business, certain *criollo* families had been successful in amassing large tracts of farm and ranch lands.[38] At the same time, others prospered in the area of trade and manufacture, largely because of the monopolies they enjoyed thanks to the restrictions the Spanish Crown imposed on commerce between the colonies and Europe. Indeed, as most economic historians now agree, prior to the Bourbon reforms, the Mexican economy underwent a sustained period of growth during the seventeenth century and into the first half of the eighteenth century.[39] In effect, by the mid-eighteenth century the viceroyalty had come to possess an economy as large and vibrant as that of North America, and probably healthier than that of Spain itself.[40]

The Bourbon reforms stand, therefore, as an attempt to capitalize on this economic expansion, extracting a larger portion of the wealth produced in New Spain in order to improve the situation of the metropolitan economy.[41] From the 1750s on, *criollo* families and individuals saw their power and wealth threatened by Bourbon policies designed to reduce their participation in political institutions and to extract taxes from them more aggressively.[42] It is my hypothesis that in the face of this turn of events, they came to see themselves as members of an economic and political class with interests existing in a relationship of increasing antagonism to those of the colonial bureaucracy. In spite of the control they exerted over the greater part of the economic exploitation of the region, they were repeatedly frustrated by administrative decisions that affected them negatively, primarily as a result of the Bourbons' attempts to reassert centralized control over the viceroyalties (Pietschmann 46–59). This situation produced a breach between the state and civil society, and a greater concentration of the activities of educated *criollos* in the latter sphere.[43] It is within the context of this struggle that, I contend, *criollos* sought to achieve a level of authority in the intellectual sphere parallel to that which they exerted in those of agriculture and trade. By the mid-eighteenth century, members of *criollo* society envisaged control of the areas in which knowledge and legislation were articulated not merely as a desirable goal in itself, but also as part of a general strategy that would enable them to acquire legitimacy in colonial society and accumulate wealth more efficiently, unimpeded by metropolitan interference.

In positing the development of such a strategy, I am not suggesting that *criollos* conceived of alliances with the different indigenous and *mestizo* groups inhabiting the territories of New Spain.[44] Rather, I propose that it afforded *criollos* the means through which to outmaneuver Spanish administrators and exploit the labor of those sectors for their own increasingly differentiated purposes. In my investigation, therefore, the concept of a *"criollo* archive" serves as a device with which I track the complexities of this symbiotic unfolding of economic and intellectual regimes.

I do not mean to imply that educated *criollos,* in their capacities as clerics, pedagogues, and/or lawyers, always maintained the idea that the indigenous and *mestizo* populations existed solely to be exploited, or that every trace of their presence should be effaced from all legitimate forms of culture. It is important not to underestimate or dismiss the utopian aspects of the ideologies that grounded the actions of many clerics and religious orders, and that were manifest in their dealings with members of other ethnic groups, even if such interventions derived from a classically paternalistic and hierarchizing conception of social relations.[45] Significantly, the project of producing written accounts of the cultural achievements of pre-Hispanic societies is a central feature of the work of many *criollo* intellectuals, particularly that of Eguiara y Eguren. However, it is my concern to determine the degree to which the inclusion of indigenous and subaltern elements in the textual production of these *letrados* was only deemed permissible as long as it was mediated by them, and incorporated into the rewritings of Mexican cultural history that articulated, and were articulated by, the emergent and protean subject-positions specific to those *criollos.*[46]

At the same time, in my investigation I use the concept of the "archive" to designate not just discursive representations but also institutional dynamics, in order to track the unfolding of spaces and forms of power. Specifically, I propose that in seeking to consolidate a measure of control over the production of knowledge, *criollos* establish and inhabit a contradictory space of modernity in which a cultural sphere acquires a limited autonomy with respect to the infrastructure of political power, within the context of an emerging division of interests between the Spanish-controlled institutions of the state, on the one hand, and a largely *criollo* civil society, on the other. It is my hypothesis that the texts of Eguiara y Eguren and Landívar construct not so much the ideal of "Mexico" as a separate nation, although such a utopian projection does help shape the *criollo* archive, but the materialization of a sphere of knowledge production administered and guarded by an educated class that attempts to establish itself as a discrete entity, shaping its own self-regulating system of values and norms. Both writers project the image of an "imagined community," but in a form that diverges from Benedict Anderson's model (*Imagined Communities*). I posit, rather, that it is an "imagined community" without a state, a formation that emerges in the murky area on the fringes of the apparatuses of colonial government, in the space of a burgeoning civil society.[47]

I speak of a "contradictory modernity" to the extent that in these texts the development of critical discourse and the trajectory of the relationship between the state and civil society does not neatly conform to the idealized model of eighteenth-century Western European societies offered by Jürgen Habermas.[48] Rather, it is a matrix that resembles José Antonio Maravall's conception of the Baroque as the first, contradictory, form of Hispanic modernity, in which residual and emergent formations are inextricably bound up with each other (*La cultura* 55–127). This does not mean that no project of change is articulated, but that such a task is not projected by autonomous groups of middle-class individuals, a relatively small constituency within colonial society.[49] Instead, these actions are realized by subjects situated ambiguously between traditional social formations and emergent modes of thought that have the potential to disrupt the continuity of those formations. That is, the members of the very same religious and educational institutions that form the core of the hegemonic order, together with the key figures of a *criollo* economic elite, conceptualize the transformation of existing modes of knowledge, economy, and politics.[50]

Eguiara y Eguren and Landívar stand as exemplary products of the two primary institutional bodies of higher education in eighteenth-century New Spain, the Real y Pontificia Universidad de México and the Jesuit college system, respectively. Additionally, after completing their studies they later worked as educators within the same institutional infrastructure in which they had received their formation. The works of these figures are shaped by the paradigms of knowledge promoted by those institutions and the struggles around those paradigms that unfolded within and outside the universities and colleges in the light of the new philosophical and scientific developments of the eighteenth century. Of significance also is the fact that both composed their works in Latin. As scholars such as Ignacio Osorio Romero have shown, within the culture of the time *criollo* intellectuals would have been as comfortable writing in Latin as they were in Castilian.[51] However, I see this choice also as an important gesture within the process of the unfolding of the discursive formation of the *criollo* archive, to the extent that mastery of Latin served as a marker of intellectual achievement and prestige (Osorio Romero, *Conquistar* 7–8).

Born in Mexico City, Juan José de Eguiara y Eguren trained for the priesthood at the seminary of San Ildefonso and studied philosophy at the Jesuit Colegio Máximo de San Pedro y San Pablo. Having received his degree in theology from the Real y Pontificia Universidad de México in 1712, he served as a substitute professor at the same institution between 1713 and 1722. In 1723 Eguiara y Eguren became a permanent professor of philosophy, and of theology the following year. In 1738 he achieved the position of head professor of theology, and in 1749 was made rector of the university. A long career in the clergy culminated in his appointment, in 1751, as Bishop of Yucatan. However, in 1752 he rejected the position and dedicated himself primarily to the task of compiling the *Bibliotheca Mexicana,* an undertaking in which he was still engaged when he died in 1763.[52]

The Real y Pontificia Universidad de México had been created initially to help facilitate the process of the establishment of religious orthodoxy in the viceroyalty of New Spain. From its inception its primary role was to build a corpus of clerics who would serve to maintain the ideological foundations of the new regime (Gonzalbo Aizpuru, *Historia de la educación en la época colonial. La educación* 60–61). Conceived after the model of the University of Salamanca, the institution's curriculum comprised elements of both scholasticism and the humanities (Gonzalbo Aizpuru, *Historia de la educación en la época colonial. La educación* 71–73; 96). Making up the university's program were the faculties of Theology, Canonical Law, Civil Law, Medicine, and the Arts. Courses in rhetoric and Latin grammar figured in the curriculum, but both these disciplines lost ground within the university over time as the prestige of the Jesuit education system in these fields rose, with the result that students tended to take such classes in the order's colleges (Gonzalbo Aizpuru, *Historia de la educación en la época colonial. La educación* 96–99). Nevertheless, knowledge of Latin grammar remained, even into the eighteenth century, an essential requirement for anyone wishing to pursue advanced studies at the university, since all such courses were taught in Latin.

Through the seventeenth and eighteenth centuries, the university continued to function as one of the institutions that helped maintain the ideological order of viceregal society. It generally preserved an atmosphere of rigid orthodoxy that was challenged only occasionally by exceptional figures such as Carlos de Sigüenza y Góngora, professor of mathematics and astrology in the second half of the seventeenth century (Gonzalbo Aizpuru, *Historia de la educación en la época colonial. La educación* 59; 64–65; 108).[53] Such, then, was the environment that prevailed at the institution into the 1700s, even as the new ideas emerging in Enlightenment Europe were filtering into the viceroyalty through other channels (Gonzalbo Aizpuru, *Historia de la educación en la época colonial. La educación* 121).

In the face of this situation of intellectual stagnation, Eguiara y Eguren appears to have developed the project of the *Bibliotheca Mexicana* primarily outside the immediate structures of the university. True, it was largely thanks to his position within the university that he was able to become acquainted, either directly or via correspondence, with an extensive network of scholars. These contacts undoubtedly facilitated the labor of gathering information about a wide range of institutions, authors, and works associated with the various regions that made up the viceroyalty. Nevertheless, the project of the catalogue seems to have been carried out in an ambiguous sphere, a form of civil society in the process of being articulated by members of a group increasingly isolated from the mechanisms of the state. Additionally, the relative degree of freedom from institutional interference Eguiara y Eguren enjoyed in realizing the enterprise was enhanced by the inheritance left to him and his brother by their father, which had enabled them to import a printing press from Europe. Ultimately, the catalogue produced by Eguiara y Eguren and his assistants stands as a manifestation of the general shift in the orientation of colonial historiography during the eighteenth century away from an orthodox imperialist, universalist model, and toward a more specific focus on the different regions of colonial Spanish America, with a particular concern for the histories of indigenous peoples in the pre-Hispanic period (Stolley 349–61). It is this mode of historiography that I take to constitute one of the key discursive formations of the *criollo* archive.

A more dramatic shift in *criollo* intellectual thought can be found in the figure of Rafael Landívar, who was educated at the Real y Pontificia Universidad de San Carlos de Guatemala and within the network of Jesuit colleges in Guatemala and New Spain. Specifically, it was the Jesuit education system, or at least its premier institutions in Mexico City, that, during the eighteenth century, came to stand in for an absent public sphere, in a political regime where the division between the state and civil society was in a process of flux. To this extent, the initial stages in the unfolding of a form of modernity in the region were largely engineered by members of the Jesuit order, a pattern of development that diverged significantly from the liberal model of the Enlightenment.[54] Precisely, one of the groups that the members of the emergent public sphere sought to displace in Europe became, in the Spanish colonies, the architect of a limited range of the very intellectual transformations that the *philosophes* promoted, in particular, empiricism, experimental method, an aesthetics based on clarity of exposition and universal standards of "good taste," and a pragmatic approach to agriculture and economy. Concomitantly, and paradoxically, it was within the universalist framework of Jesuit education and economy that a discourse of differentiation and particularity was articulated, on the grounds of its status as the most legitimate regime of learning, and as the most stable and enduring agricultural and commercial matrix in New Spain and Guatemala.[55]

Landívar's descriptive poem the *Rusticatio Mexicana* simultaneously reflects and retheorizes the character of the contradictory modernity that begins to assume its amorphous shape in Eguiara y Eguren's work of intellectual history. Focused more on the fields of economy and natural history, it articulates a restructuring of existing formations, not just in terms of the modes of knowledge that can be formulated, but also in the types of social structures and subjectivities to be accorded positive value in the regime of colonial life. At the same time, the conditions that facilitate the elaboration of Landívar's poetic utopia reproduce the pattern already discerned in the figure of Eguiara y Eguren, to the extent that Landívar too is a product of an important component of the institutional framework that upheld the order of colonial society.

Having established a presence in New Spain in 1572, at the order of Philip II, charged with the task of improving the standard of the education provided for the children of functionaries and *encomenderos,* the Jesuits came to play an important role in colonial Mexico and Guatemala, initially helping to consolidate the hegemony of the Spanish state (Kerson, *Rafael Landívar* 28). Nevertheless, this image of a seamless continuity of interests gave way, over time, to a more complex matrix in which the Jesuits came to constitute a powerful cultural and economic body in the region. From the beginning of the eighteenth century, the order maintained an increasingly uneasy relationship with the bureaucratic mechanism of the Spanish Crown. This colonial inflection forms part of the series of conflicts that were to pit the nationalist programs of the emergent European nation-states against the universalist vision of the order and its simultaneous affiliations with local elites in the colonies.[56]

In the Spanish colonies this development stemmed from the deliberate policy the Jesuits chose to follow soon after their arrival in New Spain, in accordance with which they strove to establish themselves as a self-sufficient entity. Almost immediately, the first group chose to set up not only a system of colleges, but also a network of farms and ranches capable of supporting the centers of education and their members (Riley 4–12; 36–74). Traditionally, it is for their feats in education that the Mexican Jesuits have been given most credit, both by the colonial society of the time and by modern historiography. Their success was, in large part, due to the efficient application of the *ratio studiorum,* a curriculum drawn up in the latter part of the sixteenth century and repeatedly reworked until the completion of the definitive edition of 1598/99.[57] The program of the *ratio studiorum* offered a rigorous formation in Latin and written culture, incorporating also a dynamic regime of public activities, such as debates, poetry recitals, and the performance of plays, all of which afforded students opportunities to put their skills into practice. From the first moments of their presence in the viceroyalty, at a time when there was only a limited mechanism for children of the privileged classes to receive comprehensive instruction, the Jesuits acquired increasing popularity among *criollos* as the purveyors of the best education available in the colonies.[58]

Under the leadership of Pedro Sánchez (1525–1609), the Colegio de San Pedro y San Pablo was founded in 1573 in Mexico City. Following the rapid achievements of this first college, the three seminaries of San Gregorio, San Bernardo, and San Miguel were established, all four institutions then being combined to form the Colegio de San Ildefonso. Classes began there in 1582, although it was not officially opened until August 1, 1588, becoming a Colegio Real on January 17, 1618 (Kerson, *Rafael Landívar* 31). More important still, however, was the Colegio Máximo de San Pedro y San Pablo (not to be confused with the earlier institution of the same name), on which construction began in 1575. Modeled after the Universities of Alcalá and Salamanca, this college gradually emerged as the center, not only of the Jesuit network, but of the whole system of public education in New Spain.[59] It offered instruction at all levels, housed the Jesuit professors, and served as the training ground for the teachers who were to staff the twenty-eight colleges set up across the viceroyalty over the course of the first century of the order's activities in the New World.

Toward the middle of the eighteenth century, the Colegio Máximo became the site of a move to incorporate modern ideas into the traditional Jesuit curriculum. Inspired by the teachings of José Rafael Campoy (1723–77), a generation of elite Jesuit students gravitated toward new methodologies and problems.[60] Among them was Landívar, who attended the Colegio Máximo from 1750 to 1755, furthering his education and studying for the priesthood. At the time when Landívar was at the college, it was undergoing the aforementioned transformation in its approach to learning, following Campoy's dissemination of the ideas of modern thinkers such as Descartes, Bacon, Gassendi, Locke, and Newton. This involved the development of a paradigm of knowledge that reconciled the doctrine of scholasticism with the new epistemology, which placed greater emphasis on empiricism and experimentation.

Clearly a product of this new curriculum, the *Rusticatio Mexicana* is notable to the extent that it articulates a breach of the regime of textual authority and stylization normally associated with Jesuit pedagogy, and points toward an intellectual framework founded on empiricism and neoclassical aesthetics, in accordance with which emphasis is placed on the denotative and communicative function of language.[61] In Landívar's poem, language serves less to suppress the material reality of the colonial space behind a stylized veneer but, instead, comes to form part of a more pragmatic dynamic in which the text is conceived as a medium for producing theoretical knowledge that can facilitate practical intervention in physical environments.[62] Effectively, then, Landívar's creation is more than an idealized pastoral or an exercise in intellectual virtuosity. Rather, its interest derives from the fact that it is a work engaged with the material world, the components of which it seeks to catalogue, shaped by the emergent discourse of natural history and by the accumulated experience of the Mexican Jesuits in the sphere of agriculture.[63]

In impressive detail, the *Rusticatio Mexicana* projects the image of an economy and a society run in accordance with the values of efficiency, artisanry, and collective labor. The thematics that binds these elements together is a concern about what will form the basis for the organization of societies in America following the removal, in 1767, of the ordering matrix provided by the institutional infrastructure afforded by the Jesuits. Up to that point, the Jesuits had overseen the development of *criollo* society through the dissemination of the order's ideological principles, on the one hand, and the practical work of its educational institutions and agricultural concerns, on the other. In the face of the disappearance of the Society's mediating agency, then, the *Rusticatio Mexicana* theorizes a new utopian order administered by *criollos,* decoupled from the authority of both the Jesuits and the Spanish state. In Landívar's hands, the *criollo* archive mutates, gathering knowledge about the physical geography and economy of the colonial world, a knowledge that will form part of the basis for discourses of local identification and association.[64] Within this broad scheme, the *Rusticatio Mexicana* offers a totalizing representation of the environment of the region, cataloguing its different parts in such a fashion as to stage a performance of *criollo* intellectual mastery. At the same time, Landívar's poem reconstructs a utopian landscape in which *criollos* could see themselves constituted as subjects bound together by a collection of shared practices and in the visualization of certain natural tableaux. In this fashion, therefore, through his poetic articulation of knowledge about the economy and natural history of New Spain and Guatemala, Landívar attempts to establish the intellectual ground for the position of an autonomous *criollo* subject emerging from between the widening cracks in the regimes of the Spanish state and ecclesiastical authority.[65]

In this introduction I have attempted to sketch a historical and philosophical outline of a particular conjuncture in which the intellectual foundations of a *criollo* subject are theorized during the eighteenth century. From this starting point I will proceed, in the rest of this book, to reconstruct the process of this subject's emergence through my analyses of the works of Eguiara y Eguren and Landívar. The task of the chapters that follow will be to trace how this process comes to be inextricably linked to projects oriented around the gathering and presentation of knowledge about the cultures, economy, and natural environment of New Spain and Guatemala.

Part 1
Juan José de Eguiara y Eguren and the *Bibliotheca Mexicana*

Framing the *Criollo* Archive

Knowledge and Legitimization: Juan José de Eguiara y Eguren and the *Bibliotheca Mexicana*

The *Bibliotheca Mexicana* is the first attempt to organize systematically a heterogeneous range of authors and texts into the form of a Mexican intellectual tradition. It is both product and agent of the process through which a sense of shared identity and interests comes to be envisaged in New Spain. Written in Latin, it was compiled under the directorship of a cleric and high-ranking educator at the Real y Pontificia Universidad de México, Juan José de Eguiara y Eguren. Organized alphabetically,[1] the work was primarily intended to be a comprehensive biobibliography, detailing the individuals, texts, and institutions of importance within the history of the region, from the period of conquest to the moment when publication began in 1755. It is supplemented by a series of prologues, written by Eguiara y Eguren, which offer an archaeology of pre-Hispanic Mexican indigenous cultures. However, the death of Eguiara y Eguren in 1763 brought the project to an abrupt end, with only the sections comprising the entries under A through C completed.[2]

It is significant that this project of producing a totalizing, encyclopedic catalogue of Mexican literary and cultural production in the pre-Hispanic and colonial periods was never finished. In this sense, the *Bibliotheca Mexicana* stands as a cipher for *criollo* subjectivity and authority in an era of widening schisms within the colonial order. Within such a context, I perceive in the text an attempt to found an autonomous *criollo* subject-position, one in which *criollo* subjectivity alternately coalesces and disperses in heterogeneous fashion. This *criollo* subject-position is hypothesized as guarantor of, and as being predicated upon, a corpus of knowledge in which a dominant Spanish cultural regime is opened up to a supplementary semiosis comprising *criollo* and indigenous elements.

The horizon of the collection of texts that constitutes the *Bibliotheca Mexicana* is the constitution of a body of knowledge and the subject who would appear to organize and support it. The work is a response to the European prejudice that there could be no *criollo* knowledge nor, by extension, subject, and the coetaneous tendency to represent America as a space of pure nature, a gap standing in an irreducible opposition to Europe, conceived as the locus of culture. Faced with such a framework, the *criollo* must open up the frontiers of the colonial discursive regime in order to articulate knowledge not only of its main Spanish sources of authority but also of that which lies beyond its threshold: the literary and scholarly production of American-born individuals and the peoples they represent.

In the labor of the collation of these types of texts, I discern the movements of a *criollo* subject in gestation, coalescing and cohering as it catalogues the scholarly achievements of American-born Hispanics but at the same time has to distend and open itself up in the act of eulogizing native American artifice, and absorb it into a unified edifice of Mexican culture and identity. At the site of this very tension, and in the contradictions that the movement between different symbolic fields produces, I will locate and describe the coordinates and mutations of the *criollo* subject in the struggle for authority and power.

The *Bibliotheca Mexicana* came into existence as a response to a particularly denigrating account of Americans' physical and intellectual capabilities written by Manuel Martí, a Spanish cleric, which was first circulated in published form in 1735.[3] In response to a request sent to him by a young Spanish student seeking advice regarding his plans to travel to America in order to further his education, Martí had written a letter in which he portrayed the New World as a cultural wasteland. His principal observations were that its inhabitants were by nature ill-disposed toward learning and that the region did not possess educational institutions capable of offering those inhabitants a level of education commensurate with European norms. Martí's provocative text is, however, but one among many disparaging representations of America's nature and its inhabi-

tants produced by a variety of Europeans over the course of
the preceding two and a half centuries. It is important, therefore, for modern readers to situate the *Bibliotheca* within the
context of these polemics[4] and resist the temptation to see
it, anachronistically, as a text projecting a fundamental break
with the structure of the imperial state of which New Spain
formed a part. Indeed, much of the contradictory logic of the
work is bound up with Eguiara y Eguren's ambiguous intellectual positioning in a kind of pan-Hispanic cultural space, a
factor that leads him to defend the entire Spanish-speaking world
against its European detractors.

The complex nature of Eguiara y Eguren's cultural investments is an element that has perhaps been oversimplified by
critical work on the *Bibliotheca Mexicana.* The project tends
to be read from a position that might be said to blend the ideologies of nationalism, humanist idealism, and classical philology.
In this fashion, Eguiara y Eguren is seen as a forerunner of modern Mexican nationalism, one step in a seamless narrative of
identity that can be traced back to pre-Hispanic times. This position is articulated by Federico Gómez de Orozco in his prefatory remarks about Agustín Millares Carlo's critical edition of
the prologues of Eguiara y Eguren's work. He refers to Eguiara
y Eguren as an

> ilustre personaje de nuestro período colonial y a quien de-
> bemos por muchos motivos una deuda de gratitud, especial-
> mente por haber sido él el primero en destacar, con deliberado
> propósito, el movimiento cultural de México, reseñando lo
> que fué ese aspecto antes de la conquista española y en dos
> y medio siglos de dominio colonial, poniendo de manifiesto
> que, aquí como en Europa, no eran raros los talentos, ni su
> aplicación al estudio, pues también en él produjeron obras
> de mérito y positivo interés, que merecieron el honor de ser
> reproducidas en nuevas ediciones europeas. (9)

> illustrious personality from our colonial period, to whom
> for many reasons we owe a debt of gratitude, especially for
> having been the first to highlight, with a deliberate purpose,
> the cultural movement of Mexico, reviewing what this as-
> pect was before the Spanish conquest and for two and a half
> centuries of colonial domination, manifesting that, here as
> in Europe, talents were not unusual, nor was their applica-
> tion to study, since in it they also produced works of merit

and positive interest, which were worthy of the honor of being reproduced in new European editions.[5]

Gómez de Orozco makes it clear that the motivation for the publication of the edition is derived, in large part, from the desire to retrieve this project of information-gathering and establish it as a foundational stone in the construction of a storehouse of knowledge that serves to form the basis of a Mexican intellectual identity (12–13). In his own introductory sketch of Eguiara y Eguren, Millares Carlo gives an overview of the most important observations that have been made by different scholars about the techniques involved in the composition of the *Bibliotheca* and about the formal organization of the text itself. These remarks are drawn largely from the critiques of Eguiara y Eguren's work made by José Mariano de Beristáin y Souza in his catalogue of 1816,[6] and by the historian Joaquín García Icazbalceta, who in 1886 published a bibliography of works published in Mexico during the sixteenth century.

Millares Carlo opens his comments by noting that Eguiara y Eguren was primarily a theologian and educator during his lifetime, although he is today known more as a bibliographer (31). In fact, the interventions he made in colonial society as a religious orator and as a learned theologian at the Real y Pontificia Universidad de México would have been considered to have been of equal, if not greater, significance by his contemporaries than the *Bibliotheca* itself.[7] If one considers Eguiara y Eguren's intellectual production as a whole, one discovers that the majority of his published works are, as Millares Carlo notes, "quodlibetos, pláticas, oraciones sagradas, panegíricos y elogios fúnebres" (31; "quodlibets, sermons, sacred prayers, panegyrics, and funeral eulogies").

After establishing this intellectual picture of Eguiara y Eguren, Millares Carlo proceeds to summarize the critical remarks that have been made about the *criollo* scholar's work. Although they are articulated by individuals from different stages of history, certain themes recur in their arguments. In the early part of the nineteenth century, Beristáin denounced Eguiara y Eguren's imputed "barroquismo" from the position of the new rationalist subject produced by the dissemination of Enlightenment thought in Mexico. Writing in the latter part of the nineteenth century, García Icazbalceta commented that the vehement tone of the ripostes to Manuel Martí that Eguiara y Eguren delivers in his prologues, together with the apologetic, or panegyric, character of his descriptions of individuals, institutions, and texts, detracts from the tone of objectivity that scientific thought dictates should be maintained in the presentation of any catalogue of data (Millares Carlo 34–35). Millares Carlo, for his part, largely reproduces the reservations expressed first by Beristáin and, later, by García Icazbalceta about the criteria used by Eguiara y Eguren to assemble his work. These include the organization of the catalogue according to the first names of individuals, and the translation of the titles of works into Latin.

Millares Carlo also assumes the critical standpoint of the modern subject of Enlightenment in endorsing García Icazbalceta's remark that the exaggerated tone of Eguiara y Eguren's observations and eulogies undermines the intended effect of objectivity. This perspective is developed still further by Gómez de Orozco, who places great emphasis on the complicated style and structure of Eguiara y Eguren's sentences. In his prologue to the edition, he notes the following contradictory features of Eguiara y Eguren's writing:

> a pesar de su sapiencia, de la gravedad de sus elucubraciones filosóficas, de su oratoria sagrada, tan aplaudida por sus auditorios, y de sus serias y doctorales argumentaciones teológicoescolásticas, se nos presenta impregnado de barroquismo, ese barroquismo que, como polvo que flotara en la atmósfera, lo contaminaba todo y le imponía su huella inconfundible, desde las artes plásticas hasta las costumbres y el espíritu; porque, en realidad, así fué. Aunque hoy nos parezca pueril y curioso, caracteriza una época, fué norma de vida de varias generaciones y marca una etapa en la evolución del espíritu humano. (13)

> [In] spite of his wisdom, the gravity of his philosophical formulations, his sacred oratory, which was so applauded by his audiences, and his serious and doctoral theological-scholastic arguments, he presents himself as saturated with baroquism, that baroquism which, like dust floating in the air, infected and imposed its unmistakable trace upon everything, from the plastic arts to customs and the spirit; because, in reality, that is how it was. Although it may appear puerile and curious to us today, it characterizes a period, was

> the norm of life for several generations, and marks a step
> in the evolution of the human spirit.

In effect, both Gómez de Orozco and Millares Carlo preserve the convention of reading the Hispanic colonial period
through the modern theoretical category of the Baroque, and
situate the *Bibliotheca Mexicana* within that framework, reading
it as displaying the ornate aesthetic style that is held to have
pervaded most levels of cultural expression and social organization in the colonies long after it had been displaced in the
metropolis.[8] In seeking to reformulate the terms of analysis, I
will explore the hypothesis that the project of the catalogue
constitutes an attempt to reconfigure, textually, the structures
of the regime of empire, and envisage a society in which *criollos*
would exert more power in the construction of cultural and
political realities. Eguiara y Eguren seeks to achieve this through
the application of a modern technology, specifically a totalizing and rationalizing form of organization, that of the catalogue.[9]
However, the materials that he tries to assemble in this manner are firmly rooted in existing cultural and political configurations, with the result that he produces something that
straddles the uncertain terrain between the dominant epistemological and political order, on the one hand, and an emergent
formation in which the principles sustaining that order begin
to be reconfigured.

Ernesto de la Torre Villar offers the most comprehensive and
systematic treatment to date of the figure of Eguiara y Eguren
and the *Bibliotheca Mexicana* in his introduction to a new bilingual edition of the text. In a much more sustained fashion
than the scholars referred to above, Torre Villar subsumes the
variety of activities in which Eguiara y Eguren engages under
the master signifier of nationalism.[10] In the first place, the discussion of Eguiara y Eguren's work as a sacred orator (Torre
Villar cvii–cxxiii) leads Torre Villar to read into it a concern
to reconstitute the ideal of a unified Christian people under the
aegis of a form of nationhood. Torre Villar remarks that the work
of Eguiara y Eguren and his associates "significa tanto la
construcción de una nación cristiana cuanto la creación de una
patria común" (cxxiii; "signifies as much the construction of a
Christian nation as the creation of a common fatherland"). Such

an interpretation is correctly conscious of Eguiara y Eguren's religious orthodoxy.[11] Nevertheless, Torre Villar does not sufficiently interrogate the implications of this ideology, failing to analyze to what extent it encodes a manifestation of the dualistic movement that I take to be characteristic of much *criollo* discourse. In part it expresses a commitment to the ideal of reimposing a transnational unity over the divisions produced by the emergence of Protestantism. At the same time, it embeds within that master narrative a strategy for uniting *criollos* around a reformulated cultural and literary canon in the struggle being waged over spheres of cultural and political power with the apparatuses of the Spanish state.[12]

Torre Villar makes the *Bibliotheca Mexicana* central to a retroactive weaving of disparate elements into a narrative of protonationalism. Torre Villar notes that Eguiara y Eguren seeks to distinguish his own work from earlier American responses to the kinds of criticisms articulated by Martí. In contrast to Diego de León Pinelo's rejoinder to Justus Lipsius, which had tended to function at a merely personal level, Eguiara y Eguren produces a text that transcends such a dynamics of reaction through its totalizing and implicitly prescriptive scope (Torre Villar ccxxviii). The *Bibliotheca Mexicana* would be a catalogue of individuals and texts that, over the course of several centuries, had come to synthesize an image of cultural commonality and consistency. Torre Villar expresses this in the following terms:

> En ese inmenso catálogo comprensivo de varias centurias y de miles de individuos, sería posible descubrir el desarrollo de la mentalidad que reinaba en tierras americanas y que distinguía a sus habitantes de los de la metrópoli. El significado del término *Biblioteca* que Eguiara daría a su obra sería éste, significado que tenía no sólo un valor cultural y ético, sino también político, pues tendía a mostrar la diferencia espiritual y cultural de una comunidad, su anhelo de agruparse en torno de valores y esencias comunes, su deseo de mostrar su libre acción pensante, de enorgullecerse de su obra creativa, de mostrar su independencia intelectual, sin desconocer los aportes recibidos. (Ccxix)

> In that immense catalogue covering several centuries and thousands of individuals, it would be possible to discover

the development of the mentality that reigned in the American lands and that distinguished its inhabitants from those of the metropolis. The significance of the term *Bibliotheca* that Eguiara would give to his work would be this, a significance that had not only a cultural and ethical value, but also a political one, since it tended to show the spiritual and cultural difference of a community, its longing to group itself around common values and essences, its desire to show its free thinking activity, to take pride in its creative work, to show its intellectual independence, without being ignorant of the contributions [it had] received.

In this description, Torre Villar adds greater nuance to his thesis of protonationalism. He specifies how such a discourse is being articulated in the *Bibliotheca,* indicating the materialization of what might be termed a Mexican—read *criollo*— "public sphere." Over the course of the rest of this chapter, I will propose a slightly different reading. This reading involves, first, a critique of the type of recuperative interpretation that, consciously or unconsciously, reads Eguiara and his associates as the unambiguous precursors of Mexican nationalism. In the second place, I will seek to explore the erasures and appropriations encoded in the concept of "nation" that is projected in the *Bibliotheca.* In the context within which he moves, Eguiara produces a work that is bound to emergent *criollo* interests. Thus, the *Bibliotheca Mexicana* is informed by a variety of intellectual investments that pertain to the shifting terms of a struggle around the articulation of intellectual, and, therefore, political, authority in New Spain, a struggle in which knowledge and power are inextricably intertwined.

As a point of departure, I will argue that the act of reconstituting Eguiara as a kind of foundational stone of Mexican nationalism tends to foreclose the possibility of discerning other ideological elements in his work, such as his religious orthodoxy and a commitment to a kind of cultural pan-Hispanism predicated on a continuing loyalty to the concept of a world united under the aegis of a "universal monarchy," the center of which would be the Spanish Crown. In addition, I will look at the system of hierarchies and exclusions upon which I hypothesize Eguiara's conception of the "Mexican nation" to be based.

It is my hypothesis that Eguiara is concerned to construct a textual grid that would form the archival basis of an *essence.*

Nevertheless, in the very act of trying to manufacture a sense of a commonality, or homogeneity, within Mexican intellectual and cultural tradition, he opens up contradictions. This dynamic functions first at the level of the exclusion, or mediation, of some of the very elements that were constitutive of that tradition. In the second place, it occurs at the level of the inclusion and appropriation of indigenous artifacts and texts, that is, the cultural capital of groups whose physical presence tends to be subsumed and effaced within the process of the projection of structures of power in the viceroyalty, which is articulated by the discourses of *criollo* subjectivity and the *criollo* archive.

Staging Legitimization: The *Aprilis Dialogus*

The *criollo* archive is a heterogeneous and mobile corpus, a curious mixture of images and symbols drawn from differing cultural and intellectual codes. In its motion one can observe the mutations of a *criollo* intellectual subject in the dynamics of formation. The very structure of the *Bibliotheca Mexicana* is a product of the *ad hoc* character of the processes involved in the construction of the *criollo* archive and its subject. The difficulty involved in attempting to achieve any kind of closure in these processes can be discerned in the long sequence of twenty prologues that Eguiara accumulates in prefacing the work, and in the fact that the catalogue itself was ultimately left incomplete.

The heterogeneous composition of the *criollos'* nascent intellectual culture is a function of the position they occupy in eighteenth-century viceregal society. That is, they have not yet become constituted fully as a discrete, self-sufficient class, with a consciousness of a common mission and program. Rather, they are engaged in a process that is still in gestation, that is being theorized in diverse realms, means, and forms of association, and that is being constructed in different spheres. In scholarly circles, *criollos* form and maintain friendships with Spanish-born intellectuals with common interests. At the same time, they seek to advance their careers within the administrative structures through which the viceregal administrators maintain order in the colony, fostering professional alliances and cultivating

European intellectual disciplines, particularly civil and canon law.[13]

A significant intellectual collaboration is that which develops between Eguiara y Eguren and the Andalusian Jesuit Vicente López. The importance of their interaction is borne out by the parts of their correspondence that have survived to the present (Eguiara y Eguren, *Bibliotheca* 5: 623–48), and by the inclusion of a dialogue composed by López as a form of preface to the *Bibliotheca*. Written in Latin, López's text bears the title *Aprilis Dialogus,* translated into Spanish as *Diálogo de abril,* or, alternatively, as *Diálogo abrileño* (Eguiara y Eguren, *Bibliotheca* 1: 19).

López had traveled to New Spain in 1709 and, through his interaction with Mexican members of his order and others involved in the work of educational institutions such as the Real y Pontificia Universidad de México and the Colegio Máximo de San Pedro y San Pablo, had become very impressed with their achievements and capabilities in the areas of classical and theological scholarship. The *Aprilis Dialogus* would be his most explicit contribution to the literary defense of the intellectual worth of the *criollos*. It plays a key role in the construction of the *criollo* archive, as the source of the intellectual authority that Eguiara y Eguren seeks to assemble. This role functions in a variety of fashions, all of which come together under the projection of Mexico as a scenario in which humanist scholarship can flourish.

In the first place, López brings to the text the authority and prestige associated with the position of the Jesuit order, in its capacity as the organization whose intellectual institutions were most open to, and informed by, the most advanced forms of knowledge production. In the second place, López's work contributes to the consolidation of *criollo* legitimacy by staging an appraisal of the products and infrastructure of the Mexican intellectual spheres, within the parameters of cultural value established by various strands of European humanism. The legitimacy of this sphere is projected through the fictional depiction of the successful functioning of humanist pedagogy and practices in a Mexican scenario. The representation of such a setting is effected through the careful assembly of various elements into a harmonious image of organicity. These elements are: a humanist articulation of the classical genre of the dialogue; the depiction, and transportation to Mexico, of characters representing the most important centers of humanist authority; and the invocation of the rhetorical figure of the *locus amoenus*.[14]

The distinction between "nature" and "culture" is one of the foundational antinomies of Western thought. It is central to key writings on aesthetics, law, politics, and society throughout the early modern period, ranging from Spanish missionaries' descriptions of native peoples to Thomas Hobbes's reflections on the rationale for the state as organizing principle in and over modern society.[15] One of the principal contradictory components of this antinomy is the tension between a postlapsarian privileging of the state of nature over civilization, on the one hand, and the elaboration of a hierarchy in which European subjects enjoy power and authority over that which is non-European by virtue of the latter's ignorance of the ideas and practices of humanistic learning and Christian belief in which the former are embedded, on the other hand.

This is the problematics identified as the starting point for the *Bibliotheca Mexicana*. Martí had identified America as a *solitude*—"solitudine"—a wilderness, or empty space, bereft of culture. Here, the interrelated concepts of the pastoral and solitude are stripped of the positive connotations they bear in stoic thought, as a locus for reflection on both the material world and the divine.[16] One of the tasks of the *Bibliotheca Mexicana* is to recast the terms of the conceptual framework articulated by Martí and other Europeans, and re-present America as a space amenable to the cultivation of eloquence and knowledge. This task is begun in the *Aprilis Dialogus*.[17]

Vicente López uses the dialogue form in classical fashion, creating a text in which a wider variety of topics could be addressed than could be treated in a complex and nuanced fashion. He utilizes the form to treat the question of the dignity of America and its inhabitants. The dialogue is conducted between representatives of the most celebrated centers from which the ideologies and practices of early modern humanism were disseminated: a Spaniard, a Belgian,[18] an Italian, and "alii Apollinis, et Minervae alumni" (López 1; "other students of Apollo and Minerva"). The only explicit *criollo* presence is not a human character, but comes in the form of the fictional Mexican setting,

which the Italian describes using the following quotation from
Virgil's *Eclogues* (3.55):

> . . . In molli consedimus herba,
> Et nunc omnis ager, nunc omnis parturit arbos,
> Nunc frondent, silvae nunc formosissimus annus
> . . . dicite (López 1)

> . . . We have sat down on soft grass, / Now all the fields turn
> green once more and every tree now ripens its fruits; / Now
> the forests give forth their foliage; we are in the season of
> spring. / . . . Tell . . .[19]

As the title of the dialogue suggests, certain specific elements
have been added to the topos of the *locus amoenus.* At the most
immediate level, the invocation of the month of April as the
moment in which the dialogue is set appears to be a reference
to the date when the first volume of the *Bibliotheca* was published.[20] It is, at the same time, clearly part of the invocation
of the fictional space of the *locus amoenus,* being a month associated with the springtime. Nevertheless, it is also part of a
large-scale conceptualization of America, and in particular,
Mexico, as a place in which humanist scholarship is being
reelevated to the state of vitality it enjoyed in Europe during
the fifteenth and sixteenth centuries. That is, the eighteenth-
century intellectual culture of New Spain is projected as a scene
in which standards of erudition and eloquence similar to those
set in motion by humanism in Western Europe during the Renaissance are being attained.

Appropriately, therefore, it is the Italian character in the dialogue who offers his opinion about the trade of goods between
Spain and America. He states:

> Si quid novi est ab Aeuropa; audivi enim ex Hispania naves
> ad portum Veraecrucis appulsas, solentque inde ad nos usque
> raras ac peregrinas librorum merces convehere, quas auro
> quovis Mexicani coemant: quo pacto fit ut quidquid in magna
> illa ingeniorum altrice Aeuropa cultores literarum scribendo
> inveniunt, elaborant, perficiuntque, utilissimo, nimirum, et
> honestissimo commercio facile ad nos perveniat; et dubitari
> possit auro ne magis, et argento americani Aeuropam, an
> Aeuropa suis libris mexicanos ditaverit. Quanquam in hujus-

modi negotiatione, et in advectis a Septentrione mercibus
hispani fraudem, dolumque malum, non semel detexerint.
(López 1)

If there is something new from Europe; well, I heard it said
that the ships which come to the port of Veracruz from Spain
usually bring us, from there, rare and surprising merchan-
dise of books which the Mexicans buy for a certain price;
in this manner, it is achieved that all that which the cultiva-
tors of letters discover, elaborate, and perfect, through a most
useful and honest commerce, in that Europe, which is a rich
wet-nurse of talents, comes to us. And it can be doubted
whether Americans have enriched Europe more with their
gold, or Europe the Americans with their books; although
in this form of business and in what is taken over there from
America, the Spanish have not infrequently discovered bad
frauds and deceptions.

The ambiguous benefits Europe and America have received
as a result of the processes of conquest and colonization are
mentioned briefly. Nevertheless, the Italian avoids developing
any critical commentary on this dynamic, electing, instead, to
acknowledge the authority of the Belgian interlocutor in the
fields of trade and communications.[21] The debaters avoid any
interrogation of the moral problems raised by the violence of
the conquest and economic exploitation of America, and the
discussion moves on to the issue of what use the inhabitants
make of the cultural goods they have been afforded by the various apparatuses of European colonialism. These are represented
metonymically here in the figure of the book.

The discussion of intellectual culture in the viceroyalty develops out of a reference to the aforementioned Martí, the man
whose letter provoked Eguiara y Eguren's anger and provided
part of the impetus for the *Bibliotheca Mexicana*. The criticism
of his negative remarks about American reality is articulated
through the voice of a Spanish character, who indicates his
willingness to enter into an open exchange of opinions about
the matter (López 4–5). The implicit criticism of European
intellectual prejudice is focused at the level of Martí the individual, rather than as an attack on peninsular values and thought
in general. The Spaniard swiftly defers to the legitimating authority of the Belgian interlocutor, stating:

> Imo potius aude, effareque voce ista, ac belgico pectore: nam propterea tibi in dialogo isto ante alios loqui concessimus, quod sciremus te belgam esse, ex natione, scilicet, cui nihil sit probitate antiquius, nihil veritatis studio amabilius. Ob quas animi dotes, et in scribendo judicii sine affectatione maturitatem, estis vos Belgae chari, vel nationibus exteris, et orbi literarum quam qui maxime commodi, et utiles. (López 4–5)

> Take heart, and raise this voice from your chest; since for that we grant you the first voice in this *Dialogue* before the other speakers, knowing that you are Belgian, that is, of the nation which has nothing more pristine that its integrity, nor anything more lovable than the study of truth. And because of these adornments of the soul, to which is added maturity of judgment without affectation in the use of the pen, you Belgians are most esteemed by any of the foreign nations, and by the world of letters, as those of greatest utility and advantage.

Having been invoked as a source of intellectual authority, whose performance is enhanced by the favorable conditions of the Mexican *locus amoenus,* the Belgian engages in a rebuttal of Martí's opinions. The criticism of Martí also contains, however, an implicit eulogy of Spain as a nation. A narrator intervenes to observe that Martí's ignorance is all the more surprising to those listening to the Belgian, given that he was born in Spain and educated in Rome (López 5). At the same time, this exchange serves to endorse the ideal of a universal humanistic culture—open to Europeans and Americans alike—the proponents of which derive their authority not from their geographical origins, but from the depth of their acquired learning, and the skills they show in the use of that learning.[22]

By extension, the worth of Mexico and Mexican cultural production is inextricably bound up with its subjects' successful acquisition and development of the theories and practices associated with this ideal. The overall prestige of the region's intellectual culture will be manifested not only in the performance and achievements of individual authors, but more through the workings of a matrix comprising educational institutions, scholars, and the texts they produce.

The Belgian informs his fellow discussants of how Eguiara y Eguren assembled the *Bibliotheca,* and they are given some time to read it (López 11). The next day they awaken and re-convene in a fictional environment that is pleasant and condu-cive to the production of an elevated level of intellectual debate. It is, significantly, as if the experience of reading Eguiara y Eguren's work of erudition has manufactured the necessary infrastructure for such debate. The narrator describes the scene in the following terms:

> Postera autem ubi dies exorta est, cum a potione indica con-vivae omnes recentes essent, e villa, rusticationis gratia in subjectum pratum descendunt, qua tenuis, ac placidus rivulus permeabat. Tunc Italus:
>
>> Eccur non murmur, et cantum aqulae discurren-tis sectabimur, qui nos ad fontem suum deducet, in quo forte sub alicujus arboris umbra, ubi Sol coeperit aestuare, inceptum heri sermonem claudemus.
>
> Et quidem divinasse visus est Italus. Modico enim spatio decurso, ventum est ad fontem, ex quo rivulus emanabat; eratque loco facies aspectu mirabilis, variis peregrinisque plantis, et stirpibus consita densis etiam arboribus inumbrata, in quibus plures, et apprime canorae aviculae nidificabant. Ut qui aderant nec Ciceronis Academiam requirerent, aut Tusculanum; nec ipsius Alonensis decani villam cui descri-bendae omnes ille orationis lepores, et charites advocavit. (López 11)

> No sooner has the next day dawned, when the companions were still savoring the flavor of the chocolate on their lips, than they went down to a meadow which stretched below the villa, [and] through which a narrow and pleasant brook moistened the meadowlands, in order to spend a day in the country. Then the Italian said: why don't we follow the mur-mur and song of the brook until it takes us to the spring from which it flows; there, perhaps, under the shade of a tree, when the sun begins to warm up, we can finish the conversation we began yesterday. And it seemed that the Italian had fore-seen [it], since after walking a little they arrived at the spring from which the brook came. The place was of a beauty worthy of admiration, abundant in varied and extraordinary plants, strewn with bushes and shaded by the leafy tree tops, where songbirds were beginning to weave their nests; in such a manner that those present did not long for Cicero's academy nor his country house in Tusculum, nor the dean of Alicante's

> own villa, which he [the dean] described using all the beauties
> of style and even the Graces themselves.

The act of reading the *Bibliotheca* has transported the humanists to a Mexican *locus amoenus,* a place that is propitious for study and intellectual discussion. This is an uncertain imagined space, one that juxtaposes a European discourse of cultural formation with a material reality upon which it has been transposed, but which, nevertheless, periodically threatens to undermine and rupture the organicity of that discourse. López does not just re-create, in his dialogue, the neoclassical scenario of early modern European depictions of fictional countrysides. Rather, he injects into this figure a representation of American nature as a positive force, favorable to the elaboration of culture, not a dark environment that is hostile to human interests.[23] The strange and varied animals and plants are shown to be conducive not only to high levels of agricultural production, but also to intellectual work.[24] At the same time, the Italian interlocutor argues, the human minds emerging out of this environment do not flourish precociously and then rapidly decline, as many Europeans writing about America had maintained, but live long and fruitful lives, in many cases continuing to develop and disseminate their learning into their sixties and seventies (López 19–21).

Notably, in much the same manner as the Belgian, the Italian character functions here as a master sign, denoting a source of supreme authority in human and divine letters. While the Belgian provides most of the information about Mexico and its inhabitants themselves, the Italian character acts as the moderator of the discussion of humanistic knowledge, in his capacity as a modern descendant of Rome, the republic that assumed the role of cultural center after the ancient Greeks. He is introduced in the following terms by the Spanish character: "quia primae in judicando Italis tribuuntur, ex quo ipsi veterem illam Graeciam suis literis expoliarunt, placet eidem Apollini, ut initium sermonis Italus ducat" (López 11; "since in this matter of judgments the Italians triumph, as they were the first to wrest Greece's literature from it, it pleases Apollo himself that it should be the Italian who conducts this talk").

The construction of the image of the *locus amoenus* is further developed through the comparison of Mexico City with ancient Athens, an identification made by the Belgian character. He informs his listeners and readers that it is commonly agreed that the airs of Mexico are particularly favorable to the cultivation of the intellect. He continues his re-creation of the genesis of Eguiara y Eguren's project in the following terms:

> Audiebat praeterea noster scriptor, legebatque, in famosis quibusdam libellis exagitari, proscindi saepius, ac lacerari Americanos imo in ultimam aliquando barbariem relegari, ac ne angulum quidem illis in Republica literarum relinqui. Quare optabat, non supremum (quod isti suspicantur) sed aliquem, si literatorum Senatui, populoque placeret, genti suae locum concedi, in quo sedate ac sine tumultu, suas Minervae oleas, suas lauros Apollini excolleret et irrigaret. Et erat certe cunctorum, qui hic habitarunt, sententia, et consensu, justissima viri postulatio, et minime contemnenda petitio. Propterea quod alendis ingeniis, inter diversas orbis plagas nulla mexicano coelo sit aptior. Ut qui maxime Athenas illas veteres, urbemque Mexicum cognoverunt et contemplantur, pares aut simillimas faciant, aeris, ac coeli benignitate, quibus plerumque suum acumen, acies, et magnitudo constat ingeniis. (López 15–16)

> Moreover, our author heard and read in certain famous satires how Americans were frequently scorned, wounded, and lacerated, [and] even more, how they were relegated to the final extreme of barbarity, without being allowed even a corner in the republic of letters. Because of this, he longed for his nation [to have] not the most exalted place (to which they aspired) but any [place], if it pleased the senate and the lettered citizens, where she [the nation] could plant her olives to Minerva and her laurels to Apollo calmly and without anxiety, and water them appropriately. And by the unanimous decision of all those who lived here, that was, certainly, the very just postulation of our author and the plea which cannot, in any way, be refused because, among the varied climates of the globe, none is more suitable to the inspiration of people of talent than the sky of Mexico; so that those who have become familiar with ancient Athens and now contemplate Mexico City consider them to be very close in similarity for the gentleness of their skies and their airs with which they sustain and refine the shrewdness, ability, and grandeur of their wits.

Having established the climatic and geographical conditions that favor Mexico as a place for the cultivation of minds, the

Belgian proceeds to delineate the cultural factors that further enhance that process. He first states that certain inherent, natural qualities enable Mexicans to succeed in their studies: "Mexicanorum indoles apta, docilis, et ad scientias omnes et literas modulata" (López 16; "the suitable and docile disposition of the Mexicans, shaped for every kind of sciences and letters"). Then, he describes the institutional infrastructure that helps them acquire these forms of knowledge. He paints a picture of the education privileged Mexicans are given, from early schooling through colleges and universities, where there is offered "a teneris unguiculis bonarum artium, sublimiorum facultatum, cultus disciplina, et sub magistris in unaquaque scientia doctissimis, liberalis educatio, sedulaque institutio" (López 16; "the liberal education and careful instruction which, from their tender years, they receive from teachers who are very learned in fine arts, in the highest faculties and in all the disciplines of culture"). Then, he gives details of the centers of advanced learning, that is, the institutions of the various religious orders active in New Spain.[25] In these places, which only a limited number of outstanding scholars are allowed to enter in order to further their studies, scholars achieve high levels of erudition in Latin, Greek, and in the history of matters pertaining more specifically to life in the American continent:

> Sunt, qui postea quam contentione summa, et labore ex omni cum graecae, tum eruditionis latinae campo flores primos, et succos libaverint, apum instar multo nectare cellas, et alvearia sua distendunt, favosque conficiunt dulcissimos, quos aliis gustandos insumendosque relinquant. Sane quicumque cum fide, ac pro dignitate res Americas literis commendarunt, ex historiis, aut commentariis jam ante in America elucubratis, abunde profecerunt. (López 17)

> There are some who, after much struggle and work, have tasted the finest nectars of erudition in both Greek and Latin, and, just as the bees know how to do in fields of flowers, fill their cells with beautiful liquid, and spread out and make very sweet honeycombs where they leave others the taste of their labor and flavor. In truth, those who have written with honor and loyalty, and worthily, on the matters of America in histories, or in commentaries that have been composed in America for a long time now, have been very abundant and of great benefit.

After giving this account of the institutions of learning, and the work that goes on inside them, the Belgian character completes his picture of a self-sufficient order by reflecting on some of the other environmental features that facilitate the cultivation of knowledge in Mexico. He notes that Mexico has enjoyed a long period without wars, affording a stability that permits the unhindered pursuit of knowledge and culture. There is an implicit reference to the continuing instability and fragmentation produced by the struggle for military and economic influence waged between the emerging nation-states of Europe.[26] At the same time, this gesture suppresses from the text any mention of the scattered threats to this order posed by popular indigenous and *mestizo* uprisings.[27] The Belgian remarks:

> Denique cum Hispani sponte, et ingenio in Martis, et Minervae stipendia ferantur, evenit ut in pacatissima urbe bellis circumquaque longe silentibus, mexicana juventus omnes illos naturae igniculos, animique vires traducat ad literas; ut quominus armis eo magis doctrina, et pacis artibus evadat insignis. Itaque cum Mexicani singulari Dei optimi maximi munere ad capessendas scientias omnibus aut naturae, aut gratiae praesidiis instructi sint, et ornati, nihil video quod non suum illis inter ingeniosos literarum cultores locum merito designemus. Et quidem si velimus sedere ad calculos, temporisque rationes subducere, intra duo illa saecula, in quibus americani scientias, artesque liberales excoluerunt, culturae atque operae fructus respondit, messisque eruditis non contemnenda. (López 17)

> Finally, although the Spanish are naturally and intrinsically inclined toward the rewards of Minerva and Mars, a thing has come to pass, that since there is no bellicose activity in this most placid city and in its most far-flung environs, Mexican youth transfers all these fires of the soul and calls of nature to the study of letters, and while less experienced in the handling of arms, they are more distinguished in the sciences and arts of peace. And thus, given that Mexicans, by the singular benefit of the most excellent and greatest God, are decorated and provided with all the aids, either of nature or grace, [necessary] to learn all the sciences, I see nothing of which they are not worthy, nor can we exclude them from [the ranks of] the most ingenious cultivators of letters without clear reason. In truth, if we start to calculate

and take account of time, in the centuries which the Americans have taken to cultivate the sciences and the liberal arts, the fruits correspond to the cultivation and the sowing, [being] in no way contemptible in the harvests of erudition.

He suggests that two factors, primarily, have prevented much of the scholarship produced within this environment from being more widely disseminated. The first of these is a result of the predominance of economic over cultural transactions between European travelers and America. Qualifying the statements of the Belgian, the Italian cites the fact that most Europeans come to Mexico interested only in commercial trade, and, seeing it merely as a place from which to take raw materials to be sold in Europe, never carry back with them information about, or manifestations of, the cultures and scholarship produced in the viceroyalty (López 13–15). The second problem mentioned is the shortage of printing facilities in the viceroyalty. Since they were never published in book form, many manuscripts have been destroyed by the ravages of time, have been lost, or have survived without there being any record of their authorship (López 17–18).

At the end of the interchange between the Belgian and the Italian, the interlocutors complete the task of consecrating Mexico City as a site in which the highest forms of culture and learning are practiced and disseminated. After the participants in the dialogue have voted upon the issue of the worth of Mexican intellectual culture, their approval is expressed in the following terms:

> Itum igitur in sufragia, ac nemine refragante, decretum: vel si omnia alia deessent, ex sola *Bibliotheca* doctoris Eguiarae constare, ac perspicuum esse Senatui *Hispanos sive qui in Nova sive qui in veteri nascuntur Hispania gentem esse de omnibus scientiis, et artibus optime meritam; qui contra senseris, dixeris, mussitaveris, scripseris, violatae Reipublicae literariae, et falsi criminis reus esto, poenas luito; huncque ipsum, tu censor urbis, omni eruditorum tribu moneto.* (López 25)

> Taken thus to a vote, it was unanimously decreed that, in the absence of other documents, Doctor Eguiara's *Bibliotheca* alone would be sufficient argument, testimony, and proof for the senate that *the Spanish, be they born in old*

Spain or in the new one, are people of the greatest reason,
worthy in every kind of arts and sciences, and that whoever
might say, murmur, or write anything against this would,
by injury to the Republic of Letters, be accused of the crime
of slander and given the corresponding punishments. You,
censor of the city, will make this known to the entire tribe
of the erudite.

Together, the participants in the dialogue declare that the Belgian should be charged with the task of taking the information about Mexico back to Europe, since he is the one who has spent most time there, and because of the association of Charles V, recognized as the founding patron of Mexico City, with the region of the Low Countries (López 25). The work of legitimization is completed with the Belgian character's summary of the impressions he will convey in Europe about Mexico City. First, he praises the viceregal capital for its climate, architecture, china, and silverware (López 26). Secondly, he evokes those factors that support its claim to the status of a universal city. He emphasizes the fact that it has citizens from Africa, Europe, and Asia, varied goods, and maintains "solius catholicae religionis, et pietatis cultum, et studium" (López 26; "the sole pious cult and devotion to the Catholic religion"). In addition, he extols the virtues of its canal system, the cleanness of its air, the lake, and the flora that surround the city (López 26). However, the feature that is singled out as being of the greatest importance is the painted image of the Virgin of Guadalupe, the grandeur of which has been enhanced by the church the Mexicans built in her honor four miles from the city. He comments on the inspiration the Mexicans derive from this vision in the following terms:

Pictura demum ipsa nullam adeo aetatis injuriam sentit, ut ab anno Christi sexquimillesimo tricesimo primo vivat idem color, et spiret adhuc virginea in facie decor ille, et majestas quibus cum olim e divini artificis prodiit ingenio. Quare hoc Virginis simulacro fortunatos se Mexicani ducunt, et inclytos; cum praesertim eorum votis regina clementiae adspiret mirifice. (López 28)

Finally, that painting does not feel the damage of time; for since the year 1531 A.D. it has maintained the same brightness of color, and still exhales from its face that virginal

> decorum and majesty with which it was then born out of
> the hands of Divine artifice. For this reason, the Mexicans
> feel very happy and ennobled by the image of this Virgin,
> especially when this Queen of Clemency miraculously re-
> ceives their vows and requests.

Significantly, following this outpouring of eloquence and erudition, the final testament to the magnificence of the center of Mexican cultural production is the very inadequacy of linguistic expression to the task. When he is asked by the Belgian to say a few lines of poetry in honor of Mexico City, the Italian states that he cannot find words adequate to represent its beauty and grandeur. The dialogue closes with some words spoken by the Spaniard, who appears to stand for the figure of López himself, given the autobiographical details he offers about the education in human and divine letters he has received in the city over the course of the preceding forty years (López 28).

The favorable positions of the Belgian, the Italian, and the Spaniard thus sanction Mexico as an intellectual *locus amoenus,* an appropriate site for the production of knowledge. In the *Aprilis Dialogus* López has prepared the terrain upon which the *Bibliotheca Mexicana* can be constituted. The arguments of the contributors to the humanist dialogue indicate that *criollos* have made good use of the scholarly resources at their disposal and are capable of constructing works of great erudition. The text of the *Bibliotheca Mexicana* will afford an illustration of that erudition.

Chapter Two

Supplementing Authority

The Prologues to the *Bibliotheca Mexicana*

While the *Aprilis Dialogus* establishes Mexico as a utopian site for the production of knowledge, erudition, and texts, the *Bibliotheca* itself involves an unending quest to produce and uncover texts, and to accumulate them in a location perceived by the European intellectual subject as pure materiality, a space defined by its blackness, by an absence of discourse. Its very structure is a symptom of this problematic, since the catalogue is not of itself complete, but has to be supplemented by other documents, or palimpsests.[1] Thus, the *Dialogus* is followed by a series of prologues in which Eguiara y Eguren plays out his attempts to overcome that image of lack. Over the course of these prologues, he articulates the protean outline of the *criollo* subject as it moves between manifestations of both Hispanic and indigenous cultural production.[2] At the same time, through the inclusion of the prologues, especially those that deal with the pre-Hispanic cultures of the region, Eguiara y Eguren acknowledges, implicitly, the uncertainty of the grounds on which the *criollo* will seek to stand as synecdochic representative of the heterogeneous field of Mexican society and culture.

In his first prologue, Eguiara y Eguren sets out to explain why he has embarked on his task of writing. The *Bibliotheca* is not presented as an unsolicited and, therefore, presumptuous display of intelligence and erudition, but as a text whose existence has been required and demanded by another, as a truth that will displace a fiction comprising a series of falsehoods. The criterion that Eguiara y Eguren invokes in his explanation of his decision to compile the *Bibliotheca* is not overtly one of rebellion, but of the necessity of combating ignorance, of producing legitimate knowledge. As is usually the case with colonial writings, the text of the work is offered as a kind of service. It is the sense of duty to the Spanish Crown and to the maintenance of its good image that requires Eguiara y Eguren, as political subject, to undertake a project of such dimensions. Proceeding from the invocation of the rhetorical figure of false modesty, and in an explicit criticism of Martí, Eguiara y Eguren proceeds to state his messianic commitment to the production of knowledge in the following terms:

> Ad amicos eruditione una et iudicio pollentes delata re, audendum nobis esse et totis viribus connitendum est constitutum, iactaque in Deum fiducia, pro eiusdem honore ac gloria meditatam BIBLIOTHECAM excolere palamque dare, quae nationi machinatam nostrae calumniam ab decano alonensi contundat, coerceat, obterat et in auras et fumum abiciat.
>
> Etsi enim ipsam eruditi quique et prudentes viri cuiusvis nationis et gentis litteris expolitae, despicatui habituri sint, explosuri, nec sine cachinis audituri aut lecturi, verendum est tamen, ne similes aliqui Emmanueli Martino inveniantur, omnem qui eruditionem suam et doctrinam ponentes in latinae et graecae linguarum cultura, poeseos amoenitate et romanarum inscriptionum veterum eruderatione, cetera negligant omnia et nescientes prorsus notissimas doctis viris historias et res, una cum alonensi decano gradiantur sententia praeiudiciisque ducti et fuco ab eius Epistola facto, eosdem errores imbibant et evulgent. (*Prólogos* 59)

> But having communicated about our project with friends [who are] outstanding equally for their intelligence and enlightenment, we decided that we should throw ourselves into the enterprise, devote all our efforts to it and, with confidence placed in God, complete the conceived catalogue and publish it, with the goal of obliterating, stopping, flattening, and turning into air and smoke the slander raised against our nation by the dean of Alicante.
>
> We know well that any wise and erudite subject of an educated nation will look at such a slander with disdain and censure, and that he will not hear or read it without loud laughter; but it is always to be feared that other Don Manuel Martís may appear who, having entirely devoted their erudition and sleepless nights to the cultivation of Greek and Latin languages, to the charms of poetry, and to the exhumation of old Roman inscriptions, have paid little attention to the rest, and that knowing nothing at all of the histories

and things well-known by many learned men, might go and join the dean of Alicante in his opinion, and allowing themselves to be dragged along by the prejudices and deceptive appraisals of his letter, might end up participating in identical errors and throw themselves into spreading them.

Eguiara y Eguren's argument involves a paradoxical, Janusfaced move that implies, simultaneously, the relativization of metropolitan knowledge and, at the same time, the invocation of a form of totalizing erudition. Within this schema, it is no longer sufficient to be familiar with the textual basis of the humanists' universal culture, represented by Eguiara y Eguren's reference to skills in Greek and Latin. Rather, to be truly universal, one has to possess knowledge of America also, rewritten now not as a material void, but as a space filled with texts.

Eguiara y Eguren's first act, in his theoretical preface to the catalogue itself, involves not a defense of the intellectual work of the contemporary group of *criollos* of which he forms a part, but a re-writing of the image of the American indigenous subject. This does not imply a eulogy of the culture of his indigenous contemporaries, a move that would require him to allow them access to a central position of sociocultural agency. Rather, the work of the text is to mark out such a role as the exclusive terrain of the *criollo* sector in the struggle over multiple spheres of authority in the viceroyalty. As a living, material reality, the indigenous subject must be denied access to such a position of presence. That which is marked as indigenous can only exist within the framework of the archive, in the form of the signs, representations, and artifacts left behind by individuals and groups now long dead.[3] Only the *criollo* intellectual can possess the authority to reactivate and give life to the cultural matrix produced by indigenous subjects, since this is one of the principal manners in which he can demonstrate a greater, and, therefore, legitimating, breadth of knowledge and erudition than his European counterparts on the indigenous subjects themselves.

The establishment of this transcendent level of knowledge and authority is achieved in two steps, in the second prologue (Eguiara y Eguren, *Prólogos* 60–69). First, the reference to the archival writings of pre-Hispanic peoples—in particular, those of the Aztecs and Tlaxcalans—sets up a stark contrast between the learning displayed in the indigenous texts themselves and Martí's ignorance of them. Eguiara y Eguren seems to make an implicit parallel between Martí's knowledge of the ancient texts of Greece and Rome and his own call for a familiarity with the ancient manuscripts of the pre-Hispanic civilizations. He notes:

> Totus ferme ut erat Emmanuel Martinus in eruderandis ve-teribus orbis veteris monumentis ac romanis inscriptionibus et antiquitatibus, orbem novum fastidire visus est, et quae in ipso scitu sunt dignissimae antiquitates penitus ignorasse, quas si unquam rescivisset, mitiori credimus calamo usus fuisset et atramento, non iam de hispanis hominibus in America mexicana natis aut degentibus, sed vero etiam de indis ipsis aliquando scripturus. "Quo te vertes," inquit, "apud indos, in tam vasta litterarum solitudine?" (*Prólogos* 60)

> Entirely devoted to the exhumation of the venerable monu-ments of the Old World and of Roman antiquities and in-scription, Don Manuel Martí appears to have looked at those of the New World with disdain, and to have been wholly ignorant of the antiquities that exist here, [which are] very worthy of being known. If he had had some knowledge of them, he would have written with a more moderate pen and ink, not now about the Spaniards who have been born or live in the lands of Mexico, but about the Indians themselves. "To where will you turn your eyes," he inquires, "among the Indians, in the middle of such a great wilderness [bereft] of literary studies?"

Eguiara y Eguren maintains that the ancient Mexicans' ig-norance of alphabetic languages is not sufficient reason to label them as being bereft of culture, as peoples ignorant of the sci-ences, books, and libraries (*Prólogos* 61–62). He thus establishes his authority, in the second place, through the act of writing about these pre-Hispanic texts, in the unfolding of his own eru-dition, constituting himself as an expert in a field of which Martí and most other Europeans have little knowledge, and about which, therefore, they are not sufficiently authorized to speak. Here, Eguiara y Eguren demonstrates his familiarity with both the original texts themselves and the works written about them by Spanish and *criollo* clerics. The discussion of pre-Hispanic cultures covers the text of prologues 2 through 7.

What is articulated in these six prologues is not so much a transparent image of pre-Hispanic cultures, but a "learned" discourse on those cultures. It is not a form of disinterested scholarship, but of an archivism that abrogates a role for itself in the struggle over interpretation. Eguiara y Eguren inserts himself into an already long body of scholarly writing about the American indigenous other in order to acquire for himself the authority vested in the genealogy of texts he shows himself to have read. The struggle for legitimization, to establish an interpretive ground, is endlessly waged across two interwoven narratives. Eguiara y Eguren seeks to establish the configuration of a legitimate framework for knowing the non-European other. In this fashion, he seeks to garner authority for his own exhaustive knowledge of both texts and material realities over the truth-claims made in the agglomeration of Europeans' descriptions of the American world. At the same time, he is engaged in a paternalistic and interested defense of pre-Hispanic peoples' own paradigms of knowledge.[4]

This latticelike structure of narratives unfolds in such a way as to make it impossible to separate the indigenous cultural artifacts and practices described, from the metacommentary on the texts written about them by learned scholars since the Conquest. All the features that Eguiara y Eguren describes are categorized through the taxonomies and evaluative criteria of early modern European literary-philosophic culture. The Mexicans are shown to have cultivated not only pictographic writing, but also "poesim, rhetoricam item et oratoriam, arithmeticam, astronomiam, et id alia" (*Prólogos* 63; "poetry, rhetoric, oratory, arithmetic, astronomy, and other things"). They also are judged to have a culture equivalent to those of the most esteemed ancient civilizations, to the extent that they developed a system for representing and recording history. Eguiara y Eguren describes this in the following terms:

> Quo enim pollebant ingenio haudquaquam obtuso eorum primates viri sacerdotio insignes atque muneribus, litterarum vice figuras et imagines admovebant rebus signandis aptissimas, easque lapidibus quandoque insculpebant aut lignis, saepius pinguiori chartae, emporeticae nostrae simili, aut pellibus alutis, ceu membranis mollibus commendabant coloratas atque distinctas, et his quidem notis usus illis erat

nihil non memoriae commendare scitu dignum, unaque diem, mensem et annum origine et in Americam nostram commigratione. (*Prólogos* 63)

The by no means dull intelligence which characterized their principal men, who were distinguished by their priestly role and their public duties, enabled them to understand figures and images in the fashion of letters and in different colors, most appropriate to the significance of the objects, engraving them in stones or wood, or drawing them on thick paper, similar to that which is used among us in wrappings, and, at times, on finely worked skins or soft parchment; and in this manner they committed to posterity everything they considered to be worthy of memory, and together with it, the day, month, and year of their origins and their immigration to America.

Eguiara y Eguren refers to three kinds of texts here, all the while emphasizing the significance of scholarly work done by several generations of Mexican-born scholars in interpreting and conserving them. Notable among the pre-Hispanic texts are the *Circuli Picturati,* which the ancient Mexicans used to measure the passage of time, and which contain important information about the origins of their civilization. Of interest also, notes Eguiara y Eguren, are the codices, which were central to the practice of predicting future events, known by their Mexican name, *Tonalamatl.* At the same time, Eguiara y Eguren identifies the work of philological investigation and recuperation of such texts by the viceregal scholar Carlos de Sigüenza y Góngora as an integral part of the history of the archive that he is constructing. Sigüenza is praised for having rescued many pre-Hispanic texts and artifacts from the oblivion into which they had been cast during the initial period of conquest, and for having tried to interpret them, thereby reestablishing a link of continuity with Mexico's lost antiquity.[5]

This theme of a scholarly mission of reestablishing a link with the lost origins of Mexican civilization is further developed in Eguiara y Eguren's comments on a third kind of indigenous text: those that pertain to the recording of festivals, religious days, the names of children, and the rites and ceremonies bound up with marriage. He observes that many of these volumes were burned by the initial wave of Catholic priests and friars in Mexico who, on seeing the large numbers of pictures of strange animals, birds, herbs, flowers, men, and symbols, thought they were the products of witchcraft and idolatry, and were unable to understand the real significance encoded in the pictures (*Prólogos* 65). Eguiara y Eguren acknowledges the labor of conservation performed by certain indigenous scholars at that time, stating:

> proptereaque diligenter ubique quaesita, flammis concredita fuere lacrymabili antiquitatum americanorum et historiae iactura, quae certe fuisset irreparabalis, ni indorum aliqui sacris nostris addicti nec scriptorum suorum nescii, clam illa habuissent in lucemque non diu post adducta religiosis aliquibus patribus commostrassent et aperuissent, quibus usui fuere pro historiis adornandis plenissimis, indis ipsis et Mexici et alibi Americae nostrae Oedipos agentibus, et Sphinges maiorum suorum ac hieroglyphica declarantibus. (*Prólogos* 65–66)

> [S]eeking them diligently everywhere, they consigned them to fire, occasioning a lamentable loss to American history and antiquity, which would have been irreparable, were it not for some Indians who were devoted to our beliefs and knew their own writings, [who] brought them to light shortly after, and showed them to some priests who used them to adorn their chronicles; in this manner, the Indians were to act in Mexico and other places of our America as new Oedipuses, discoverers of the sphinxes and hieroglyphs of their ancestors.[6]

Eguiara y Eguren does not solely focus on the books themselves, but also on other elements of pre-Hispanic Mexican modes of representation. In particular, he defends the medium through which indigenous peoples produced their knowledge of their world, that is, pictographic writing. In the third prologue, he discusses the debate over whether this form of representation can be read as hieroglyphics. Having made reference to Athanasius Kircher's opinion that Mexican pictographic images do not qualify as language, Eguiara y Eguren proceeds to relativize this European conception of communication that gives priority to alphabetical writing over all other kinds, on the premise that pictures themselves cannot convey ideas, only the actions or events they represent (*Prólogos* 70).[7] He cites a series of Spanish and *criollo* scholars who accord Mexican pictographs the same communicative status as their ancient Egyptian equivalents.

He remarks on the unintelligibility of many of the surviving pictographic representations, even those used among the popular sectors of pre-Hispanic societies (*Prólogos* 71–72). The symbolic production of the Mexicans is valued primarily, therefore, for its opaqueness, for presenting the cultured reader with texts loaded with a structural and interpretive difficulty similar to that which is consecrated within the discourse of the Spanish and colonial Baroque, as manifested in the poetics of *conceptismo* and *culteranismo*.[8] Eguiara y Eguren seeks to establish intellectual hierarchies within Mexican pictographic representation that might be analogous to those existing within European intellectual traditions. He notes that, in accordance with a hierarchical system not dissimilar to that which informs Spanish literary production, the authority of Mexican pictographic texts is directly proportional to the difficulty of the style in which they are expressed. As in the case of the aesthetics of "dificultad docta" ("learned difficulty"), the most highly valorized text is one that would be the least intelligible to the popular classes.[9] Eguiara y Eguren emphasizes, in particular, the fact that the pre-Hispanic peoples intended these texts to serve as the basis of a historical archive of their societies, the development of such an archive indicating possession of a knowledge of antiquity. In this fashion, they meet part of the criteria required for a people to be considered civilized according to humanist principles. Eguiara y Eguren writes:

> Ad haec, cum pictoriae arti excolendae multi ex officio incumberent pro cuiusque indole et genio, characteres tamen scribere, annales condere sacraque et publica memoriae commendare sapientiorum duntaxat erat et sacerdotio insignium. Tandem, cum luxui et ornatui tabulae picturatae inservirent, colorata tamen et imaginibus distincta volumina historias concernebant, leges, sacra et quae memorabimus alia, a vulgi captu, nisi praeceptorum vox accederet, longe remota.
>
> Hoc etiam iis mexicanorum libris pretium addiderat, quod chronologiam pictis imaginibus traderent et exactam saeculorum seriem una cum historia ob oculos ponerent, in quo visi sunt sapientissimos aegyptiorum facile superasse. (*Prólogos* 75)

Moreover, while there were many who, according to their
ability and temperament, applied themselves to the art of
painting, the writing of characters, the elaboration of An-
nals, and the transmission of sacred and public matters to
posterity were only for the wise and those [endowed] with
the distinction of the priesthood. Lastly, the painted tablets
provided splendor and decoration, while the volumes with
images contained the histories, laws, sacred ceremonies and
other things mentioned, all very removed from the intelligence of the plebs, without the intervention of the voice of
a teacher.

One thing which increased the merit of these Mexican
books was that they have handed down, through painted
images, the chronology and exact sequence of the centuries of their history, in which they undoubtedly surpassed
the wisest of the Egyptians.

The third feature of Eguiara y Eguren's defense of Mexican
pictographic documents is predicated on the idea that they enable the scholar to have a more complete knowledge of the
origins of the societies that produced them. He uses his more
nuanced and more detailed reading of one of these documents
to establish the image of a form of *criollo* philology superior
to its European equivalents. Significantly, he focuses on Kircher's
superficial reading of an illustration that represents the foundation myth of the Tenochtitlan. He is referring, of course, to
the image of an eagle, with outstretched wings, perched on
top of a cactus, in the middle of a lake. This leads him into
the formulation of a rhetorical question, followed by a critique of Kircher's interpretation. Eguiara y Eguren remarks
indignantly:

An is qui depictam obtuetur aquilam expansis alis insistentem
lapideae arbori spinis obsitae (indigenis dictae "tunal") quae
in medio lacu visitur, divinare citra docentem poterit, id em-
blema esse oraculi dati venientibus olim indis e septem ur-
bibus, extruendae civitatis "Tenoxtitlam," eo paludis, ubi
insidentem arbusculo aquilam aliquando tandem offenderent?

Mirum proinde non est, si versatissimus in extricandis
hieroglyphicis vir sagacissimusque Kircherius, nostris desti-
tutus historiis, et in eis exercitatorum voce et auxilio, nil
praeterea sub eo symbolo subodoratus fuerit, quam quae iis
ipse verbis expressit. "L Tenoxtitlam repraesentat arma quibus utebantur in acquisitione loci 'tunal.' N aquilam significat,

quae ibidem nidulabatur. O habitationem sive mansionem
eorum." Quae sane omnia nil acuminis et arcani continere
nemini dubium est. (*Prólogos* 76–77)

He who sees an eagle painted with wings outstretched,
perched upon a tree of stone covered in thorns (called "tunal"
by the indigenous [people]), standing out in the middle of
a lake, might not he divine, without anyone showing him
the mystery, that it is a representation of the Oracle given
to the ancient Indians, coming from the seven cities, ordering them to found that of Tenochtitlan on that spot in the
swamp where they came to find an eagle perched upon a
bush. Consequently, it is not amazing that a man so well-
versed in the interpretation of hieroglyphs and so wise as
Kircher, but destitute of our histories and of the advice and
help of those who are expert in them, should not have sus-
pected that there was anything under the mentioned symbol other than what he expressed with these words, "the L
of Tenoxtitlan represents the arms which they used in acquiring the site of the 'tunal.' The N signifies the eagle which
made its nest there, the O, their [the Indians'] mansion or
house." Which [interpretation], there is no doubt, certainly
contains no ingenuity or mystery.

Importantly, Kircher's reading is perceived to be bereft of
subtlety and of any grasp for the recondite, that is, one of the
key features of Baroque aesthetics, as manifested in the metaphorical rationale of *conceptista* poetry and the syllogistic logic
of scholasticism.[10] In addition, Eguiara y Eguren delegitimizes
Kircher's reading by invoking a concept that is central to the
intellectual program and pedagogy of humanism, that is, the
notion of not reading ancient writings through glosses, but of
returning to the original ancient text itself.[11] What is striking
here is not the presence of the practice itself within Eguiara y
Eguren's work, but its application to pre-Hispanic Mexican texts
in much the same manner as it would have been applied to Greek
and Roman antiquity, or the Bible. Eguiara y Eguren observes
that Kircher would not have been mistaken in his reading if he
had had access to the actual codices written by the Mexicans
themselves ("nostris," *Prólogos* 77).

Eguiara y Eguren concludes the defense of pictographic texts
by acknowledging that Kircher achieved a good understanding of the ancient Mexicans' religious beliefs, or idolatry, as a

result of information he culled from his fellow Jesuits in New Spain. However, his chief purpose here is less to praise Kircher's scholarship than to use it to corroborate a thesis about the origins of the ancient Mexicans, one that links them with another ancient pagan civilization esteemed for its laws and culture, if not for its religious beliefs: the Egyptians. This thesis is important again for simultaneously consecrating colonial Mexican scholarship and establishing the intellectual legitimacy of pre-Hispanic cultures. Through the analysis of pre-Hispanic monuments, the methods they used to measure time, their external appearance, their political and religious practices, various scholars had come to see similarities between ancient Mexican society and that of Egypt. Among these scholars, Eguiara y Eguren accords transcendent importance, as noted above, to Sigüenza y Góngora, and, in particular, to his *Teatro de virtudes políticas,* which, Eguiara y Eguren says, concludes: "pluribus edocens mexicanos ab aegyptiis progenitos, a queis una cum sanguine cetera hauserint, et quod propius argumento nostro est, characteribus hieroglyphicis litterarum instar fuisse usos" (*Prólogos* 79; "[W]ith many proofs that the Mexicans are the descendants of the Egyptians and drew from them not only their blood, but everything else, and used hieroglyphic characters for letters, which fact is of concern for our topic"). On this basis, Eguiara y Eguren is able to bolster the argument that many Mexican pictographic representations merit the status of hieroglyphs, and are not just drawings or paintings.[12]

This defense of pre-Hispanic pictographic writing in Mexico then moves from one kind of text to a series of others. First, Eguiara y Eguren refers to the *monumenta* ("monuments" or "records") that remain as evidence of the highly developed status of pre-Hispanic Mexican culture, particularly in its Aztec manifestations. Maintaining his quest to bestow not only that culture, but also his own text, with the authority of erudition, he introduces these *monumenta* by referring to the numerous scholars who have written about them, including Fray Juan de Torquemada and José de Acosta (*Prólogos* 79–82). The objects that he counts as monuments are mentioned in a passage quoted from a summary of a description of Mexico City contained in Juan Francisco Gemelli Careri's work, *Giro del mondo* (cited in Eguiara y Eguren, *Prólogos* 82). In it, the author, who had visited

Mexico and spent some time at its university,[13] is quoted as stating that the city is comparable to any in Italy because of the magnificence of its buildings, the beauty of its women, and its large population of around one hundred thousand (Eguiara y Eguren, *Prólogos* 83). The gloss of Gemelli Careri's work cites particularly its pictures of two *monumenta,* the first being a complete chronology of the Mexican people from their origins up to the Conquest, and the second being the cycle of the centuries that they used to measure time, both composed of symbols and hieroglyphs (*Prólogos* 83). It also singles out two pyramids dedicated to the sun and moon, noting that the stone of which they were constructed had allowed them to survive the violence done to them by the Spanish. The text continues with a criticism of the Spanish, according to which the latter are depicted as being cloddish and having little sensitivity for culture, and an affirmation of the work of cultural archaeology and conservation carried out by Mexican *criollo* and indigenous scholars after the Conquest. Eguiara y Eguren's citation of a passage from the gloss ends with a reference to these labors. It is worth noting, again, that his construction of a genealogy of Mexican scholarship and intellectual tradition is articulated from the standpoint of a discourse of pan-Hispanism, which he seeks to reconfigure from within. Not only does he censure Martí, but he also inveighs against the prestigious scholars of Leipzig for the prejudiced impressions they hold of Hispanic intellectual culture in general, thus reemphasizing the notion that his own work is a service to the Crown. He writes:

> "Vindicavit haec omnia ab interitu quem hispanorum ruditas minabatur" (haec scilicet est repetita ab exteris in nos cantinela, et ab alonensi decano plenis buccis iterum atque iterum decantata) "Juan de Alva, dominus de Cetzieazgo, etc., qui ex regibus Tezcuci descendebat; explicavit vero eadem D. Carolus de Siguenza et Gongora, cathedraticus et professor matheseos Universitatis mexicanae in sua *Cyclographia,* qui et idem edidit alium tractatum sub titulo *Libra Astronomica . . ."* (*Prólogos* 83)

> "All these [records] were saved from the ruin with which Spanish ignorance threatened them" (this is certainly an old song that is repeated against us foreigners, and which the dean of Alicante chants again and again at the top of his

voice) "by Juan de Alva, a cacique chief, etc., who was descended from the kings of Texcoco; their meaning was explained in his *Cyclographia* by Carlos de Sigüenza y Góngora, professor of mathematics of the University of Mexico, who also published another treatise under the title of *Libra Astronomica* . . ."

The construction of the trope of an intellectual origin continues in a section devoted to the description of the educational institutions of the pre-Hispanic civilizations. In this case, Eguiara y Eguren relies wholly on the historical sources of accounts given by famous writers, both from Spain and from other parts of Europe, to refute the depiction of the ancient Mexicans as barbarous and ignorant (*Prólogos* 84–85). In referring to the education given to young Aztec males from age five onward, he cites principally the Belgian Justus Lipsius, and Gerardo Mercator, quoting the latter as noting the Mexicans' awareness of the importance of children's education for the smooth running of the private and public affairs of their society (*Prólogos* 86). As regards more advanced forms of education and scholarship, he refers to the centers set up by the Texcocans, and the arts practiced in them, particularly under the patronage of Nezahualcoyotl. Eguiara y Eguren remarks:

A Torquemada et Betancurtio etiam habemus, praeter gymnasia mexicanensia in ipsa urbe imperii capite condita et frequentata, alia quoque floruisse apud tezcucanos, potissimum regnante Nezahualcoiotl, qui imperatori mexiceo suberat. Nam ut erat insigni prudentia, huius opera Academiae instar constitutus fuit coetus poetarum et musicorum, magno apud tezcucanos numero eorumque etiam qui astronomiam colebant et historias ornabant, artibusque aliis sese exercebant, ut collatis rebus atque discussis, in dies exercitatiores evaderent et doctiores, dato ipsis praeside filio suo Xochiquetzaltzin nomine. (*Prólogos* 87–88)

From Torquemada and Betancur we also know that aside from the Mexican gymnasia established and frequented in the capital of the empire itself, among others those of the Texcocans flourished, particularly during the reign of Nezahualcoyotl, who was under the authority of the Mexican emperor. Such was his wisdom that by his own work and with his son named Xochiquetzalzin as protector, there was formed, in the fashion of an Academy, a nucleus of poets

and musicians, who are very numerous among the Texcocans,
as well as astrologers, historians, and those who cultivated
other arts, so that by conferring among themselves and discussing their affairs, they might become more experienced
and wiser with each day.

Eguiara y Eguren emphasizes Nezahualcoyotl's cultivation
and encouragement of what he calls poetry ("poetica") and song
("canticum"). This observation leads him into the final part of
his discussion of the activities of pre-Hispanic peoples, namely,
the intellectual arts they cultivated. These spheres of artifice
are subsumed under the categories of poetry, oratory, medicine,
and laws (*Prólogos* 88). The common thread that links these
activities for Eguiara y Eguren is the idea that the ancient Mexicans possessed forms of society, organized according to rationalizing principles. Significantly, what is described as poetry
is portrayed as a type of oral expression, existing in conjunc-
tion with pictographic representation. This form of oral expression is carefully fitted into the genre of epic poetry. This mode
of articulation is valued in a similar fashion to folklore, as a
means of producing and maintaining the history of a people.

At the same time, the Texcocans' own work of cultural archivism is represented as a practice to be connected seamlessly
to the later work of ethnographic scholarship carried out by
Europeans on Mexican native peoples after the conquest.
Eguiara y Eguren thereby establishes an impression of continuity between the intellectual work of Spaniards and *criollos*
in New Spain, understood here as part of a specifically Mexican tradition, and the indigenous societies' own modes of producing knowledge of their surroundings and experience. He
remarks:

> Non is solum, quem mox diximus, rex tezcucanos Musis
> litare excipereque festive canentes usu tenuerat, sed et alii
> reges et imperatores politissimique mystae et sapientes, poeti-
> cis enim numeris delectati, epica carmini concinebant praea-
> longa puerisque addiscenda tradebant, ut praeteritarum rerum
> memoriam dulcedine metri conditam in ipsos facili negotio
> instillarent et ad posteros etiam transmitterent deque praesen-
> tibus, qua aetate carmina fundebantur, illos docerent. Atque
> his artibus historiam Americae omnem et characteribus pictu-
> ratam in voluminibus et repetitam canticis, sartam tectam
> ad adventum usque hispanorum servarunt, qui demum in-

dorum consuetudine et usu vivaque doctiorum voce eruditi, libros europaeorum more confecerunt quam plurimos et historias absolutissimas. (*Prólogos* 89)

The Texcocan king, of whom we now spoke, was not the only one to make offerings to the Muses and gaily receive their devotees, but there were other kings and emperors, as well as very cultivated priests and wise men. Delighting in the charms of poetry, they composed long epic songs, and later communicated them to their children so that they might learn them and that they might easily instill in them, expressed with the delightfulness of poetry, the memory of past events, transmit it to posterity, and show them temporal events through the poems composed about them. And with these arts they maintained intact the entire history of America, painted with characters in their books, and repeated in their songs, until the arrival of the Spanish who, instructed through their daily contact with the Indians and by the living voice of the learned, wrote numerous books and very complete histories in the European manner.

The importance accorded to the art of public speaking by the ancient Mexicans enables Eguiara y Eguren to attribute to them the cultivation of a practice analogous to the humanist discipline of rhetoric. Thus, he reformulates the question of the standing and legitimacy of indigenous languages in relation to European alphabetic languages. In this fashion, he dismantles the terms of European intellectual discussions of native American media, according to which indigenous modes of expression were relegated to the level of transparent pictorial representations, bereft of the nuances of meaning created by writing and the conventions of its usage. Above all, Eguiara y Eguren valorizes the techniques involved in producing elegant and varied speeches, something that again fits neatly into the range of skills that humanists had sought to develop.[14] Ultimately, the question of the written aspect of languages is subordinated to that of their oral performance and usage:

Egregium itidem operam exhibuere in ornato dicendi genere, quod et magistri multo usu exercitationeque sibi fecerant familiare, et iis tradebant iuvenibus, quos rhetoricis efformabant praeceptis oratoresque olim initiandos, divite supellectile loquendi copiosissimo et elegantissimo idiomate accurate instituebant.

> Hinc natae fuere orationes minime incultae quae in his-
> toriis mexicanis hispanorum calamo scriptis leguntur ab indis
> profectae, nec ab hispanice narrantibus scribentibusque con-
> fictae, ut opportune animadversum voluit P. Acosta indicando
> postmodum loco. (Eguiara y Eguren, *Prólogos* 90)

> They showed equal care in the decoration of speech, which
> their teachers made familiar to them with much practice and
> exercise. They taught the precepts of rhetoric to the young
> so that once formed as orators, they were furnished with the
> powerful recourses of eloquence, favored by their abundant
> and most elegant language.
>   Proof of this were the by no means uncultivated discourses
> to be read in the Mexican histories written by the pen of
> the Spanish, which were produced by the Indians, as Father
> Acosta wished to observe in the place to be indicated later,
> and not invented by the Spanish in their narrations and
> writings.

The recuperation of indigenous forms of knowledge and their
deployment extends into a discussion of the area of medicine.
Eguiara y Eguren comments upon the Mexicans' use of medicinal flowers and herbs to produce treatments for ailments.
Citing Antonio de Solís y Rivadeneyra's description of the gardens of Moctezuma in his *Historia de la Conquista de México,*
he represents indigenous medicine not as an irrational, mystical activity, but as a systematic series of practices, involving
experimentation with a variety of plants from different regions,
and carried out by individuals specialized in the preparation
of remedies for illnesses (*Prólogos* 90–91).

A parallel rationality is observed in the system of laws with
which the Aztecs governed their society. Here Eguiara y Eguren
makes a typical legitimating gesture, noting that had this system of political government been combined with an observation
of the norms of the Catholic religion, there would have existed
the necessary foundation for their vast empire to have lasted
for a longer period. In a move often made by *criollos* of the
period, he establishes an implicit analogy between pre-Hispanic
Mexican societies and the esteemed ancient pagan civilizations
of Greece and Rome (*Prólogos* 91–92). Eguiara y Eguren concludes the sixth prologue with an exposition of indigenous
societies' development of skilled forms of manual labor, par-

ticularly in the use of feathers and various kinds of animal skins (*Prólogos* 92–93).

In the seventh prologue, Eguiara y Eguren concludes his recuperation of indigenous culture, arguing that the textual evidence he has accumulated indicates that the ancient Mexican peoples deserve to be placed within the pantheon of cultured nations. The key to the summation of his thesis is his interpretation of a statement about the wisdom of Moses cited from an ecclesiastical text. In it, Saint Stephen is quoted as remarking that the Old Testament patriarch was educated in all the forms of knowledge of the Egyptians, which are divided into two tiers (*Prólogos* 94). The first tier, which was accessible to all, comprised geometry, arithmetic, astrology, and music. The second, more exalted tier was, transmitted through the more difficult medium of hieroglyphs, the secrets of physics, theology, and the science of government. Since the Mexicans were no less familiar than the Egyptians with the disciplines in both tiers, Eguiara y Eguren notes, they merit inclusion within the constellation of ancient cultures used as models and sources of authority by the administrative and pedagogic institutions of the Spanish Crown. In this manner, he recuperates the artifacts of pre-Hispanic societies as a series of texts that the *criollo* intellectuals were required to know. The practice of cultural archaeology facilitates the reconstruction of a historical narrative of continuity linking the scholar with a lost origin, in a narrative that tends to suppress the problem of racial divisions and hierarchies that separate him from his indigenous and *mestizo* contemporaries in colonial Mexican society.

This device allows Eguiara y Eguren to proceed smoothly toward a defense of Mexican culture during the viceregal period. In this fashion he moves to bind together the heterogeneous components of Mexican cultural production into a seemingly harmonious whole. This organic corpus will underwrite the authority of the *criollo* intellectual subjectivity elaborated through the course of the text. The defense of post-Conquest Mexican culture is developed in the subsequent eleven prologues (the eighth through the eighteenth). In building his case, Eguiara y Eguren constructs what amounts to a history and sociological description of the cultivation of letters in Mexico over the course of two centuries. This undertaking serves to refute Martí's dismissal of America as a vast wilderness, bereft of the civilizing presence of letters ("tam vasta litterarum solitudine"). Eguiara y Eguren opens this part of his text by affirming that the ancient native inhabitants of the continent were not the real object of Dean Martí's observations:

> Quoniam vero non indos ille veteres cogitavit, sed novos indigenas in iisque et hispanos in America natos et alibi genitos viros in ipsam ascitos, quos ad unum omnes quam longissime dissitos credidit a Minervae sedibus et pomoeriis, eiusdem ut in hisce rebus ignorantia scribendique temeritas aperiatur et propulsetur, e re nostra est. (*Prólogos* 100)

> However, since [Martí] was not thinking of the ancient Indians when he wrote that, but of the new natives, and of the Spanish born in America, and those men born in other parts who had come to it, considering them all together to be dispersed from the house and grounds of Minerva, it is our task now to uncover and refute his ignorance of these things and the temerity of his writings.

Eguiara y Eguren begins his defense of post-Conquest literary culture, in the eighth prologue, by detailing the number and variety of educational institutions existing in the viceroyalty, beginning with the Real y Pontificia Universidad de México, founded by order of Charles V in 1553. He states that in that university, and in those of Santo Domingo, Guatemala, Havana, Caracas, and Yucatan, just as in Europe, education is provided in all the principal disciplines, and at the same levels, even up to that of the doctorate (*Prólogos* 100–01). In addition, he mentions the colleges, seminaries, and other kinds of schools that provide instruction for the young. Eguiara y Eguren boasts that these institutions exist in abundance, claiming that there are no less than sixty in Mexico City alone. He notes, moreover, that this pedagogic infrastructure is reinforced and made possible by the highly developed network of ecclesiastical institutions spanning New Spain's vast territories, comprising two archbishoprics, twelve bishoprics—the majority of them employing large numbers of lay clergy—and eighteen monastic provinces devoted to teaching and to the gathering of historical texts and artifacts (Eguiara y Eguren, *Prólogos* 101).

Having provided details of the educational centers themselves, Eguiara y Eguren writes of the teachers who work within them, in response to Martí's rhetorical question to his young correspondent: "'Quem adibis non dicam magistrum, cuius praeceptis instituaris, sed auditorem?'" (*Prólogos* 102; "'Will you find, dare I say it, teachers, who will teach you the precepts, or even an audience [for those precepts]?'"). Eguiara y Eguren steps in to rebut Martí, insisting that Mexico has an abundant quantity of teachers: "Adibis sane quem malueris e sexcentis magistris, a quo efformeris. Nam intra mexicana pomoeria semper offendes doctores centum plus minusve, quo autem tempore scribimus haec, centenario maiorem eorundem consessum invenies, qui infulis redimiti, e voto tibi et sententia litteras instillabunt" (*Prólogos* 102; "You will certainly find him by whom you prefer to be educated out of six hundred teachers. For in the Mexican lands you will always encounter a hundred doctors, more or less, and at this time in which we write, and an assembly of a hundred more of them, who will instill in you plainly and according to your wishes the knowledge of letters").

Eguiara y Eguren proceeds to list the number of professors to be found teaching in each of the important disciplines. In the Real y Pontificia Universidad de México, twenty-three professors teach rhetoric, philosophy, mathematics, medicine, Roman and canon law, and theology (*Prólogos* 102). At the Colegio Máximo of the Society of Jesus, twelve professors instruct young men in grammar, rhetoric, philosophy, and theology, while nine professors fulfill a similar role at the Seminary College of the Metropolitan Cathedral. In addition, many others work in the monasteries and colleges of the Dominicans, the Augustinians, the Franciscans, the Mercederians, and the Carmelites. Outside of the capital, Eguiara y Eguren singles out the variety of teachers to be found in Michoacan, Oaxaca, Durango, Guatemala, Yucatan, and, in particular, Puebla (*Prólogos* 103). Finally, he remarks upon the system of exams, which requires scholars to deliver oral discourses and write theological dissertations, both in Spanish and in Nahuatl, in order to compete for the highest posts in the universities and colleges.

The mention of these feats of scholarship serves as a point of transition, as Eguiara y Eguren turns, in the ninth and tenth prologues, to the description of books and libraries published and assembled by Mexicans since the Conquest. Here, Eguiara y Eguren dissects Martí's statement to his young correspondent that he will not be able to find any books or libraries in Mexico (*Prólogos* 107). Again, the rebuttal is founded as much on a critique of the Spanish scholar's philological weaknesses as it is on an exposition of Mexican achievement. Eguiara y Eguren turns Martí's criticism back against him, arguing that it is not that there are no books or libraries in New Spain, but that the dean of Alicante has been deficient in his studies, to the point that he is unaware of the numerous Mexican texts that have been important enough to have had editions published in Europe as well as in America (*Prólogos* 108–11). Among the works he cites in this connection are Antonio Rubio's *Logicam mexicanam,* Marcos Salgado's *Cursum medicum mexicanum,* Bernardo de Balbuena's *Grandeza mexicana,* and the writings of Sor Juana Inés de la Cruz, all of which had either been included in bibliographies such as that of Nicolás Antonio, or were commonly known to those who moved in Spanish university circles. He studiously notes that Martí himself had collaborated in the composition of Nicolás Antonio's work and was familiar with other catalogues that make mention of texts produced in New Spain.

In this part of his critique, Eguiara y Eguren seeks to establish a distinct subject-position for Mexican literary expression and learning, and for the writings of its citizens, still within the framework of a universal humanist culture. At the same time, he endeavors to consecrate Mexican literature and scholarship as legitimate objects of knowledge and, thus, as part of the ground of this intellectual subjectivity. Eguiara y Eguren writes:

> Ad haec animadversione dignum existimamus, doctum virum Emmanuelem Martinum tritas ab eruditis frequentissime viris bibliothecas editas penitus neglexisse, dominicanam et franciscanam, Societatis Iesu et carmelitarum, *Alphabetum augustinianum* et *Epitomem* Pinelianam aliasque collectiones iam pridem vulgatas, quae cum codices mexicanos multos obiciant legentibus, nunquam ab eo libatas fuisse sunt argumento. Quis vero crederet, virum elegantissimum et rarioribus inhiantem codicibus, ne salutasse quidem *Orbem terrarum scriptorum calamo delineatum* (quo de infra)

mexicanos, ut omnium nationum, libros non invidentem? (*Prólogos* 110–11)

Moreover, we believe that it is worth noting that as learned a man as Manuel Martí should have neglected catalogues which are frequently handled by scholars and in which [notice] is given of Dominican, Franciscan, Jesuit, and Carmelite [writers]: the *Alphabetum Augusitinianum* and Pinelo's *Epitome,* and other collections already published which he must never have looked at, since they inform readers about numerous Mexican books. Who would believe that a man so refined and so covetous of rare tomes should not even have paid reverence to the *Orbem terrarum scriptorum calamo delineatum* (of which [we will speak] below), in which Mexican books, just as those of other nations, are not despised?

The validity of Eguiara y Eguren's remarks is bolstered by quotations from the works of European writers who, in this case, have extolled the virtues of Mexico's printing presses (*Prólogos* 111–12). Having brought forth the names of important works produced by Mexican authors, Eguiara y Eguren thus moves into a description of the material infrastructure that enables and fosters the production of such books in New Spain.

In the tenth prologue, he initiates an account of how books are gathered together in the viceroyalty's libraries and private collections. He begins by stressing that the libraries are unable to rival the royal collections in Madrid and Paris, or that of the Vatican, in terms of both their holdings of ancient texts and the number of their books (*Prólogos* 114). However, he carefully establishes that Mexico possesses many libraries that fulfill the criteria for the *Ideae bibliothecae universalis* formulated by the French scholar Pierre Blanchot.

Having cited the favorable remarks made about Mexican libraries by such European travelers as Francisco Gemelli Careri and Pedro Cubero Sebastián, he then proceeds to list the different public institutions that meet or surpass Blanchot's criteria, placing special emphasis on those of the Real y Pontificia Universidad de México and of the Dominican, Franciscan, Jesuit, Carmelite, and Mercederian orders (*Prólogos* 116–19). In addition, he makes reference to the numerous private collections of professors, preachers, *oidores,* lawyers, doctors, and members of religious orders. Most outstanding among this group is the library of

Sor Juana Inés de la Cruz, which he believes to have contained around four thousand books (*Prólogos* 120). After completing this inventory of Mexican libraries, Eguiara y Eguren hails the fact of their compilation as an achievement of vast proportions in view of specific problems of finance and distribution. Most significant in this respect is the fact that the shortage of books in Mexico means that European merchants are able to sell the books they bring to America at prices three or four times higher than in Europe (Eguiara y Eguren, *Prólogos* 121). Given such difficulties, the Americans' cultivation of letters is portrayed by Eguiara y Eguren as being all the more worthy of admiration.

At this point, Eguiara y Eguren is able to fix a position of *criollo* intellectual subjectivity. He focuses on the human subject of letters, and of knowledge, the final component and, ultimately, the guarantor, of the mechanism of viceregal Mexican culture. His discussion of this element begins in the eleventh prologue, which bears the heading "De americanorum ingenio et in litteras amore ac studio" (*Prólogos* 124; "Of Americans' wit and their love and study of letters"). The evidence he brings forth in this part of his argument corresponds again to the logic of a humanist universalism. In order to give his claims more validity, he declares that he is going to rely not on the testimony of the subjects of that wit themselves but on the observations of Europeans who have taken the trouble to travel to America and actually see it with their own eyes. This invocation of the authority of experience is part of Eguiara y Eguren's continuing attack on the authority and legitimacy of the opinions of those who, like Martí, have had no direct experience of the objects of their denigrating remarks. He writes:

> credimusque a sapientibus viris auditum non iri eos qui, Andabatorum more, clausis oculis, quos in Americam minime coniecere, nec probatis instructi monumentis aut auctoribus eruditi, iaculis nos impetere et de nobis iudicare tentaverint.
>
> Reliquum est ergo, ut idoneis usuri testibus, viros doctos et graves audiamus, qui apud Europam nati, in consuetudinem nostram venerint et longo americanarum rerum usu et experimentis res ipsas imbiberint, mox alios optimis usos testimoniis et fide dignis instrumentis, parce exhibeamus. (*Prólogos* 124–25)

[A]nd we believe that wise men ought not to listen to those who, going blindly, like blindfolded gladiators, never saw America, and did not acquire knowledge of approved documents or of learned authors, but attacked us with their darts and tried to voice opinions about our things.

Therefore, it remains that we listen to suitable people, to learned and serious men who, having been born in Europe, came to our lands and imbibed our customs after a long time of contact and experience. Then we will briefly give account of others who used the best evidence and most reliable documents.

The common theme in the first part of the defense of Americans' wit and devotion to letters is that of the favorableness of the area's climate for study. He cites one source's comment that not only are Americans possessed of a lively mind, but also that outsiders' intellectual capacities are enhanced when they spend time in Mexico or Peru (*Prólogos* 126). This notion, already treated in López's prefatory dialogue, is further developed through the inclusion of quotations from various sympathetic accounts of the New World written by Europeans. These quotations serve to combat the constructed image of America as a natural wilderness that is hostile to the cultivation of humanist artifice. This is most forcibly brought out in Eguiara y Eguren's citation of the work of the Spanish Jesuit Jerónimo Pérez de Nueros, in which the practice of identifying Mexico with the ancient European centers of erudition is repeated. He quotes him as stating:

Hinc Hesperiae gentis sub natali Americae solo, auspicata caeli irroratione irradiatio neque solis feliciter fecundata, genia et ingenia perpendenti, acrique et vivido, florido pariter, compto et amoeno mentis acumine ad omnigenae litteraturae studium, ipsa favente et fovente natura, illam conspexeris exornatam, idem quod de Athenis debuccinavit fama, aequiori forsan iudicio constitutus arbiter de America testaretur. (*Prólogos* 131–32)

The influence of nature, with the humidity of its climate and the irradiations of its sun, has favorably endowed the Spanish born on American soil with a measured wit which is at once brilliant, fervent, charming, and very apt for the study of all kinds of letters, with the help and favor of nature itself, to the extent that an impartial judge of America would apply to it, perhaps with even greater reason, the same opinions which fame voiced about Athens.

The topic is further developed in the twelfth through the fourteenth prologues, in which Eguiara y Eguren seeks to disprove the theory that American minds flourish and reach their peak precociously, only to decline just as rapidly afterward. He cites Feijóo in support of his argument, noting that the Spanish thinker argues that *criollos* flourish more quickly in literary arts because they are made to start learning grammar and rhetoric at the age of twelve, or even younger, and progress to the study of philosophy and the higher faculties soon after (*Prólogos* 135).[15] Eguiara y Eguren then proceeds to develop his own explanation of the solid foundations of Americans' wit. First, he denies Feijóo's claim that *criollo* students only acquire knowledge of philosophy by reading prescribed books, without the direction of skilled teachers. He relates that they are taught in a classroom setting and that teachers put together courses specifically for their use. Eguiara y Eguren remarks that evidence of this more developed system of education is to be found in the numerous manuscripts of course curricula that are included among the entries to be found in the catalogue of the *Bibliotheca* itself (*Prólogos* 136–37).

In addition, Eguiara y Eguren notes that the students' intelligence is enhanced by a greater rationalization of the educative process, to the extent that the study year is longer at Mexican centers of study than in Spain, since vacations have been shortened and other kinds of interruptions have been reduced. This regime serves to help the *criollos* exploit to the maximum their aptitude for the sciences, all poetic genres, and scholastic problems (*Prólogos* 137–38). Eguiara y Eguren legitimates his ambitious claims about the intellectual abilities of Americans through reference to the comments of Antonio Peralta Castañeda, a theologian from the esteemed University of Alcalá de Henares, who had served for some time in both an ecclesiastical and educative capacity in Puebla. He paraphrases the Spaniard's recollections in the following terms:

minorem quidem scholarium numerum esse in gymnasiis angelopolitanis, quibus ipse praeerat, quam esse soleat in

> complutensibus, apud quos imbiberat litteras, provectorum
> tamen in scientiis copia istis illos anteire seque assuetum
> magistris gravissimis Compluti respondere in palaestra cer-
> tantibus, non semel Angelopoli, ut propositas a discipulis
> suis obiectiones dissolveret, impeditorem factum nec absque
> negotio nodis se eis expediisse. (*Prólogos* 139)

> [A]lthough the number of students he had in his charge at
> the school of Puebla was less than is usual at Alcalá, where
> he had absorbed letters, they were, however, more advanced
> and made greater progress in the study of sciences, and he
> adds that although he had dared in [the University of] Alcalá
> to argue in debates with the most learned teachers, more than
> once in Puebla he had difficulty refuting the objections pro-
> posed by his pupils, and scarcely extricated himself from
> the knots of their arguments.

He corroborates Peralta Castañeda's statements with the descriptions offered by other European commentators, particularly Feijóo. Eguiara y Eguren insists that he does not seek to bestow
upon the inhabitants of the New World the status of the highest wits in the world. Rather, he invokes the thesis that all nations
are potentially equal in wit, an argument based on an inverted
logic of false modesty that allows him to place Americans on the
same plane as their Old World counterparts (*Prólogos* 141–42).

Having established the solidity of Americans' early intellectual formation, Eguiara y Eguren sets out to demonstrate that
they do not subsequently lose their faculties prematurely after
reaching the ages of thirty or forty (*Prólogos* 142). He states
that there are numerous educators at the Real y Pontificia Universidad de México who have become professors emeriti, a status
that can only be acquired after twenty-five years of service, at
which point most are over fifty years of age. Moreover, he notes
that not only are there many men over sixty or seventy who
are still active in the academies, but that there are others of the
same age engaged in ecclesiastical functions, such as giving
sermons and hearing confession. Among those still living, he
mentions the esteemed Dominican Juan de Villa Sánchez, who
continued to give sermons, write, and publish books in Puebla
into the 1750s, although he was by then a septuagenarian (*Prólogos* 144). He then lists a series of men who continued to have
outstanding careers well into old age (*Prólogos* 144–49).

The treatment of this topic carries over into the fourteenth prologue, in which Eguiara y Eguren offers fuller descriptions of the achievements of some of the individuals whose names figure in the main body of the catalogue (*Prólogos* 150–63). Having offered a list of the most outstanding individuals, he then develops other arguments against the thesis of the premature deterioration of American minds. He observes, first, that there are individuals who abandon serious study when they attain an ecclesiastical position, mainly in order to be able to fulfill the broad duties that are subsequently required of them (*Prólogos* 160); second, that people of all nations, not just those of Mexico, are often obliged to curtail their scholarly interests in the face of other obligations; third, that many *criollos* are prevented from achieving fame in letters by poverty or because slow communication means that news of their work takes an inordinately long time to reach the Spanish court (*Prólogos* 161–62).

After rebutting the imputation of the early decay of American wits, Eguiara y Eguren returns to the aspersions cast by Martí and others about the ability of *criollos* to produce works of erudition. Over the course of prologues fifteen through eighteen, he turns his attention to the negative comments of another Spanish scholar, the Jesuit Father Pedro Murillo Velarde. Eguiara y Eguren notes that Murillo Velarde has written favorably of Americans' memories, eloquence, wit, and linguistic fluency (*Prólogos* 164), but has also claimed that in spite of this, and the existence of flourishing academies, colleges, and universities, America has produced nothing of the level of achievement one might expect after two hundred years of literary endeavor. Eguiara y Eguren expresses doubts that the Spanish priest meant to imply that there had been no outstanding minds, especially since he himself, in his *Geographía histórica* of 1752, had extolled the wisdom and writings of Mexicans such as Sor Juana Inés de la Cruz (*Prólogos* 166–67). Here Eguiara y Eguren constructs his argument very carefully, as if seeking to give Murillo Velarde the benefit of the doubt:

Nulli credimus, visis a Murillo tot scriptoribus eorumque plurimis excultissimis, verba sibi excidisse immaturos etiamnum nostratum foetus existimanti. Sed ut nostram de eo ita

scribente sententiam promamus, credimus quidem voluisse
sibi hactenus ab America non prodiisse alicuius auctoris
multa grandia volumina, quae cum Thomasianis, Scoticis,
Suarezianis, Kircherianis, Caramuelianis et similibus certent
atque contendant. Et hoc quidem ut sponte fatemur, sic etiam
credimus argumento non esse acerbae adhuc Minervae nostrae, quod maturitas non a pomorum multitudine iudicanda
sit, sed a dulcedine eorundem et suavitate; nec profecto plurimis etiam elapsis saeculis speramus fore olim, ut ingentibus
et praegrandi numero voluminibus Minerva americana tandem aliquando maturitatis indicem et exemplar datura sit.
(*Prólogos* 167–68)

We cannot at all believe that Murillo, with knowledge of so
many writers and of the most cultivated, should have written that among us no offspring has come to maturation. In
our opinion, what he really wanted to say was that until now
our authors have not produced works to be compared and
to compete, in volume, with those of Saint Thomas, Scotus,
Suárez, Kircher, Caramuel, and others like them. We con-
cede this, without allowing that for this reason our Minerva
is not matured, since it should not be judged by the large
number of its fruits, but by their sweetness and pleasant-
ness; nor do we despair that, with the passage of the centuries, the American Minerva will come to produce notable
books which, by their importance and number, will give a
sign and example of its maturity.

Eguiara y Eguren underscores this statement by reiterating
the fact that the production of books in New Spain has constantly been hindered by the absence of good printing presses
of the kind available in Europe (*Prólogos* 168).[16] He mentions
other practical problems that prevent Mexicans from publish-
ing large numbers of high-quality books. Eguiara y Eguren
argues that the distance separating authors from Europe, and
from the best publishers, prevents them from overseeing the
printing process and making sure that their works finally appear in a more polished form. Eguiara y Eguren himself adds
that the cost of labor and of paper—which must be brought from
Europe—involved in producing books at the few printing presses
actually existing in Mexico is so high that it would astonish a
European who had not visited the New World (*Prólogos* 169–
70). To illustrate this, Eguiara y Eguren describes the problems

that would present themselves if one were to attempt to print an edition of the kind of handwritten multivolume chronicles that had commonly been produced by the various religious orders in America. Citing the example of Fray Antonio de la Calancha's thirty-two-volume *Corónica moralizada del Orden de San Agustín en el Peru* (1638), he remarks:

> quae si Limae procuderentur, opus esset amplius centum triginta mille argenteis uncialibus; quinquaginta vero ut minimum, si edenda in Hispania essent, apud quam nisi pessime cudi non possent, nescientibus scilicet operis et correctoribus europaeis tres illas linguas americanas, queis et hispana libri illi constant. Quibus de causis insignia quidem opera apud Americam lucubrata, vel in angulis delitescunt bibliothecarum, vel fodicata corroasque a tinea perierunt. Accedit, libros editos distrahi praeterquam inter nosmetipsos non posse citra maiora impendia, quorum vitandi causa vix a mexicanis ad peruanos et vicissim volumen transmeat. (*Prólogos* 170)

> [W]ere this work to be printed in Lima it would cost more than one hundred and thirty ounces of silver, and in Spain fifty thousand, at minimum, and, in spite of the considerable expense, the printing would be most wretched, since the European printers and correctors do not know the three American languages, besides Spanish, in which those books are written. From this can be seen the reasons why so many notable works, which have been composed in America, lie hidden in the corners of libraries or have perished, perforated and gnawed by worms. It can be added that the published books cannot be sold among us due to their great expense, as a result of which they hardly circulate between Mexico and Peru, and vice-versa.

Eguiara y Eguren concludes his generous interpretation of Murillo Velarde's remarks about Mexican minds, and his carefully worded revision, by making reference to the opinion of an unnamed friend, who maintains that the Spaniard had actually meant that he had been unable to find an individual who had produced a work of large-scale erudition. The description of this ideal scholar corresponds, significantly, to the image of the omniscient subject of the type of knowledge presented in the genre of the encyclopedia, a form that assumed growing importance in the gathering and presentation of knowledge during the eighteenth century. Eguiara y Eguren paraphrases this interpretation of Murillo Velarde's observation in the following terms: "Murillo scilicet fuisse in optatis masculum apud americanos ingenium aliquod, cui acceptum Minerva referret systema apud litteratos insigne, aut datum publice eruditionis vastissimae documentum, vel quod portento simile haberetur aliud specimen et encyclopediam" (*Prólogos* 171; "That is to say, Murillo wanted there to be some excellent wit among the Americans, to whom Minerva would ascribe some distinguished work, recognized as such by men of letters, or which would be held, like a sign, as an example of encyclopedic knowledge"). This enables Eguiara y Eguren to reintroduce the agency of his catalogue, in the sense that it not only offers a detailed exposition of American wits, but is also proof, in itself, of the triumph of an idealized subject of erudition. Thereby, it fills out the lack that Murillo Velarde is reputed to have observed in New World cultural production (*Prólogos* 171).

The subsequent two prologues (the sixteenth and the seventeenth) carry on the work of providing information that corroborates and supplements the descriptions of books and manuscripts in the catalogue itself. In the sixteenth prologue Eguiara y Eguren provides biographies of two learned Mexican scholars, Pedro de Paz Vasconcelos and Antonio Calderón. He concentrates on conveying the kinds of data of which Europeans could have no knowledge unless they had actually traveled to America. He traces the course of the two scholars' achievements in oratory, poetry, Latin, philosophy, theology, and law, within the educational institutions where they studied and taught. The key factor in their biographies is that neither left to posterity any published trace of their scholarship, Paz Vasconcelos because he was blind, Calderón because he felt that to publish his own work would be an act of intellectual vanity inappropriate to a true Christian (*Prólogos* 177).

In the seventeenth prologue Eguiara y Eguren provides details of the student career of Antonio Lorenzo López Portillo. As an addition to the description of professorial excellence provided in the sixteenth prologue, this section serves to give an indication of the trials involved in the process of a student's pursuit of scholarly excellence in viceregal Mexico. The prologue contains descriptions of the four oral doctoral exams that this student took and passed with flying colors. During the first of these, at a public ceremony at the University of Mexico, in which he was seeking a title in civil and canon law, López Portillo recited from memory the four books of Justinian's *Institutionum,* clarifying any interpretive problems emerging from the text and questions put to him by his examiners (*Prólogos* 178–79). Eguiara y Eguren adds that four years later, in 1754, however, López Portillo would surpass his performance in that first test of his academic skills. First, on May 28, he successfully undertook an oral defense of his knowledge of courses in philosophy and theology (*Prólogos* 180–81). Second, on the morning of June 6, he demonstrated his knowledge of the Decrees of Pope Gregory IX, and of scholarly commentaries about them, successfully handling the questions of professors possessing expertise in canon law (*Prólogos* 181–82). In the afternoon, he showed his understanding and knowledge of civil law, responding to more questions from senior professors. Third, on June 11, he answered more questions and problems of points of law, originating from his reading of the works of Antonio Fabri. Eguiara y Eguren's eyewitness account of these proceedings gives a good indication of the principles of higher education and scholarship that shaped the production of knowledge at this time in the viceroyalty:

> Tandem undecima iunii mane et vespere productioribus moris et confertiori litteratorum hominum multitudine adstante, Antonii Fabri *Opera omnia* undecim voluminibus comprehensa, uno excepto codice Fabriano forensi, prout adpromisserat, tuitus est, detexuit, composuit, non segnius ac praecedentes egerant magistri et doctores, rectore gravissimo clarissimisque antecessoribus Universitatis in omnem partem Antonium moventibus et qua interrogationibus, qua syllogismis, qua longe datis oratione soluta ratiocinationibus (qua etiam methodo praecedentibus diebus pro suo quisque genio usus fuerat) in examen adducentibus subtilissimas Fabri opiniones resque intricantissimas et penitissimas, quas Portillus omnes ad unguem se habere monstravit, responsionibus unicuique datis eruditis et plenis, sive forma, ut dicimus, scholastica sive oratoria, ut se ad dicentium modum aptaret peraeque facilis ac facundus illa methodo atque ista, ut qui familiarem sibi fecerit Marcum Tullium et amoenioris litteraturae auctores, in quibus otia sua collocavit et quietem. (*Prólogos* 182–83)

Finally, on June 11, in the morning and afternoon, for a longer
time, and in the presence of an even larger crowd of men of
letters, he defended, expounded, and commented upon the
complete works of Antonio Fabri, with the exception of his
forensic code, as he had promised, being questioned, no less
energetically than by their predecessors, by the teachers,
doctors, a most venerable rector, and by most renowned professors of the university who, moving through all parts of
Antonio's text, with questions, syllogisms, and with reason-
ings expressed without limitations (a method used by objec-
tors on the preceding days according to their own procedures),
brought under examination the most subtle opinions of Fabri,
and his most involved and most recondite points, finding
that Portillo knew them thoroughly and gave erudite and
complete answers to each one, whether in the form that we
call scholastic, or in that which we call oratorical, adapting
and matching himself to the mode of the speakers, and with
equal facility in one method or the other, as one familiar
with Marcus Tullius and other authors of finer literature, to
the study of whom he devoted his leisure and relaxation.

Eguiara y Eguren notes that the faculty of the university
swiftly resolved to accord López Portillo the titles of doctor
of philosophy, theology, civil and canon law. Stating that he
hopes that the young scholar will soon produce something to
be included in the catalogue of the *Bibliotheca,* Eguiara y Eguren
seeks to establish that a tradition of Mexican literary scholarship is being continued into the future (*Prólogos* 183). Having
consolidated this textual image of Mexican scholarly study and
oral performance, he concludes the seventeenth prologue by
posing a rhetorical question as to whether it can still be argued
that there are neither devoted teachers nor students of letters
in New Spain. At this point, he is ready to move into the final
phase of the construction of the picture of Mexican erudition.
To the representation of universities, libraries, teachers, students, and texts, he will now add a description of the different
sciences, or fields, in which "nostri" (*Prólogos* 186; "our
people") have excelled.

In the eighteenth prologue, Eguiara y Eguren gives an account of the intellectual disciplines in which *criollos* have produced works. First, he covers the area of religious texts, referring
to the commentaries that have been written on the books of
scripture (*Prólogos* 187–90). Within the realm of this supreme

science, he details the different spheres of scholarship in which texts have been written, including works of scholastic (or speculative), mystical, and polemical theology. In addition, he mentions the writings produced in the form of sermons and catechisms.

Having spoken of the queen of the sciences within the traditional ordering of the disciplines, Eguiara y Eguren proceeds to list the other disciplines that the Americans have cultivated. First, he mentions the large bodies of texts written on matters pertaining to the different kinds of law. Second, he notes that a large number of treatises have been published on questions of medicine, and related matters of anatomy, botany, and surgery (*Prólogos* 190–91). In the third place, he states that numerous authors have written texts about the natural history of the Indies and theoretical pieces about problems of farming. Fourth, he notes that many have dedicated much time and effort to mathematics. The fifth discipline he discusses here is philosophy. He describes the work of learned Mexicans who have focused particularly on the key components of the traditional framework of the discipline, specifically Aristotelianism, Thomism, Nominalism, and Jesuit writings in the field. Moving down the hierarchy of the disciplines, he comes to the related spheres of rhetoric, grammar, human letters, and poetry, all of which, he states, have been brilliantly cultivated by large numbers of *criollos,* most specifically by the authors he cites here as examples, Bernardo de Balbuena and Juan Ruiz de Alarcón (*Prólogos* 192). The seventh field covered comprises the texts relating the history of the region and critical writings on questions of politics (*Prólogos* 194).

The eighth and final area he treats is one in which *criollo* scholars have demonstrated learning and skill at least equal to that of their European counterparts. This is the linguistic work that has been undertaken in gathering information about the many and difficult languages spoken by indigenous peoples in America. Eguiara y Eguren emphasizes the degree of erudition and wit that these labors have required, adding that they have yielded knowledge that Europeans have not been able to emulate. He concludes the eighteenth prologue with the following remarks:

Quae sane opuscula quanto ingenio constent, studio atque
labore, nemo non viderit, modo sciat, ut hispanos genitos
in Europa, ita etiam in America natos unum cum lacte a
matribus trahere hispanum idioma, americana vero tam ipsis
peregrina et ignota esse quam europaeis. Enimvero qui animum intenderit ad incondita idiomata pronunciatuque diffi-
cillima et cognitione, maioris scripta illa operae atque negotii
dicet, quam essent plura hebraice, graece, chaldaice et orien-
talibus linguis iam pridem cultissimis concinnata, librorum
ope et insignium magistrorum subsidio. (*Prólogos* 195)

Nobody will fail to see the wit, devotion, and effort that such
works involve, if one only considers that the Spanish, both
those born in Europe and those in America, have learned
the Spanish language at their mothers' breasts, those [lan-
guages] of America being as strange and unknown to them
as any other European tongue. Anybody who focuses his
attention on these confused languages, which are most difficult to pronounce and understand, will have to say that those
writings are of importance and greater works than many of
those composed in Hebrew, Greek, Chaldean, and Oriental languages, which were made to be most cultivated long ago with
the help of books and the collaboration of eminent teachers.

The mention of scholarship in the area of indigenous languages leads Eguiara y Eguren into the final step in the construction of a prefatory framework for the *Bibliotheca*. In the
nineteenth prologue he presents a picture of the culture of indigenous people in America during the period in which a select few
had received formation in Hispanic letters.[17] Here, he actually
makes reference to subjects who are part of an active, contemporary conjuncture, and not just to the cultural production of
their pre-Columbian forebears, which he has incorporated into
the archive of *criollo* (self-)knowledge. Nevertheless, their construction and active participation as legitimate subjects of erudition are represented as processes still to be overseen and
administered by *criollos* within the general project of the construction of a Mexican republic of letters.

Eguiara y Eguren begins by reiterating that the pre-Hispanic
societies were able to communicate their ideas by means of
pictures, a practice that was to be used initially in the practice
of religious confession with Spanish priests (*Prólogos* 196).

He then proceeds to give an overview of texts offering testimony as to the capacities and disposition of indigenous subjects through the process of their education in, and incorporation into, letters. Through reference to the accounts of various ecclesiastical figures, he notes that they tend to surpass their Spanish and *criollo* counterparts in their ability to become proficient in the study and use of Latin and Castilian (*Prólogos* 197). Furthermore, he observes that they are humble, obey their teachers, and are kinder and friendlier to their fellow students than are Spanish youths. Eguiara y Eguren then gives details of the institutions that were set up specifically to provide education for indigenous subjects, although he is less forthcoming about the principles of social control and organization that have determined the activities of these colleges. He places special emphasis upon the work of the most prestigious center, the Colegio de Santa Cruz de Tlatelolco, founded and run by the Franciscans under the auspices of Charles V in the sixteenth century.[18]

The achievements of the Franciscan teachers receive high praise in view of both the results of their teaching and their efforts to preserve the indigenous languages and cultures:

> Nec porro ii oleum et operam perdiderunt elementa litterarum prima tradentes, grammaticam, rhetoricam, dialecticam, physicam et alias liberales artes, quod eas omnes indi citra negotium hauserint et in singulis mire proficerint ac magistris ipsis et institutoribus praeceptores se dederint idiomatis mexicani et Oedipos egerint pro aperiendis scriptas antiquis characteribus gentis historias et pristinarum monumenta rerum mexicanensium. (*Prólogos* 199)

> And good proof that those teachers did not waste time and effort in teaching the rudiments of letters, grammar, rhetoric, dialectics, physics, and other liberal arts, is the facility with which the Indians learned them all, the marvelous advances they made in all, offering themselves at the same time as teachers to their own teachers in the learning of the Mexican languages and acting as Oedipuses in showing how to uncover the histories written in their ancient characters and the records of earlier Mexican matters.

Eguiara y Eguren notes the assistance some of the members of the first generation of natives educated in letters gave to

Sahagún in the composition of his *Diccionario histórico mexicano*. He adds that many others who subsequently learned Spanish and Latin produced translations of Spanish and Latin texts into their own languages, and cooperated with Franciscan fathers on other similar works. Furthermore, many also learned the art of typography and actively participated in the printing of books (*Prólogos* 200).

There would be, however, many more Indians fully versed in the art of letters, Eguiara y Eguren relates, were it not that the colleges for indigenous youths fell into decline over the course of the seventeenth century because of a lack of economic support, and that attempts to revive them have met with failure during his lifetime (*Prólogos* 201). He concludes his description by referring to the successes of many indigenous students in the eighteenth century, achieved in spite of the limited possibilities open to them. First, he notes that there are some, of noble birth, who have acquired a scholarly education, and then gone on to work within ecclesiastical institutions (*Prólogos* 201). Second, he describes the skills developed by Ignacio Antonio de Sandoval in the areas of music and painting. In the third place, Eguiara y Eguren negates some Europeans' claim that all Indians merely pretend to be committed to Catholicism while they continue to practice their traditional mythical beliefs under a veil of secrecy (*Prólogos* 204). In response, he argues that all nations, even those that have fought most aggressively in Europe in defense of the Catholic faith, have included dissenters and heretics among their populations.

In the twentieth prologue, Eguiara y Eguren concludes his presentation of his biobibliographical catalogue by explaining the rationale for the choice of the title of *Bibliotheca Mexicana*. He begins by justifying his delimitation of the scope of the work within the boundaries of what is called "Mexico." Eguiara y Eguren states that this is, first and foremost, a consequence of the fact that Manuel Martí's barbs touched Mexicans specifically (*Prólogos* 205). Second, he argues that he does not feel himself to be adequately qualified to write about literary matters in the other principal territory in colonial Spanish America, that is, the viceroyalty of Peru. He cites the problem of the distance that separates the two regions, remarking that there is very little maritime commerce between them, with the result that he has limited access to texts produced in the South. Eguiara y Eguren then defines the geographical scope of his work:

> BIBLIOTHECAM itaque sistimus MEXICANAM *sive eruditorum historiam virorum, qui in America Boreali nati vel alibi geniti, in ipsam domicilio aut studiis asciti, quavis lingua scripto aliquid tradiderunt, eorum praesertim qui pro fide catholica et pietate amplianda fovendaque, egregie factis et quibusvis scriptis floruere editis aut ineditis.* (*Prólogos* 206)

> Therefore, we have established the *Bibliotheca Mexicana, that is, the history of the erudite men who, having been born in North America or in other places, belong to it by residence or by their studies, and wrote something in any language, and especially those who have achieved eminence through their exceptional accomplishments and through any class of published or unpublished works, directed toward the progress and nurturing of the Catholic faith and piety.*

Eguiara y Eguren notes that he is acting in accordance with the use of "Mexico" as the term by which this northern region is known, although he points out that this involves a misleading metonymical use of the name of its largest and most famous city. He observes that the region as a whole includes places as diverse and as far-flung as the area comprising Caracas and its surroundings, which can be included as part of "Mexico," since it falls within the administrative purview of the diocese of Santo Domingo (*Prólogos* 207). At the same time, he excludes such places as Carolina, Virginia, New England, Louisiana, and Canada, since they are under the rule of other European monarchies, and New Spain has little contact with any of them.

He also includes the contributions of some individuals born in other nations, particularly Spain, arguing that their participation in the history of the cultural life of the viceroyalty is no less the object of Martí's denigrating comments than is that of the *criollos*. In this fashion, he reiterates his defense of a form of pan-Hispanism in such a fashion as to project, simultaneously, the outline of an autonomous *criollo* intellectual subjectivity. Eguiara y Eguren negotiates this Janus-faced identification with both local and imperial frameworks with careful reasoning:

Iam vero cur in Bibliotheca Mexicana et natos apud Americam nostram viros et alibi genitos atque domicilio vel studiis in ipsam ascitos comprehendimus, non una nobis ratio est, nam et alonensis decanus una omnes calumnia impetivit et una eos omnes politica societas et respublica litteraria coniungit, et, quod caput est, hispani in America geniti, ut stirpem et genus ducimus ab hispanis apud Europam natis, ab ipsis itidem litteras primum traximus et doctrinam, cum Universitati mexicanensi, condendae operam dantibus, tum religiosis ordinibus constituendis, fidei iuxta ac pietatis at litterariae quoque rei causa. Aliarum etiam nationum homines, quos vel studia in nostris gymnasiis imbibita vel perpetua aut longa apud nos commoratio civitate donarunt, quibus etiam nominibus nostrates habentur geniti in Hispania permulti, nefas esset dimitere aut minus splendide pertractare. (*Prólogos* 209–10)

More than one reason has moved us to include in the *Bibliotheca Mexicana* both the men born in our America and those who, having been born in other parts, belong to it by residence or by studies. For the dean of Alicante's false accusation attacked all [of us]. All [of us] are united in one political government and in one literary republic and, which is more important, we, the Spaniards born in America, derive our stock and origin from those who were born in Europe, and from them we first learned letters and sciences. It was they who devoted their labors to setting up the University of Mexico and who brought the religious orders, looking to bring us to faith and piety, as well as to the study of letters. It would have been unjust to have silenced or to have less clearly treated the men of other nations who either were educated in our schools or acquired the right of citizenship for having spent an uninterrupted or long period among us.

Eguiara y Eguren overcomes these contradictions in much the same fashion as does Vicente López, by having recourse to the concept of the republic of letters, invoked as a utopian ideal that binds humanists across geographical boundaries. Informing these remarks are the ideology of humanist universalism and Eguiara y Eguren's belief that its structures and principles are so all-embracing that they will afford a position for the subjects of any "nation" within them, precluding the notion of some radical break with the infrastructure of Spanish empire.

Finally, he carefully outlines one more feature pertaining to the demarcation of subjectivity in the *Bibliotheca,* explaining what he means when he specifies the *natio* or *patria* of each individual. The first of these nomenclatures appears to move somewhere between the Latin sense of "genus," "race" or "people" and the emergent idea of the subject of the European nation-states:

> Nationem scriptorum et patriam, si quidem fieri poterit, indicabimus, quam multoties praeteritam faciemus, diligentiae nostrae subductam. Mexicanos natione quos legeris, scito hispanos esse in America natos, nisi conceptis verbis expressum videris ab indis parentibus illos esse procreatos, ut propterea mirum tibi non esse debeat, apud BIBLIOTHECAM nostram mexicanos natione dici hos ipsos, qui in aliis bibliothecis hispanis dicuntur. Utrumque enim e vero credas. Hispani enim sunt, si genus spectes et sanguinem, quod hispanis genitoribus usi, et insimul mexicani natione, quippe natale solum Mexicum habeant aut mexiceam Americam. (*Prólogos* 211–12)

> Whenever possible, we have indicated the nation and homeland of the writers, but in many cases we had to omit it because it did not come to our notice. It should be known that those whom we note as being of the Mexican nation are those who were born in America, unless we expressly say that they are the children of Indian parents, for which reason you should not be surprised that in our catalogue we call Mexican some who in other catalogues are called Spanish. For both criteria are true. For they are Spanish, if one bears in mind their race and blood, since their parents were Spanish, and of the Mexican nation, for having been born on the soil of Mexico or of Mexican America.

Having dealt with the questions of geographical, cultural, and racial identity, Eguiara y Eguren proceeds to address more explicitly philological or structural concerns. He anticipates that three kinds of criticisms will be made of the *Bibliotheca.* First, he states that he will be faulted for having included data about unpublished manuscripts in addition to the information he gives about published works (*Prólogos* 212). In the second place, he feels that he will be criticized for having included the names of minor authors. Third, he believes that some will argue that an unnecessarily large amount of information has been provided about the religious background and affiliations of the individuals mentioned.

Eguiara y Eguren responds to the first possible objection by stating that in giving the names of manuscripts he is only following the example of European catalogues of the writers and works of nations, religious orders, and other kinds of institutions. In addressing the second criticism, that he has included works and authors of little importance, he argues that even in the most apparently inconsequential books one can find something intriguing or of historical significance (*Prólogos* 216).

Addressing the third problem, Eguiara y Eguren repeats the argument that the most prestigious catalogues written up to this point have already set a precedent of providing biographical information about the writers included in them (*Prólogos* 217). In addition, he reiterates the topic of the state of ignorance in which many Europeans exist with regard to matters concerning America, exemplified for him in the remarks made by Martí. In view of the large body of false information published in Europe about the viceroyalties, which have been depicted as places characterized by a geographical and climatic environment inimical to the successful cultivation and dissemination of letters, Eguiara y Eguren argues that it is even more necessary for him to provide fuller biographical information about the writers mentioned (*Prólogos* 218).

To conclude this discussion of the dynamics that have surrounded the composition of the catalogue, Eguiara y Eguren stresses the fact that it is a work in progress. He begins by describing the problems that have prevented him from producing a more complete work. In the first place, he cites the fact that he was restricted in the amount of time he could devote to the task by ill health and his obligation to continue his activities in other spheres (*Prólogos* 222). Second, he reiterates his complaint that many manuscripts have been lost as the result of the little effort that has been made to preserve them, and of the constant shortages of paper that have prevented many from being published in book form. Third, he states that many archives and libraries have lost much of their holdings, after being either ransacked or damaged by fire (*Prólogos* 223). He closes by making a call to his readers to assist him in overcoming these adverse circumstances by corresponding with him, and sending him information about authors and works he may have omitted from the catalogue as it stands at the moment of the publication of its first volume. Eguiara y Eguren writes:

> Sed priusquam hinc abeamus, eruditos nostros rogatos volumus suum ut quisque in opus commune symbolum dignetur afferre, certos nos de iis facientes opusculis, editis aut ineditis, quae vel apud se habent vel alcicubi esse aut aliquando fuisse certo dignoverint, queis una cum auctoribus suis opportuna subsellia dabimus, eorum a quibus id officii receperimus, ut par est, memores, grati adversus ipsos animi significatione palam exhibita, prout hactenus fecimus, iis praesertim qui a nobis per litteras requisiti, suis nos syllabis sunt dignati, passim commemoratis. (*Prólogos* 224)

> But, before finishing, we want to ask all learned persons to deign to bring their contribution to this labor by communicating to us information about those little works, published and unpublished, that they might have in their possession or might know to exist or to have existed in other places, with the certainty that we will find a place for them in this work and that, as is only right, we will acknowledge those who have done us such a favor, showing them our gratitude publicly, as we have continually done up until now, especially to those who, having been asked by us in letters, did not disdain to favor us with their recollections.

In this fashion, Eguiara y Eguren identifies the task of cataloguing the production of *criollo* letters as a continuing project, ever unfolding into the future. Although he is firmly rooted in the intellectual framework of scholasticism, placing emphasis on established texts over rationalizing impulses toward the demystification of their authority, he haltingly sketches the position of an autonomous *criollo* subject-in-process, straddling the principal educational institution of the Spanish Crown in Mexico—the Real y Pontificia Universidad de México—and the still unclear contours of a Mexican civil society, evoked in terms of Eguiara y Eguren's appeal to possible collaborators for his project and to the eventual readers of his text. The call to future assistance, coupled with the acknowledgment of the impossibility of textual finitude, indicates his location between two intellectual paradigms as he crystallizes the logic of a *criollo* origin and the concept of an archive of great texts, authors, and institutions dedicated to the reconstruction of the genealogy of that origin. As archivist, Eguiara y Eguren thus sifts through the texts of the past and fashions them into an object, a ground, on the basis of which a form of *criollo* subjectivity will project, move, and assume its shape.

Chapter Three

The Fragmentary Archive

The Catalogue of the Bibliotheca Mexicana

The *Aprilis Dialogus* and other prologues to the *Bibliotheca Mexicana* serve to ground the position of the *criollo* subject, and its knowledge. In both their formal organization and their thematics, they mobilize the contradictions that structure the thought of that subject. While they serve to posit the locus of its theoretical autonomy and organicity, they simultaneously demonstrate its investment in, and tension with, the semiotic matrices of indigenous, *mestizo,* and Spanish cultures. The catalogue itself constitutes an attempt to impose a totalizing order over such contradictions. Nevertheless, in its very logic and structure it tends to reproduce, and exacerbate, the very same contradictions in the body of knowledge it presents.

The focus of the text now turns exclusively to the cultural and intellectual history of the regions comprising New Spain since the Conquest. While in the earlier, supplementary, parts of the work, a certain heterogeneity was maintained—particularly, in the separation of the discussions of indigenous and Hispanic cultural production into different prologues—there is now a concern to gather these conflicting elements together into a cohesive, organic whole. Organized in alphabetical order, the catalogue is an attempt to present information about all the most important educational institutions and individual missionaries, poets, and scholars in the history of the viceroyalty of New Spain.[1] Taken as a whole, its main project is to depict the material and discursive workings of humanist and ecclesiastical culture, and the ordered, rational civilization they are held to have produced in the region over the course of more than two centuries. In the labor of synthesizing the often disparate aspects of this matrix, one can discern again the motion and mutations

86

of a subject moving between a series of contradictions and discontinuities in the face of which it seeks to establish an order, both in its corpus of knowledge and in its own position as gatherer and presenter of that knowledge. At the same time, the very unfinished state in which the catalogue was published serves to underline the incompleteness and flux that characterizes the structure and work of the *criollo* subject of knowledge.

In keeping with the incomplete quality of the *Bibliotheca Mexicana,* I will not attempt an exhaustive analysis of the published parts of the catalogue—letters A through C—but will focus on certain lines of narrative that organize the project, and the problems they set in motion. The first recurrent feature of the *Bibliotheca* comprises the reconstructions of the histories of the viceroyalty's institutions of higher education. As a result of the truncation of the project, only the University of Mexico is described in detail (Eguiara y Eguren, *Bibliotheca* 3: 1–11). The second principal component is composed of the descriptions of the lives and literary and scholarly works of individuals who have made significant contributions to the history of the viceroyalty. These individuals can, in turn, be grouped in a series of fields that have importance for the cultural history of the Conquest and post-Conquest.

The first group is made up of explorers, such as Columbus, and the principal agents in the conquest of native peoples and foundation of Mexico City, most notably Cortés. A second criterion for the inclusion of certain individuals pertains to their achievements in a variety of areas of scholarship, most particularly theology, law, philosophy, the natural sciences, classical languages and literatures, and various native languages of the regions of the viceroyalty. The third rationale for inclusion stems from the production of eloquent works in Latin or Spanish, primarily poems and sermons, by canonized writers such as Bernardo de Balbuena. The fourth main group that merits inclusion in the *Bibliotheca* is composed of missionaries, of various orders, who played significant roles in the conversion of different native peoples to Catholicism, particularly in the most remote and inhospitable regions on the northernmost fringes of the viceroyalty, or on islands such as the Philippines. Although each of these groups is more or less conceptually discrete, the entries devoted to many of the individuals described are not confined to a single category. Most particularly, in the entries that deal predominantly with the third and fourth areas of endeavor, there are frequently overlaps, with the information presented under the purview of descriptions of great labors and works in the different areas of knowledge.

The project of fitting such disparate elements into a coherent, organic scheme leads Eguiara y Eguren into a dialectic of contradiction and projected resolution. The key factors in the construction of projected forms of association between the different components will be twofold: the descriptions of the histories and power of institutions; and the narrative of the civilizing and unifying effects of the discourses of literary humanism and Catholicism.

Subject and Institutionality

In apparent contradiction with the alphabetical logic of the organization of the *Bibliotheca,* the first entry in the catalogue is devoted to the Real y Pontificia Universidad de México. Eguiara y Eguren justifies opening with a description of the university's history by its status as the *alma mater* of many of the authors included in the catalogue (*Bibliotheca* 3: 1). Specifically, he accords primary importance to this institution as the central agent in the dissemination of civilizing and unifying knowledge and skills throughout the history of the viceroyalty. In foregrounding the descriptions of outstanding individuals in the cultural history of New Spain with an account of the university's history and workings, Eguiara y Eguren explicitly acknowledges and emphasizes the embeddedness of *criollo* intellectual subjectivity in the mechanisms of the pedagogic infrastructure of the viceregal order. That is, the position of the *criollo* subject of knowledge is not one of autonomy and self-sufficiency, but is firmly situated within an institutional mechanism, the disciplinary structure and hierarchy of which condition and delimit the range of statements that subject can make.[2]

Eguiara y Eguren's re-creation of the university's beginnings opens with a brief account of the achievements of Hernán Cortés in the pacification of various native peoples and foundation of the new city of Mexico on the site of Tenochtitlan. Notably, only summary reference is made to the violence and destruction carried out in these actions (Eguiara y Eguren, *Bibliotheca* 3: 1–2). Eguiara y Eguren focuses, rather, on the diligent efforts made by Cortés and his principal officers in seeking to establish not only churches to facilitate the conversion of natives to Catholicism, but also educational institutions that would educate people of all nations in all the most important disciplines (*Bibliotheca* 3: 2). He notes that Cortés called for the construction of a university, a request that was fulfilled in 1553, after Charles V had signed a *cédula* in 1551 mandating the action (*Bibliotheca* 3: 204–05).

Eguiara y Eguren's relation of the circumstances surrounding the early history of the university activates the movement of the *criollo* subject of knowledge in the direction of identifications with the foundational moment represented in the actions of the *conquistadores* and the idealized period of the reign of Charles V. In this fashion, *criollo* subjectivity is able to move between the positions of its foundational conquering generation and the administrative order of the Spanish Crown, overriding the tensions between the two parties.[3] In this fashion, a genealogy is constructed in which *criollos* are to be regarded as the legitimate heirs of the order established by the *conquistadores* as one of the components of the Spanish empire in the period of its apogee.

Eguiara y Eguren then proceeds to delineate the important work of the university in promoting knowledge in a variety of disciplines and in maintaining order over a vast space and its heterogeneous population. He notes that its curriculum was structured to follow closely the models of the two most prestigious centers of learning in Spain, the universities of Salamanca and Alcalá de Henares (*Bibliotheca* 3: 205). In addition, he cites two praiseworthy descriptions of the teaching and scholarship carried out at the university once it was established. One of these is a brief statement of admiration for the minds of Americans made by a German Jesuit named Franz Xavier Scherer (*Bibliotheca* 3: 207–08). The more important account is that which Eguiara y Eguren cites and paraphrases from the dialogues of Francisco Cervantes de Salazar, one of the earliest educators at the Real y Pontificia Universidad de México, of significance primarily as a professor of rhetoric.[4] As such, he represents an important source for Eguiara y Eguren in the labor of chronicling the existence of a culture of eloquence and philology in the viceroyalty, a tradition that, by the mid-seventeenth century, stretched over a period of two hundred years. Of particular importance is a passage in which the characters Gutiérrez and Mesa comment about the role of the university in fostering the dissemination of both secular learning and Christian doctrine:

> GU. . . .Verum quod est potius, quodque Academiam vere nobilitat, quales habet Institutores? ME. Optimos. GU. Non de probitate rogo, sed de doctrina, et docendi dexteritate. ME. Industrios et in omni scientia versatissimos: vis dicam? Minime vulgares, et quales paucos habet Hispania. GU. Ecquis fuit reitantae author? ME. Caesar cujus auspiciis et ductu multa sunt ubique terrarum praeclare gesta. GU. Quibus immunitatibus et privilegiis? ME. Maximis et multis, et in omnibus a Salmaticensibus nihilo dissimilibus. GU. Multo pluribus, ac si fieri posset, maioribus digni sunt, qui est tam procul a Patria docent, et qui in tanta opulentia, et Parentum deliciis discunt. ME. Quinpotius, quod dicere debuisses, eo utrique honore afficiendi sunt, quod novum Orbem sapientiae fulgore, ignorantiae nebula, qua obscurabatur, primi omnium liberent, et Indos in fide cultuque Dei sic confirment, ut ad posteros semper firmior derivetur integritas. (Quoted in Eguiara y Eguren, *Bibliotheca* 3: 4)

> Gutiérrez: . . . But what is more to the point, and which really ennobles the university, what teachers does it have?

> Mesa: The best.

> Gutiérrez: I am not inquiring as to their quality but to their doctrine and ability in teaching.

> Mesa: Skilled and very well versed in all sciences, and, what is more, not at all ordinary and few of the like Spain has.

> Gutiérrez: And who was the author of such a great undertaking?

> Mesa: Caesar [Charles V], under whose favor and command many undertakings have been gloriously realized throughout the globe.

> Gutiérrez: With which immunities and privileges?

> Mesa: Great ones and many of them, no different from all those of that of Salamanca.

> Gutiérrez: They are worthy of many more and greater ones if possible, they who proffer teaching so far from their home-

land just as those who receive it amid so much good and
with the happiness of their parents.

Mesa: Still more you ought to have said that one and the
other must be raised up with more honor for being the first
who, with the gleam of wisdom, will free the New World
from the mist of ignorance in which it was shrouded and in
such a way that the Indians might be confirmed in the faith
and worship of God, and Catholicism might be forever transmitted to future generations, and with greater firmness.[5]

The passage emphasizes the important role to be played not
only by the labor of evangelization, but also by educational institutions in the process of the consolidation of a unified political and social order. Eguiara y Eguren interprets the writings
of Cervantes de Salazar and Scherer as utopian projections of
what the university would be in its ideal state. This enables him
then to present his *Bibliotheca* as cataloguing the evidence that
this utopia construct has been transformed into reality over the
course of two centuries. At the same time, the *Bibliotheca* is
itself described as one of the fruits of the scholarly regime set
in motion at the university:

> Ast quoniam, et quae CERVANTES haud vanus sibi vates pol-
> licitus fuerat, et quae SCHERER partim attestatur, et partim
> optat, bono a nobis in lumine collocanda veniunt in Biblio-
> theca nostra; nunc in Academia, quae eiusdem caput et prin-
> cipium agit, morati, praecipua huius ornamenta persequamur
> dicendo, e quibus Litteraria Americae nostrae Respublica
> mirabiles certe fructus accepit. (*Bibliotheca* 3: 5)

> Taking into account, then, that which Cervantes had not
> dreamed in vain and of which Scherer gives account and
> forecasts, it seemed good to us to give it a full and lumi-
> nous place in our *Bibliotheca*. Now, focusing on the uni-
> versity, which is the first letter and beginning of the latter
> [the *Bibliotheca*], let us continue and speak of its main val-
> ues, from which the republic of letters has harvested admi-
> rable fruits.

The university is thus evoked as the site that has facilitated
the construction of the position of the *criollo* scholar as the
subject of diverse disciplines of knowledge, simultaneously
articulating each and ordering the corpus as a whole. Eguiara

y Eguren lists the disciplines taught at the university, foremost among them being grammar, rhetoric, philosophy, mathematics, canon and civil law, theology, and languages. Notably, he devotes most space to the last of these fields, describing the great labor that has been undertaken by successive generations in gathering and maintaining knowledge of the principal native languages. Eguiara y Eguren emphasizes the importance of this scholarship, which is focused primarily on Nahuatl and Otomi, primarily for the role it has played in the task of evangelizing native peoples:

> Quod vero ad Idiomata spectat, sapientissime constitutum a Maioribus nostris est, ut quandoquidem tam sunt multa in hisce Regionibus, Hispanis etiam in eis natis ignota, ut pro illis discendis non modo egregia opus sit diligentia, sed industriis etiam Magistris: tamque earumdem usus linguarum necessarius, quamqui maxime ad Indos instruendos in Fide, et in omnibus Christianis juxta ac politicis disciplinis educandis: prudentissime inquam a nostris conditoribus suit provisum, ut eorum vice Antecessorum qui in Europae Academiis Sacras Linguas profitentur, in nostra gemini instituerentur pro duabus tradendis, quae communius in America nostra tenent, et quodam gaudent veluti principatu, *Mexicana,* ut vocantur, et *Othomia.* Queis factum est omnibus, ut viginti tres Antecessores suam quotidie spartam Academicis in Gymnasiis adornent, totidem praefecti Suggestibus, e quibus frequentissimis auditoribus dictando explicandoque doctrinas instillant, quae et ipsis, et publico bono sunt prosuturae. (*Bibliotheca* 3: 5–6)

> As for languages, with all wisdom it was ordered by our forefathers that, since in these regions so many languages are spoken, unknown even by the Spaniards born here, that not only does it require singular diligence to learn them, but also skilled teachers, and as they were so necessary for their common usage just as for the instruction of the Indians in the Faith and in all forms of Christian politics, most prudently our founders established that just as in the universities of Europe there are teachers devoted to the sacred languages, there would be instituted two who would teach those which are most commonly spoken in our America and which are preeminent, Mexican, as they say, and Otomi. With all this done, daily twenty-three teachers illuminate their discipline

in the halls of the university, all seated on their podia, from which they communicate, dictating and explaining, to their large audiences, the learning which is of use to themselves and to the public good.

In this fashion Eguiara y Eguren reaffirms the important role played by the university in helping to consolidate the imperial Spanish project of a society unified by a political order and faith in a single religion. Nevertheless, he has also built into his account a role for these indigenous languages as themselves constituting a basis for association, both between their native speakers and, for Mexican scholars, as objects of knowledge endowed with a prestige equal to that of the ancient languages taught in European universities. Although it is not explicitly stated, within the overall scheme of the work it seems logical to deduce that the scholars described are, for the most part, *criollos*. Their erudition and skills as linguistic mediators serve, within the framework of the university's overall mission, to consolidate the association of the different segments of the population of the viceroyalty, maintaining, but at the same time overcoming, the linguistic diversity of the region.

This vision of the unifying function of the university and of learning in the viceroyalty is further developed in Eguiara y Eguren's description of its role in the formation of the region's youth. He observes that it draws individuals not just from Mexico City itself, but from all parts of New Spain:

> Ut tamen Mater est alma Universitas Mexicana, quae cum prope adstantes, in Urbeque de gentes primaria filios, uberibus admovet, tum etiam longe positis, et alibi Civitatum, imo Regnorum domicilio gaudentibus lac Scientarum propinat, mediis scilicet Alumnis strenuis; mirum plane est quanta grandescat sobole, hominumque doctissimorum numero. (*Bibliotheca* 3: 6)

> But since the University of Mexico is the *alma mater,* just as it invites the inhabitants of the capital city and those from nearby, in the same fashion it also offers the milk of wisdom to those from far away and the inhabitants of other towns and from the farthest corners of the kingdom, when they have become advanced in studies; and it is a thing of admiration to see with how many people it is aggrandized and with how many most wise men.

The university is thus seen as one of the key components of the *ciudad letrada,* an organizing center that brings order to the dispersion of the region's population, stabilizing its heterogeneity within a single form of association. The discursive agency producing that form of association is the program of humanistic education and learning, and the generations of scholars who have come together to teach the viceroyalty's youth and devote themselves to study. Together, they are the key factors in the formation of the *criollo* intellectual subject, the material and discursive matrices out of which that subject's theorized position as organizing center has been articulated.

Narratives of Foundation: Explorers and *Conquistadores*

Eguiara y Eguren emphasizes the important founding role played by the Mexican *conquistadores,* first and foremost by Hernán Cortés, in the planning and establishment of a university in the reconstructed metropolis. This description of *conquistador* agency forms part of an unfolding narrative in which the *Bibliotheca* affirms and emphasizes the relation between the *criollo* subject of the mid-eighteenth century and the first generations of explorers, warriors, and settlers. The text articulates a discourse of legitimacy of *criollo* interests and rights to participate in the process of the determination and regulation of its inhabitants' affairs. This discourse is developed further in the entries accorded to Christopher Columbus and to important historical participants in the dynamics of conquest and colonization, particularly Bartolomé de las Casas, all of whom are fitted into the archive of *criollo* knowledge.[6]

The biography and descriptions of published works that constitute the entry on Columbus are written in an admiring tone. The section relates the navigator's achievements in discovering the Caribbean islands and the tribulations he underwent in the wake of the discovery (*Bibliotheca* 3: 492–500). Most significant is the manner in which the explorer is incorporated into the scheme of Mexican semiosis in the opening sentence of the entry: "D. CHRISTOPHORUS COLUMBUS, Natione Italus, Patria Genuensis, Novi Orbis detectione, quem ab Hispaniola auspicatus est Insula, Mexicanus jure, si quis alius, dicendus, scriptis quoque in America nostra Litteris, per utrumque, qua late porrigitur, Orbem notissimus est" (*Bibliotheca* 3: 492; "Don Christopher Columbus, Italian by birth, whose homeland is Genoa, for the discovery of the New World, which he began from the island of Hispaniola, ought, by right, to be called Mexican like no other, and for the letters written in our America, which are most famous throughout the extension of both worlds").

The text becomes refocused here on the need to reconstruct another part of its origins, a starting point for the *criollo* archive and a ground for the subject ordering it. Columbus is an important component of this edifice to the extent that he is seen to combine the skills of explorer with the verbal arts of the literary humanist, both of which are seen as possible agents in the task of binding together the heterogeneous range of spaces and peoples that make up the world. In the same vein, he is eulogized for having opened up the continent of America to the unifying labors of Christian missionaries (*Bibliotheca* 3: 492). Specifically, he is identified as "Mexican" for the action of discovering the New World and for the texts he wrote during his time there. Represented thus as an individual articulating various forms of agencies that produce unifying order and mastery, Columbus is fashioned into a model for a logic of association now oriented around *criollo* intellectual subjectivity. In addition, with regard to the dominant paradigm of Castilian subjectivity within the history of early modern Spain, the explorer's position as a peripheral subject (i.e., one not born in Spain) adds to his relevance to attempts to establish a locus for *criollo* intellectual culture and thought with respect to Old World authority.[7]

Similarly interesting is the entry that Eguiara y Eguren devotes to Bartolomé de las Casas (*Bibliotheca* 3: 363–77). The illustrious friar is, like Columbus, incorporated into the scheme of the *criollo* archive, in spite of his having been born in Spain, for his lengthy actions in defense of the native inhabitants of the New World and for his work as a clergyman. The catalogue describes him as "an adornment of our America" ("Americae nostrae ornamentum"; *Bibliotheca* 3: 363). What is most notable here is not only the identification, and appropriation, of Las Casas as a glorious figure who brings prestige to America, but also the use of the first-person-plural possessive adjective to modify the name of the continent. In the section devoted to Las Casas, this expression, made most famous much later by José Martí, is used even more repeatedly than in other parts of the work.[8] In addition, the first-person-plural possessive adjective is used in the entry to classify the native peoples of New Spain and the region of Chiapas (*Bibliotheca* 3: 365; 366). The insistence on the possessive forms in the section indicates the importance assigned by Eguiara y Eguren and his collaborators to the task of situating Las Casas within the mechanisms of the *criollo* archive.

Again the logic informing the lengthy defense of this participant in the early history of the conquest and colonization of America is bound up with the process of reconstructing origins for a genealogy of *criollo* agency and intellectual subjectivity. There are two decisive moments in the narrative composed out of the details of Las Casas's life. First, the text emphasizes the belief that he was one of the first twelve priests brought to the island of Hispaniola to see to the conversion of its native inhabitants. Particularly significant is Eguiara y Eguren's insistence on the credibility of this idea, in the face of some who have questioned it: "[a]nd if some are opposed to this idea, we nevertheless have the support of common opinion, that he was one of the first clergymen who emigrated to those first parts of our America" ("Cui et si alii placito reffragentur, collatitia tamen omnes tenent suffragatione, e primis Nostrum fuisse Praesbyteris in primatem illam Americam commigrantibus"; *Bibliotheca* 3: 364). The recuperation of Las Casas as origin is thus bound up with the discourse of public opinion, an important component of the matrices of association.

The second key moment in the narrative of Las Casas's life is the description of the issues and circumstances pertaining to his famous debate at the Spanish court with the renowned scholar Juan Ginés de Sepúlveda. The rationale developed by Sepúlveda to justify the excesses carried out by many Spaniards against native American peoples is described as being eloquent and well articulated (Eguiara y Eguren, *Bibliotheca* 3: 366). Nevertheless, Las Casas is presented as the victor in the polemic, overcoming his adversary through both his command of discourse and the ethical justness of his argument:

Evocatos inter Doctores adfuit Joannes Genesius Sepulveda Cordubensis, Theologus, et Caesari a Chronicis, vir ab eruditione, doctrina, et eloquentia maximi habitus, Antagonistae Nostri partes acturus, qui quamvis extra rationis orbitam a saevis non paucis Hispanis nullus ipse decurrentia excussaret inique gesta; duriuscula tamen emollire aggressus et propugnare viva tunc voce, deinceps etiam scriptis datis, repulsam jure passus est, Nostro ex adverso illum Libris etiam et verbis quatiente, iterumque atque iterum arietante Theoremata aequitati et humanitati non admodum consentanea. (*Bibliotheca* 3: 366)

Among the doctors summoned to combat the arguments of our man was Juan Ginés de Sepúlveda, a Cordoban, the Emperor's chronicler, a man of the highest quality in his erudition, doctrine, and eloquence, and although neither he nor anyone else could, except beyond all reason, excuse the deeds unfairly perpetrated by a few cruel Spaniards, he nevertheless made a great effort to reduce them to small things, and defended these things with such a lively voice as he did later in writing; but he was extended the rebuff that by rights was merited by our combatant [who], repeatedly striking and battering [him] with his books and words, [showed that his arguments] were not in agreement with the basic ideals of equality and humanity.

Las Casas, his position within the *criollo* archive reaffirmed through the use of the first-person-plural possessive adjective, is portrayed as overcoming one of Spain's greatest logicians and scholars of the sixteenth century through his own mastery of the arts of oral and written discourse. His skilled and ethically principled argumentation in defense of the inhabitants of the New World is thus reconstructed as a source of authority, not just for Europeans, but also for the populations of the American viceroyalties in the eighteenth century. Furthermore, Las Casas's ambivalent position with regard to the inconsistent workings of Spanish imperial policy, and the frequent abuse of it by European adventurers in the New World, uniquely situates him, in similar fashion to Columbus, as a model of subjectivity for *criollos* like Eguiara y Eguren, seeking to establish a locus for themselves with respect to peninsular matrices of intellectual and political authority.

Scholars and Poets

The greater part of the catalogue of the *Bibliotheca Mexicana* is given over to biobibliographical accounts of individuals noted for their contributions to poetry and different scholarly and scientific disciplines. Since the published section covers only first names beginning with the first three letters of the alphabet, many outstanding writers and scholars, most notably Sor Juana Inés de la Cruz, are not discussed in any detail. Nevertheless, Eguiara y Eguren and his collaborators were able to gather and present detailed information about some of the most celebrated figures in the intellectual history of New Spain. I will focus here on the entries accorded to two of those individuals: Bernardo de Balbuena and Carlos de Sigüenza y Góngora.

Born near Toledo, Spain, Bernardo de Balbuena is best known as the author of the *Grandeza mexicana,* an important poem celebrating Mexico City. The catalogue is careful to emphasize that, although Balbuena was born in Spain, he received the most important elements of his higher education in Mexico City, a detail that had been omitted from other accounts of his life and career (Eguiara y Eguren, *Bibliotheca* 3: 434–35). The entry praises the lucid depiction of the viceregal capital Balbuena presents in the *Grandeza mexicana,* and the pleasing style in which the poem is written, noting that it is the work of someone who had taken care and time to observe the city in all its detail (*Bibliotheca* 3: 435). Implicit in the eulogy of Balbuena's attention to Mexican space and culture is another criticism of the ignorance of Spaniards such as Martí with regard to America. Significantly, the praise of Balbuena's eloquence and of the organic representation of Mexico City offered in the poem is followed by a passage justifying the length of the comments devoted to its author:

> Longius forsan in hisce morati videbimur cuiquam, nisi duo quae subdimus advertenti: alterum, e re nostra esse eximium nobis hominem vindicare, quem Collegia nostra instituerint atque Gymnasia: alterum, oportere ejus itidem gloriam aperire omnem, etiam a juventute hausta, qui nostratum palam aperiedis dotibus vigilavit. Nec porro ipse Oratoria minus floruit laude, quam poetica, omnigenaque spectabilis doctrina Ecclesiastem egit insignem. (*Bibliotheca* 3: 435)

> Perhaps someone may consider that we have spent too long
> looking at these things, unless we present two reasons to
> him who reproaches us: one, to claim as one of our own an
> exceptional man, educated in our colleges and academies;
> and another, that it is right to reveal all the glory of that man
> who, since his youth, had sought to make known the gifts
> of our ancestors. Moreover, he was no less praised for flour-
> ishing in oratory than he was in poetry, and thanks to his
> broad erudition he was a very lucid and distinguished
> preacher.

Thus, Balbuena is included within the framework of the
criollo archive on two grounds. First, he is represented as having
achieved his great abilities as a result of his education in the
humanities, philosophy, and education. Second, his *Grandeza
mexicana* constitutes one of the first accounts of the achievements of the inhabitants of Mexico City in a variety of fields
of culture, most notably, architecture, education, government,
poetry, and scholarship.

One of the lengthiest entries in the catalogue is that devoted
to Carlos de Sigüenza y Góngora. This seventeenth-century
scholar assumes importance in the *Bibliotheca* primarily for
his achievements in poetry and multiple academic disciplines.
The section devoted to Sigüenza opens with the statement that
more than any other inhabitant of Mexico City, he is deserv-
ing of inclusion in the archive of his birthplace: "Don Carlos
de Sigüenza y Góngora, of the Mexican nation and homeland,
who is as well-deserving of the latter as anyone" ("D. CAROLUS
DE SIGUENZA ET GONGORA, Natione Mexicanus et Patria,
si quis illus, benemeritus de ipsa"; *Bibliotheca* 3: 470).[9]

Sigüenza constitutes a second key component in the reconstructed narrative of *criollo* intellectual subjectivity. First, he
is notable to the extent that his fame as a scholar extended
beyond New Spain into various other parts of continental Europe (*Bibliotheca* 3: 470). He corresponded, debated, and shared
information with such European scholars as Gemelli Carrera
and Eusebio Kino (*Bibliotheca* 3: 472). His reputation was such
that he was invited by the king of France to visit his court (3:
470–71). Second, his credentials as intellectual and patriot are
further enhanced, moreover, in the catalogue's account, by the
fact that he elected to continue working in the service of his

homeland. Remaining in Mexico, he was given the position
of Royal Cosmographer and assumed the role of official chronicler of affairs in the viceroyalty (3: 471). The description carefully positions Sigüenza as a figure who established for himself
a prestige that enabled him to achieve recognition not only from
the Spanish Crown but also from other sources of European
authority.

In addition, the accounts of Sigüenza's exploits in poetry,
and in various scholarly and scientific fields, consolidate his
reconstruction as a model for *criollo* intellectual subjectivity
and the task of synthesizing the heterogeneous components of
viceregal space and culture within a single body of knowledge.
First, his intellectual precocity, manifested in his composition,
at the age of seventeen, of the poem *Primavera indiana* (Eguiara
y Eguren, *Bibliotheca* 3: 470). In this work Eguiara y Eguren
finds a key contribution to the elaboration of the matrix of *criollo*
association shaped through the cult of the Virgin of Guadalupe.
Second, the catalogue relates the respect enjoyed by Sigüenza
among Mexican and European scholars alike for his knowledge
and work in the areas of theology, canon law, history, mathematics, and astronomy (*Bibliotheca* 3: 470; 472; 477).

Although the *Bibliotheca* includes a detailed overview of
Sigüenza's work in each of these areas, most attention is
accorded to his endeavors in the fields of Mexican history
and geography. Of the greatest significance in the discipline
of history are Sigüenza's studies of the civilizations and cultures
of pre-Hispanic peoples. The catalogue describes admiringly
the diligence and skill with which he gathered, translated, and
explained the hieroglyphics of ancient Nahuatl texts:

> Porro Americae cruendis antiquitatibus deditus, priscorum
> monumenta Indorum diligentissime conquisita, evolvit, et
> qua erat justissima Critica, Historiarumque accurata et multa
> lectione, revocavit ad trutinam, atque in Libros a se conditos
> varios multosque traduxit, quibus abdita et offusa caligine
> in Solem tradidit et meridiem. His conficiendis Idioma imbi-
> berat Mexicanum, et quae OEdipo eget ingenisissimo, Scien-
> tiam penitissime calluit Hyeroglificorum, Characterum, et
> Imaginum, queis Septentrionalis Americae incolae litterarum
> vice utebantur, resque ab usque ipsarum prima in hunc Orbem
> trajectione celebriores memoriae prodiderant. (*Bibliotheca*
> 3: 471)

Moreover, devoted to the study of the antiquities of America, once he had obtained with the greatest diligence the records of the ancient Indians, he studied them, and with the most rigorous criticism and assiduous readings of their histories, he submitted them to calm judgment, and translated them into various and many books, in which he brought hidden and concealed things into the midday light. In order to compose these [works] he had learned the Mexican language and the science needed by a most ingenious Oedipus, that is, to know thoroughly the hieroglyphs, characters, and images which the inhabitants of North America used as letters, in order to convey their things and record the most famous of them from their first steps in this region.

Sigüenza is celebrated for having realized a vast labor of cultural archaeology in recuperating many of the ancient Mexicans' texts and rendering them comprehensible. He is held to have reconstructed a body of texts that merit consideration as objects of knowledge. This is clearly identified as a *criollo* undertaking when Sigüenza's scholarly care and diligence are juxtaposed with the earlier actions of *conquistadores* and friars in destroying many pictographic texts during the initial period of conquest and evangelization, actions that the catalogue attributes to ignorance of the actual contents of the works (*Bibliotheca* 3: 471). Sigüenza is eulogized, by contrast, for having spent much energy and money in acquiring such volumes and for having pursued the strategy of consulting native scholars themselves descended from the ruling families of different native peoples, most notably Juan de Alva Ixtlixóchitl and Domingo Chimalpain (*Bibliotheca* 3: 472; 484). Moreover, in the descriptions of Sigüenza's various published and unpublished works, the catalogue emphasizes his achievements as the first person to have been able to understand the workings of the Aztec calendar, and for having been able to reconstruct the genealogy of Aztec rulers, which he presented in his *Teatro de virtudes políticas* (*Bibliotheca* 3: 475–76; 479–83).

No less important than Sigüenza's labors of historical archaeology are the works he produced out of his participation in official expeditions to gather information about parts of New Spain that still remained relatively unknown in the second half of the seventeenth century. The catalogue's description of Sigüenza's labors in mapping these regions, particularly those of Florida and areas around the Mississippi River, serves to construct a narrative of *criollo* mastery over the vastness and wildness of American space. First, the reader is informed of how, after the expedition had arrived in Florida in 1693, Sigüenza undertook to name the various hills in the area, even assigning his own surname to one of them, at the urging of one of his comrades (*Bibliotheca* 3: 474). Second, his organization and rationalization of this hitherto indomitable space is consolidated by the detail that a fortress was built on top of the hill to which Sigüenza—referred to here again through the use of the first-person-plural possessive adjective—had assigned his name.[10] With these first ordering actions registered, the catalogue then gives an account of how Sigüenza mapped the region:

> Recessus aperuit, Flumina, Fluvia que navigavit, Terras circunspexit conquirendorum Indorum ergo, ipsarumque notitiam hauriendi, queis agnomina dedit, non nulla inde traducta quod similes Mexicanis aliquot locis sint vise, ut qui Iztacalco, amoenissimo prope Mexicum Pago lintre multiplici quotidie frequenti, et qui Baratillo in Urbis Foro nuncupatus fuit ab haeterogeneis multis nullius pretii rebus inibi venditatis. Sacrum ut erexerat in terra Vexillum Crucis, aliisque Christianae pietatis officiis operam dederat, tabulae suae geographicae institit conscribendae. (*Bibliotheca* 3: 474)

> He uncovered the secluded area, the streams and rivers which he navigated, surveyed the lands with a view to the conquest of the Indians and to extract knowledge about them, gave them names, some of those rendered like those of Mexico, due to the similarity between them and those of that place; and thus [he called] it Iztacalco, which is a most pleasant village, near Mexico City, frequented daily by many skiffs, and which was called a market, for those who, in the city square, undertake to sell many strange things at low price. Having erected the sacred standard of the cross in the earth and fulfilled other duties of Christian piety, he undertook to compose his geographical maps.

In this fashion Sigüenza is represented as an agent of *criollo* mastery over space, having produced geographical representations that complement his knowledge of American history in both its pre-Hispanic and viceregal phases. Although the expedition was subsequently obliged to turn back, when it was attempting to navigate and chart the Mississippi, Sigüenza's labor is made to stand out for having reinserted certain areas, which had not been explored by the Spanish for a long time, into the scheme of knowledge of the viceroyalty's geography.

Missionaries

The final important subdivision of entries in the catalogue is that devoted to friars and scholars who have devoted their lives to the production of knowledge of Amerindian languages, primarily with a view to facilitating the labor of the conversion of native peoples to Christianity. As has been noted above, both in the descriptions of scholarly activities at the University of Mexico and in the accounts of the work of discursive archaeology undertaken by Sigüenza y Góngora, knowledge of indigenous languages is established as an important component of the *criollo* archive. The descriptions of the careers and works of friars, both European and *criollo,* serve to illustrate not only the legitimacy of such knowledge, but also the manner in which it has contributed to the project of ordering the various regions of the viceroyalty into an organized totality.

Although the catalogue lists multiple individuals who have devoted themselves to the tasks of learning native languages and have thus contributed to the process of conversion, I will focus here on one specific figure. Born in Antequera, in Oaxaca, Fray Agustín de Quintana was a Dominican who was sent in 1695 to work among the Mixe, an indigenous tribe that lived in an inhospitable mountain region (*Bibliotheca* 3: 334). The catalogue describes the obstacles posed to outsiders by the difficult nature of the tribe's language: "Idioma gentis difficilimum est, si quod ullum in Septentrionali America, barbarum certe, pronunciatuque asperrimum; cui tamen addiscendo tam strenue se dedit, brevi ut non modo in familiari consuetudine uteretur eo, sed vero etiam publicis concionibus ad populum habitis" (*Bibliotheca* 3: 334; "The language of that people is very difficult, like no other in North America, certainly barbarous, and very difficult to pronounce; to the study of which, however, he devoted himself so assiduously that in a short time he was using it not only in friendly conversation, but also in the public speeches he made to the people").

The catalogue relates that Quintana took over the leadership of the parish when his superior died, and carried out his duties honestly and diligently for eighteen years. This, coupled with the readiness he showed to learn and speak the tribe's language, enabled him to win the friendship of its members, so that they were more effectively incorporated into the religious and political order of the viceroyalty (*Bibliotheca* 3: 334). After he was forced by illness to return to Antequera, he dedicated himself to writing bilingual texts on Catholic doctrine, in Castilian and in the language of the Mixes, in order to facilitate the work of other missionaries in maintaining the tribe within the unifying scheme of Christianity: "nam conscribedis se Libris dedit Mixeniano Idiomate admodum prosuturis, cum Indorum institutioni, tum ministrantium ipsis Parochorum commoditati; fructusque in majori aetate tulit opimos, quos longo usu et studio Idiomatis secuerat, rigarat, accuraveratque" (*Bibliotheca* 3: 335; "[T]hus, he devoted himself wholly to writing books in the Mixe language, both for the instruction of the Indians and for the convenience of the priests who served them; and in old age he extracted from that language plentiful fruits which, by his dedication and study, he had tended, watered, and cultivated").

The catalogue informs the reader that since the Mixe language is so difficult no missionary had attempted to publish any religious texts in this language in the preceding two centuries (*Bibliotheca* 3: 335). Nevertheless, Quintana is shown to have been possessed of the diligence and scholarly skills necessary to overcome the imputed barbarousness and dissonance of the indigenous language, and make it ordered and comprehensible to Spanish speakers, in accordance with humanist linguistic principles. In this fashion, he is held to have facilitated the process of the incorporation of the tribe into the social order of the viceroyalty. Thus, the labors of Quintana and other missionaries are seen as contributing to the task of shaping the heterogeneous geography and peoples of the region into an ordered and cohesive whole, a totality that is made to seem unthinkable without the organizing framework of the *criollo* archive.

The published sections of the catalogue of the *Bibliotheca Mexicana* provide a sketch of the utopian imagining of an ideal, autonomous *criollo* intellectual subject, and of the body of knowledge that is simultaneously both ground for, and object to be organized and represented by, that subject. Together, the accounts of the contributions of educational institutions and the most celebrated poets and scholars to the cultural life of the viceroyalty constitute an attempt to articulate the matrix of a self-contained and active intellectual totality. The fact that the catalogue was never completed is suggestive of the contradictions and material problems in which *criollo* scholars and writers remained ensnared at the middle of the eighteenth century. The second main text I will scrutinize in the genealogy of the *criollo* archive is the result of an effort to confront such issues, reworking the epistemological and aesthetic framework that had informed Mexican *criollo* thought up to this point. As we will see in part 2, the *Rusticatio Mexicana* provides an interesting reorientation of this thought while at the same time opening up contradictions of its own.

Part 2
Rafael Landívar's
Rusticatio Mexicana
Expanding the *Criollo* Archive

Chapter Four

Subject, Archive, Landscape

Reconceptualizing the *Criollo* Archive

Eguiara y Eguren's *Bibliotheca Mexicana* constitutes a limit-point in the hegemony of the episteme and practices of scholasticism in New Spain. At the time of the *Bibliotheca*'s publication, the structure out of which Eguiara worked was beginning to show cracks, and was giving way to an emergent syncretic intellectual schema at the most prestigious Jesuit colleges in the viceroyalty. By the middle of the eighteenth century, the materialist and epistemological ideologies of secularizing thinkers were selectively being incorporated into the teaching of philosophy at such institutions of higher learning, producing what Mexican intellectual historiography has referred to as "eclecticism."[1]

At this point, education and intellectual production in New Spain straddled a threshold between the textualism of scholasticism and the more practical modes of thought that were emerging in the eighteenth century. The geographical regions that made up the viceroyalty could no longer serve merely as the background against which erudition was to be fashioned and created, as occurs in the texts of López and Eguiara. New forms of knowledge were being developed that were no longer marked by their evasion from, or masking of, material realities,[2] but that were derived from the practices of the observation and exploitation of such materialities. From this time on, the *criollo* archive begins to acquire a different form as it is reshaped according to the requirements and manifestations of still unclearly defined forms of modernity.

During the second half of the eighteenth century, a series of measures were set in motion with a view to imposing new

109

principles of rationalization on the administration and economic organization of the viceroyalty. Although it is perhaps tempting to read these developments through an interpretive lens that pits the forces of modernity in an unambiguous struggle against the oppressive apparatuses of tradition and Catholic orthodoxy, such an approach would be founded on a misunderstanding of the structure and functioning of colonial society. Rather, it is more appropriate to see what emerges as a conflict, not over whether or not to allow the development of processes commonly associated with the passage from traditional to modernity—most specifically, secularization and the formal rationalization of the economic, legal, and bureaucratic orders—but over how to implement and manage those processes.[3] Different projects and practices emerged in relation to the interests of various groups and institutions, which sometimes interacted and at other times came into conflict with each other. The most far-reaching and systematic of these projects was that developed by the functionaries of the Spanish Bourbon state as part of the Crown's general attempt to reassert administrative control over all its territories, in the process making them more efficient in the areas of agricultural and industrial production, and, by extension, in the payment of taxes.

Nevertheless, the imperial state was not the only agent that wielded power in the colonies. In fact, the history of its activities in New Spain and Guatemala is marked by its inability to enforce control over other groups, especially landowners.[4] The Bourbon reforms themselves represented the first real and sustained attempt to establish the state as the hegemonic presence in the viceroyalties since the second half of the sixteenth century. From the times of the earliest conflicts with the *encomenderos,* the colonial bureaucracy had pursued policies of negotiation and compromise with local *criollo* elites in order to maintain their loyalty and support, and the framework of power was not so much undermined as shaped by the practices of bribery and the sale of administrative offices to *criollos* (Coatsworth, "The Limits" 36–37). At the same time, it had relied on the leadership of the various ecclesiastical institutions to maintain order and ideological control over the populations of *mestizos* and indigenous groups that vastly outnumbered those of European ethnicity. Foremost among those were the

Dominican, Franciscan, Carmelite, and Jesuit orders. However, by the eighteenth century the actions of the Jesuits, in particular, had come to be viewed with increasing hostility by a state seeking to consolidate its hegemony and authority throughout its territories.

As a latecomer among Christian orders, the Society of Jesus had arrived in New Spain in 1572. By this stage, much of the work of evangelization and pacification of indigenous peoples had already been completed, except in the more remote frontier areas such as California, Florida, and New Mexico. Some members of the order dedicated themselves to missionary activities in those far-flung regions, in similar fashion to their comrades in the Far East and Paraguay. However, most of the order's physical and monetary resources in New Spain would come to be invested in undertakings realized in rural and urban areas already colonized and controlled. The Jesuits quickly set about acquiring land on which they constructed monasteries and colleges, administering and farming the soil around them, and setting themselves up as agrarian producers on a scale that appears to have been at least as large as that of any secular *hacendado.*[5]

On an ideological level, the central role of the Society in the viceroyalty came to resemble closely its activity in the countries of Western Europe. It established, in the major urban areas, institutions of higher education that quickly acquired prestige as the most important centers of learning in New Spain and Guatemala, next to the universities of Mexico and San Carlos. The order's educative and agricultural concerns were not kept separate, but functioned interactively in accordance with the very practical directives that guided its actions in the New World. In effect, this practicality, coupled with the systematic discipline and organization of the Society's activities, made it arguably the most efficient and productive institution in the viceroyalty, especially when viewed alongside the mechanisms of the state bureaucracy, at least prior to the period of the Bourbon initiatives.[6]

The first reform of philosophical thinking and pedagogy in New Spain is undertaken at one of the key centers of the Jesuit education system in the viceroyalty, the Colegio de San Ildefonso. At that institution a series of philosophy courses were taught, first by Rafael Campoy, and later by Diego José Abad (1727–79) from 1750 on, incorporating the new systems of thought evolved principally in the works of Descartes and Gassendi.[7] In this fashion, a generation of young Jesuits was educated within the framework of a more eclectic approach to the production of knowledge, involving an attempt to synthesize scholasticism with modern methods. Some of these scholars continued working in the realm of texts, notably in the cultivation of Latin and Greek, and the study of the classical works composed in those languages.[8] Another group moved into newer disciplines such as natural history, which Francisco Javier Clavijero (1731–87) and others found to be most appropriate to a task they were urgently concerned to realize, namely, the accurate representation of America's natural environment and its inhabitants.[9] Others combined the different skills they had acquired through their education and labors within the order, not just as scholars of textual humanism, but also as active participants in the daily business of the agricultural lands that the Society exploited for sustenance and profit.

The most outstanding example of the fusion of these different forms of practical and theoretical knowledge in a *criollo* Jesuit is provided by Rafael Landívar. Landívar was born in Santiago de los Caballeros de Guatemala (today known as Antigua). He traveled to Mexico City in 1749 in order to complete his education at what was, along with the Colegio de San Ildefonso, the other principal Jesuit learning institution in New Spain, the Colegio Máximo de San Pedro y San Pablo. He returned to Guatemala in 1765 to assume the post of rector of the Colegio de San Francisco de Borja. His career there was cut short in 1767 when he was expelled from the viceroyalty by the Spanish Crown, as a member of the Jesuit order. After an uncertain period, he settled in Bologna, Italy, where he taught at a school for Jesuit novices called the Casa de La Sapienza until 1773, when Pope Clement XIV signed a brief ordering the dissolution of the Society of Jesus. Subsequently, he shared a house with several Jesuit companions and wrote the text of his poem, the *Rusticatio Mexicana,* published first in Modena in 1781. An expanded version was then published in Bologna the following year.[10] Written in Latin, this work combines the tradition of the *criollo* Jesuits' cultivation of the classical European languages and texts with a concern to produce knowledge within the framework of the emerging scientific disciplines, specifically, natural history and economy.

Divided into fifteen books, or cantos, the second edition of the *Rusticatio Mexicana* offers a totalizing picture of the geography, nature, and agricultural and industrial production of the viceroyalty in the second half of the eighteenth century. It represents a collection of material realities that are largely effaced from the sublimated sphere of symbolic production that Eguiara catalogues and fashions in the *Bibliotheca Mexicana*. In Landívar's poem, the notion of what constitutes the *criollo* archive shifts and mutates, as the relationship between the pursuit of knowledge and the exploitation of these materialities is reconfigured. Over the course of this chapter, and the two that follow it, I will explore the hypothesis that, within the scope of this retheorization, the textual framework of scholasticism becomes cracked as Landívar pursues a pragmatic investigation into the observation and linguistic representation of nature and human artifice. This endeavor is undertaken within the framework of the Jesuit order's ventures in Mexican agriculture and industry, where their interventions had often brought about a substantial degree of diversification, efficiency, and productivity (Riley 36–62).

The small body of criticism written about Landívar's poem prior to the last twenty years tends to reconstruct the work as the expression of an exile's nostalgia for his homeland.[11] More recently, however, there have been several attempts to offer more nuanced interpretations of the poem. Graciela Nemes has read it as the work of an individual who, after receiving a relatively modern intellectual formation at an elite Jesuit institution, tries to move away from an oppressive scholastic tradition and incorporate into his work some of the forms of empiricism and pragmatism that emerge in the eighteenth century (301). She sees it as a didactic poem that chiefly functions at the level of furnishing information in the form of a "large measure of useful knowledge, topographical and biological description" (298). Although Nemes remarks upon the poet's use of Latin and his eschewal of the opaque style associated with the Baroque, her comments on the formal organization go no further than that. In effect, she reads the *Rusticatio Mexicana* from the perspective

113

of thematic analysis, without interrogating the relationship of Landívar's strategies of representation to their objects of study.[12] Neither does she engage in any close analysis of the manners in which an ideology of pragmatic interaction with the material world informs the text. For Nemes, the ideologies associated with the European Enlightenment, and its program of bourgeois liberation and hegemony, can be transplanted unproblematically to a colonial setting in such a manner as to become the basis of a future rupture with the structures of empire. She articulates an idealist vision of Landívar's undertaking, suppressing the question of the Jesuits' role in maintaining stability within the empire, in part through the promotion of practices and modes of thought bound up with the passage from tradition to modernity, and the vexed problem of the order's relationship with the Spanish state.

In the most complete study of the topic realized to date, Arnold Kerson places Landívar's poem within the tradition of Greco-Roman scholarship and literature developed by *letrados* in New Spain, particularly during the eighteenth century (*Rafael Landívar* 34–49). He traces the importance classical Greek and Roman models, principally Virgil's *Georgics,* hold for Landívar. Kerson argues that the *Rusticatio Mexicana* needs to be seen within the framework of universal literature as a text that transcends the local dimensions of its thematics (*Rafael Landívar* 260–85; 294–98).

Like Nemes, Kerson also strives to situate the *Rusticatio Mexicana* within the context of Enlightenment thought. Notably, he has emphasized the importance of the literary trope of utopia in the poem ("El concepto"). Kerson illustrates how the poem functions in part as a response to the denigrating representations of America's geography and its inhabitants written by Europeans such as Georges-Louis Leclerc Buffon, Cornelius de Pauw, the Abbé Raynal, and William Robertson ("El concepto" 363–64). He contends that when combined with his exile's nostalgia and the incipient nationalism of eighteenth-century *criollo* Jesuits, Landívar's resentment of these distortions incites him to dedicate himself to the task of creating a more realistic picture of parts of New Spain and Guatemala ("El concepto" 367). Landívar's concern, Kerson suggests, is not to reject or disavow the rationalist program that informs the writings of the aforementioned Europeans, but, rather to articulate his own version of the new modes of thought, insofar as they can be incorporated into some kind of Christian framework ("El concepto" 368). Kerson nevertheless places the work within an older tradition of didactic poetry written by Jesuits, and reiterates its clear relationship to its Virgilian model, the *Georgics*. Most specifically, Kerson focuses on book 6 of the poem, which contains a detailed evocation of the work habits and social organization of the beaver. He connects this section with the humanist utopian writing of the sixteenth century, specifically that of Thomas More. In addition, he places it in a lineage that goes back to the communities founded by Vasco de Quiroga in Michoacan, Las Casas in Cumaná, Venezuela, and the Jesuits in Paraguay during the seventeenth century ("El concepto" 370–71). Kerson also sees parallels between Landívar's depiction of a harmonious state, in which equality, peace, and personal liberty are key values, and eighteenth-century writings on these topics by thinkers like Jean-Jacques Rousseau, Voltaire, Montesquieu, Morelly, and the Abbé de Mably ("El concepto" 375).

In addition, Kerson has studied stylistic nuances in Landívar's use of the didactic mode in the *Rusticatio Mexicana*. He analyzes what he perceives to be different levels of register in the poem ("The Heroic Mode"). The first of these is what he calls the "miniature epic," a figure that Landívar adopts chiefly from Virgil's model. The miniature epic is used to evoke events and objects in a wholly serious or grave fashion, so as to posit exemplary human behavior in a variety of contexts. Kerson observes how this technique of representation is applied in book 2, where Landívar provides a detailed account of the events and effects relating to the 1759 eruption of the Jorullo volcano in the area of Michoacan. He notes that the "serious" tone is appropriate to the gravity of the circumstances evoked in this section ("The Heroic Mode" 151–56). The second mode Kerson describes is that of the "mock-heroic" epic. He sees parallels between the playful, burlesque treatment that Landívar gives some of the less lofty topics in the *Rusticatio Mexicana* and a type of parodic text that emerges in eighteenth-century Europe as an antidote to the proliferation of very dull, didactic poems written during the period ("The Heroic Mode" 157). In particular, Kerson singles out book 4 of the *Rusticatio Mexicana,* in which Landívar depicts the series of elements that pertain to the cochineal worms, and to the practice of exploiting them to produce purple dye. Kerson notes that there is a purpose behind the poet's burlesque exposure of the worms' sloth and complacency in the face of spiders and indigenous dyemakers, insofar as he is seeking to recommend the imputed values of hard work and ethical behavior over the indolent pursuit of pleasure ("The Heroic Mode" 158–62).

In a short, well-written article, John Browning has given the most complete contemporary account of Landívar's poem ("Rafael Landívar's *Rusticatio Mexicana*"). Like Kerson, he seeks to place the *Rusticatio Mexicana* within the intellectual context of its production, comparing it to other works produced by Jesuit exiles in Italy during the 1780s. Browning emphasizes the idea that Landívar seeks to insert himself into the new discipline of natural history with a view to creating scientific, totalizing pictures of Mexican reality, and displacing European representations of America already produced from within the parameters of this emergent discipline of knowledge (11–18). Browning argues that, in part, it is in order to communicate such information to an audience of fellow educated readers speaking a variety of different European languages that Landívar composes the poem in Latin (18). At the same time, Browning goes further than other critics in stating that Landívar is also writing for another implicit public, drawn from the American-born inhabitants of his native land (19). Although both Kerson and Nemes make reference to the incipient proto-nationalism they find in Landívar's text, neither addresses the question of the relationship of this and other discourses of knowledge to the material contexts of their production. Browning, on the other hand, incorporates into his reading historical information about agriculture and economics in the region of Guatemala over the course of the eighteenth century. He notes that, around the time Landívar was writing, there was a certain consciousness among more educated *criollos* of a need to diversify the area's economy because of the potential dangers resulting from its dependence on one product, indigo dye (19–21). Browning argues that Landívar is concerned about this problem, and his depiction of a variety of areas of agricultural production demonstrates a desire to promote the idea of cultivating and developing other

Subject, Archive, Landscape

marketable commodities (22–23). Uncertain as to whether to view him as a proto-revolutionary or a reformer, Browning goes as far as to suggest that Landívar was probably conscious that the kind of reforms implicit in his poem would induce a transformation of the political organization of the region, to the extent that the diversification of the economy, the development of port facilities, and freedom of trade would have weakened the Spanish state's hold on the region, and allowed it a measure of independence. Browning hypothesizes:

> Landívar must have been aware of the implications of urging his younger readers to uncover their treasure and to work for a more prosperous Guatemala. A more prosperous Guatemala would have been a more independent Guatemala, and such independence would have weakened the imperial structure. The *Rusticatio* should be viewed, therefore, not only as a work of natural history, but as an important political statement as well. (24–25)

While Browning is correct to place Landívar's textual production more explicitly in a dialectical relationship with intellectual and political developments, more work needs to be done in analyzing how the *Rusticatio Mexicana* is inextricably bound up with various aspects of the social and economic organization of the viceroyalty. The working hypothesis of the chapters that follow will be that it is misleading to read Landívar's poem either as a predominantly self-referential modern literary work, on the one hand, or solely as a treatise that effaces its own linguistic constructs and processes in order to portray, as if transparently, a pre-given referent, or content, on the other hand. Rather, I will attempt to trace how the problematics of composing an intellectual artifact and of the representation of material practice, specifically agriculture, are continuously linked and intertwined. At the same time, I will seek to trace how the dynamics of the formation of the outline of a transcendent *criollo* subject becomes inextricably bound up with the task of representing American space and framing it within scientific and aesthetic discourses.

Landívar's cultural and historical positioning determine his identity as intellectual subject. As a product of Jesuit education, in its specific Mexican manifestation, at a time when paradigms

117

of knowledge and linguistic representation are in flux, he is a curious mixture of new and old. He is not the kind of man of letters whom some critics perceive in a figure such as Espinosa Medrano, that is, a person who seeks to carve out a niche for himself as a professional writer existing in quasi-autonomy with respect to the institutions in which knowledge and power are concentrated, the church and the state.[13] Neither is he entirely a holdover from the legitimating intellectual authority sustaining the symbiotic hegemony of those two regimes, someone who owes his position to premodern relations of favor and *seigneurial* ideology. Rather, he is the product of an institution born of tradition and orthodoxy that rises and expands the scope of its sociocultural influence as a result of its ability and willingness to adapt to and assimilate the very modernizing impulses and technologies that appear to threaten the conditions of its existence.[14]

In Landívar one finds something quite different from the kind of specialist intellectual who is beginning to emerge during the second half of the eighteenth century. However, at the same time, he does not represent a continuation of the cleric who articulates a form of omniscience based on authority in theological matters. He is closer, but not identical, to the general enlightened *philosophe* of eighteenth-century Europe personified in figures such as Voltaire and Addison.[15] Nevertheless, Landívar does not fully conform to the models offered by any of these types insofar as his Jesuit formation presents him simultaneously as the subject of a general, theologically based, all-embracing humanism, and as the bearer of highly specialized forms of knowledge. It is this experience that leads him to blend, in the *Rusticatio Mexicana,* the concern to produce an aesthetic that might transcend the world of economic utilitarianism with modes of knowledge that developed over the course of two centuries during which the Jesuits had exploited agricultural and mineral resources in Mexico according to principles of efficiency. These two acts of articulation, that is, the realization of a totalizing speech act that seeks to establish the *criollo* as a subject of aesthetics, and the presentation of systematic, practical knowledge, are simultaneous and interdependent. In Landívar a discourse of subjectivity is inseparable from the process of construction of knowledge about the geography in which he was born and lived. As Charles Riley has shown, from the very beginning, the existence of the Jesuit's educational institutions is tied to the economic fortunes of the order's farms in New Spain, largely due to its local leadership's concern that they should be autonomous institutions that would not depend on large-scale private interests for their maintenance (Riley 1–35). Landívar's poem effectively synthesizes textually the knowledge the Jesuits of the region subsequently accumulated over the course of almost two centuries during which they amassed an extensive matrix of colleges and haciendas.

This interweaving of discourses can be traced through three parts, all of which tend to overlap with one another. First, in the "Dedicatoria," the "Monitum," and books 1, 2, and 3 of the *Rusticatio,* Landívar focuses specifically on the geography of New Spain, evoking some of its most awe-inspiring natural landscapes and settings. The following eight books are devoted to the detailed representation of the key areas of economic production in the viceroyalty. Finally, in the last three books Landívar deals with images that cannot be inserted into the scope of the organized productive practices of the colony, in particular, exotic animals and birds, forms of leisure, and a religious symbol.

Framing the Unknown: The Beautiful and the Sublime

Following a dedicatory poem, the "Monitum" and the first three cantos of the *Rusticatio* establish a representative image of the range of geographical scenarios that constitute the territory of New Spain. As the prefatory section to the poem, the first two pieces immediately signal a shift in the composition of the colonial text. Unlike the forewords to most colonial writings, they are directed to an implied anonymous readership of educated equals, not the higher-ranking officials to which letters and chronicles are addressed.

The preliminary poem is a dedication to Santiago de los Caballeros de Guatemala, the administrative center of the kingdom of the same name during the colonial period and Landívar's own place of birth.[16] Significantly, it is one of the few parts of the text in which prolonged mention is made of urban spaces, and in which the poet's own *patria chica* is referred to explicitly.

This part of the work indicates, in its brevity, the centrality that agriculture and rural space play in the *criollo*'s conception of identity and social organization. "Vrbi Guatimalae" offers a nostalgic description of the city that appears, at first, tinged with sadness at its destruction by an earthquake in 1773. However, this lament gives way to an exultant celebration of the manner in which its inhabitants have rebuilt it out of the ruins, thanks to their energy and expertise:

> Quid tamen haec doleo? Surgunt iam celsa sepulcro
>   limina, se tollunt ardua templa polo.
> Flumine iam fontes undant, iam compita turba,
>   iamque optata uenit ciuibus alma quies.
> Scilicet, ut Phariae uolucri, felicior urbi
>   e proprio rursus puluere uita redit.
>
> Gaude igitur, rediuiua Parens, Vrbs inclita regni,
>   excidioque nouo libera uiue diu:
> et clarum subita partum de morte triumphum
>   laudibus ipse tuum promptus in astra feram.
> Interea raucum, luctus solacia, plectrum
>   accipe; sisque loco muneris ipsa mihi.
>
>   (Landívar, "Vrbi Guatimalae" 23–34)

> But what do I grieve about? From the grave there now rise lofty houses, and temples erect themselves high up to the sky. Now the springs fill their streams, now the streets are crowded, and now a longed for and bountiful calm comes to the citizens. Like the bird Phoenix, the city recovers a greater happiness, returning to life from the very dust. Be happy, immortal mother, the most eminent city of the kingdom, and now free from new destruction, live on for a long time: with your fame born in your victory over sudden death, your triumph will be carried to the stars by me and by my eulogy. Receive, meanwhile, my harsh strains, a solace from mourning; and if it pleases you, be, yourself, my reward.[17]

In like fashion, the poem is presented as the fruit of a humanist labor to be offered in the service of a city envisaged as being the capital of a state. However, the urban center at this point recedes from the general scheme of the work, in contrast to the position customarily accorded to Mexico City in the vast majority of the poetry written during the colonial period, most notably in Balbuena's *Grandeza mexicana*. Moreover, the manner in which Santiago de Guatemala is depicted involves the representation of the processes through which it is built, rather than just the sensual exploration of its architecture and artifacts.[18] This emphasis on human constructive action, and the reaction of awe that its products inspire in the poet, sets in motion the dialectical interaction of artifice and materiality that will take the *criollo* archive into areas beyond the realm of Eguiara's archive.

In the "Monitum," Landívar sets out, in prose, five points of clarification about the composition of the poem itself, indicating a concern to represent topics in a clear and readily comprehensible fashion. First, he explains the title of his work, noting, in particular, that New Spain is generally known in Europe by the name of "Mexico" (Landívar 7). Second, he is anxious to emphasize the documentary character of the work, and the fact that he has attempted to reduce fictional and rhetorical elements to a subsidiary role, as in the brief depiction of Mexican poets in book 2 (7). Landívar writes: "Quae uidi refero, quaque mihi testes oculati, ceteroquin ueracissimi, retulere. Praeterea curae mihi fuit oculatorum testium auctoritate subscripta, quae rariora sunt, confirmare" (7; "I report what I have seen, and that which eye witnesses, [who are] in all other matters most true, have told me. Moreover, I have taken care to confirm the more unusual things, recorded by the authority of eye witnesses"). Third, he observes that he has only included a small amount of information about Mexican mining, since he considers that a fuller treatment would require more detail than is possible within the limited scope of the poem. This theme carries over into the fourth point of his "Monitum," where he states that no great significance should be attached to the ancient Greek and Roman divinities invoked at the beginning of each canto (Landívar 7–8). Finally, in the fifth paragraph, he considers a central problem involved in the representation of a world that is unknown to the vast majority of his European readers, concluding:

> Vereor tamen, ne dum ista percurreris, aliqua interdum suboscura offendas. In argumento quippe adeo difficili omnia latino uersu ita exprimere, ut uel rerum ignaris sub aspectum

cadant, arduum quidem est; ne dicam impossibile. Nihilo-
minus claritati, qua potui diligentia, ut prouiderem, plurimum
in iis, quae nunc primum in lucem prodeunt, allaboraui:
uulgata uero ad incudem reuocaui; in quibus plura mutaui,
nonnulla addidi, aliqua subtraxi. Sed uerendum est adhuc,
ne incassum desudauerim, neque eorum satis desiderio
fecerim, qui in rebus etiam suapte natura difficillimis nullum
uellent laborem impendere. Solacio tamen mihi erit, quod
hac super re Golmarius Marsiglianus cecinit:

> Heu! quam difficile est uoces reperire, modosque
> addere, cum nouitas integra rebus inest.
> Saepe mihi deerunt (iam nunc praesentio) uoces:
> Saepe repugnabit uocibus ipse modus.
>
> (Landívar 8)

However, I fear that in reading this you will at times find
some things which are obscure. Since to express it all in Latin
verse on such a difficult theme, in such a manner that it might
be understandable, even to the ignorant, is difficult, if not
impossible. In spite of everything, in order to achieve clarity I have labored a great deal, with the diligence of which
I was capable, on what here comes to light for the first time:
that which is common knowledge I returned to the anvil; I
have changed many things, added some, suppressed others.
Nevertheless, it is still to be feared that I might have toiled
in vain and not complied sufficiently with the desires of
those who, even in things which are by their very nature
difficult, do not wish to expend the slightest effort. However, of solace will be to me that which Golmario Marsigliano
sang about a similar thing:

> O, how difficult it is to find the words, and fit them to
> the meter, for things that are wholly new. Often, I will
> lack (I foresee it now) the words, often the meter it-
> self will rebel against the words.

Landívar outlines here a *criollo* problematic of representation that moves into a realm heavily laden with contradictions
and conflicts. He does not merely reproduce a defense of neoclassical poetics against the imputed lack of decorum of the
Gongorine and Quevedesque modes, such as one finds in Ignacio
de Luzán's *La poética*.[19] Rather, there is here a simultaneous
understanding of the opaque, distorting aspects of language,
on the one hand, and of the confusion that swirls around European knowledge of America, on the other. This confusion stems

from the dissemination of European writings that have distorted the image of American reality, and from the specific problems that are involved in a *criollo*'s attempts to communicate empirical knowledge about his homeland to an audience whose knowledge frameworks are differentiated from his own by language, culture, and environment. In this situation, Latin is a medium that transcends such boundaries while imposing others, enhancing communicative clarity but introducing new forms of opacity. At the same time, it is reactivated here as the language that is appropriate to the depiction of noble, elevated topics, at the very moment when it was becoming an anachronism in Western Europe.[20] Its purpose, thus, is not just to enable communication with non-Spanish speakers, but also to convey what texts written in the Romance languages have been unable to represent, natural phenomena, the appearance of which transgresses the standards of beauty associated with the more temperate and tranquil geographies of the Old World. This will be the first part of Landívar's reconstruction of the *criollo* archive.

My concern here is to attempt to situate Landívar's poem in a peculiar tension with the broader scheme of eighteenth-century statements and debates about the nature of aesthetics. Central to these discussions were two key arguments. The first of these revolved around the issue of whether poetry and art necessarily had to be produced in accordance with a system of precepts and rules, as laid down by the authorities of Aristotle and Horace, and recodified in poetics by writers such as Boileau, or whether greater account should be made of the role of the creative force of the individual imagination. The second problem stemmed from a concern to delineate which kinds of objects were suitable fare for poetry and art. Initially, in these discussions, the scope of art and poetry was to be restricted to the beautiful, that is, objects that were finite in size and immediately pleasing to the senses and the mind, and could be represented clearly and neatly in accordance with the systems of precepts mentioned above.[21] Over time, however, there developed a countervailing impulse to incorporate into art and poetry objects such as rough seas and volcanoes, the dimensions and force of which precluded their representations within the tidy parameters of the beautiful. The preoccupation with the place of these resistant, unrepresentable elements, and the corresponding problem of individual creativity, within art and poetry, therefore had to be theorized through the medium of another concept, that of the sublime.[22]

Within the Western literary tradition as a whole the sublime has been a recurring mobilizing sign, assuming greatest importance in the eighteenth century, a period in which the concept underwent a series of mutations. Consideration of the concept begins with *On Sublimity,* a text attributed to Dionysius Longinus, a statesman and critic of the third century A.D., although it was probably actually composed at some time in the first century (Russell and Winterbottom 235). Although the work was already known to some European scholars by the sixteenth century, neither it nor the concept would assume a decisive role in the development of aesthetics, art, and poetry until the French scholar Nicolas Boileau published an edition of the text, together with his commentary on it, in 1674.[23] Indeed, it was in no small part due to Boileau's prestige within French literary circles that interest in the text and its central concept increased to the point that it was to play an ever more significant role in aesthetic thought.[24]

Boileau reads *On Sublimity*'s discussion of the sublime as a statement of the characteristics and requirements of elevated style, the noblest and most prestigious of the three registers of discourse codified in ancient Greek and Roman theories of rhetoric and poetry.[25] In addition, Boileau focuses on the text's argument in favor of the exposition of ideas and images in clear and simple language, an argument that came close to his own conception of good style.[26] Conventional accounts of the history of the understanding of the concept from 1674 into the eighteenth century tend to identify a series of stages. In the first period, initiated by Boileau, *On Sublimity* is inserted into the theoretical regime of neoclassicism as a support rather than as a threat to the system of rules derived primarily from Aristotle and Cicero.[27] At the same time, the concept of the sublime initially served to accommodate the very tendencies toward excess and disruption that did not fit comfortably into that aesthetic system, with its emphasis on a neat, harmonious sense of beauty and order.[28] Specifically, Boileau, in his commentaries, seeks to subsume *On Sublimity*'s treatment of the irrational, persuasive aspects of rhetorical discourse within the scheme of neo-classicism in a manner that would not undermine the integrity of the latter's overall structure (Monk 29–36).

Over the course of the eighteenth century, the accommodation overseen by Boileau gradually ceased to play this role of reinforcing neoclassical poetics and tended to open up cracks and contradictions within its order. Although neoclassicism remained dominant in French letters, its position within other European literatures became increasingly destabilized, particularly in England and Germany, where its system of rules was constantly in tension with notions of the specific character of the national spirit and the modes of expression that were held to be peculiar to that spirit.[29] Beginning with Joseph Addison's essays in *The Spectator*, in England the sublime came to play a key role in a series of debates about taste and the decisive factors in the creation of the artistic or literary work.[30]

The second moment in the development of eighteenth-century debates pertaining to the sublime, especially in England, involves a shift of emphasis away from its rhetorical inflection—the notion of elevated style—and toward an interest in the role of encounters with unbridled, immeasurable forces, be they those of nature or of the creative powers of individual genius, in the process of the elaboration of the work of art or literature. For the purposes of my discussion, the key features of this reformulated concept of the sublime can best be summarized in the following terms. First, in the face of the changing class structures of Western European societies, and the resulting potential disruption of existing notions of criteria of value, writers from Addison to Burke and Kant were concerned to delineate which mental processes and capacities for discernment were involved in the act of identifying what qualified as pleasing, good art or literature. Second, and in close relation to the first issue, notions of what merited inclusion within the scheme of good art and literature underwent a shift. Although the century opened with the hegemony of the neoclassical concept of the beautiful firmly in place, debates about the range of what might form part of the aesthetic fact changed the coordinates of the field, largely in the face of dissatisfaction with the constraints of the neoclassical system and its central concept. At this conjunctural point, the concept of the sublime was to open up art and poetry to themes and objects the vastness and incommensurability of which excluded them from the scope of the beautiful.[31]

The third important aspect of the reconfigured sublime pertained to the process of artistic and literary creation. With its connotations of boundlessness and unruliness, the concept offered itself as a key cipher for the theorization and promotion of notions of individual creativity as a significant determining factor, over and against Aristotelian and Ciceronian systems of precepts, in the production of "great" art and poetry (Monk 1–27; 101–33). The fourth feature of the shift in the conception of the sublime centered on the dualism of art and nature. *On Sublimity* emphasized the idea that the sublime style characteristically tended to efface its very artfulness and figurativity in such a fashion as to appear natural, or artless (Longinus 164).[32] Finally, the fifth important factor in the redeployment of the sublime would be its role in the theorization of the processes involved in the production of knowledge through the workings of the faculties of the human mind. Specifically, discussion of the dynamics of the apperception and cognition of the sublime would play a key part in the reconceptualization of the character of the abstract, autonomous subject of reason that was ultimately to displace divine authority as the guarantor of thought and knowledge. This line of philosophizing was to culminate in the systematic formulations articulated in Immanuel Kant's third *Critique* (1789).[33]

While the sublime has been a significant factor in English, French, German, and North American artistic and literary thought since the eighteenth century, its position within Hispanic aesthetics has appeared to be much less decisive. It surfaces only sporadically as a mobilizing sign in the works of "enlightened" thinkers and some romantic poets, most notably the Cuban José María Heredia.[34] Correspondingly, it has been discussed in only a handful of works of scholarship.[35]

The reasons for this effacement of the sublime from Hispanic literary discourse are multiple and complex. Contingently, they might be summarized in terms of the following key factors. First, while the sublime was mobilized in countries like England and Germany in order to facilitate the articulation of elements that did not fit within the constraints of neoclassical poetics—literary forms and modes that were held to be specific to the expression of the national spirit—in Hispanic letters such a role was still attributed, albeit problematically, to Baroque registers, particularly in colonial Spanish America. Although the styles of *conceptismo* and *culteranismo* were to become increasingly discredited over the course of the eighteenth and nineteenth centuries, the sublime was rarely invoked as a more acceptable supplement or alternative to neoclassicism.[36] Moreover, the twentieth-century reconstruction of Hispanic literary history has overwhelmingly reconfirmed Baroque aesthetics in such a role, most notably in *conceptista* and *culteranista* poetry, and in the confrontations between reason and unreason dramatized in the *comedia,* especially in the works of Calderón.[37]

The second factor in the effacement of the sublime from Hispanic literatures is the contradictory manner in which modernity unfolds in Spain and Latin America.[38] As can be seen most readily in the eighteenth-century English debates, the concept of the sublime is bound up with the theorization of taste within the context of a significant reordering of class structures and of modes of literary production and consumption, and with the process of the legitimization of the notion of individual genius as the chief determining factor in artistic and literary creation. Although such dynamics do begin to surface in the Hispanic world during the eighteenth and nineteenth centuries, they do not reach the same degree of development, and it remains problematic to speak of an Enlightenment and a Romantic period as distinct and discrete stages in the history of Spanish and Spanish American literatures.[39]

It is in the face of this marginal status that is conventionally assigned to the sublime within Hispanic literatures, therefore, that I will argue here for its relevance within the context of eighteenth-century colonial Mexico, specifically in the *Rusticatio Mexicana.* Admittedly, treatments and articulations of the sublime in eighteenth-century Hispanic letters do not demonstrate the richness and diversity to be found in their English and German counterparts. Typically, the concept is mobilized largely in relation to two areas of signification: the codification and defense of the elevated style of writing; and the perception and representation of grandeur in nature. Nevertheless, it is precisely in these realms that the concept acquires interest-ing, complex, and ambiguous nuances, particularly within the praxis of the formation and mutations of *criollo* intellectual subjectivity I am attempting to map.

It is clear that some of the Mexican Jesuits who were formed during the period of the opening up of the principal colleges' curricula to modern philosophy were at least familiar with the concept of the sublime. One of the most important literary works produced by a member of the group later expelled is Francisco Javier Alegre's translation of Boileau's *Art poétique,* which he supplemented with a commentary presented in the form of exten-sive notes (Alegre 1–132). In one of the notes to Boileau's text, Alegre makes explicit reference to the text attributed to Longinus. Alegre does not discuss Boileau's own edition of *On Sublimity,* nor the French scholar's exegesis of the treatise. Nevertheless, the intensive quality of his scrutinization of the *Art poétique* and his demonstration of knowledge of Longinus's text indicate that he was very probably acquainted with it through that edition and also, that he was, therefore, aware of the concep-tualization of the elevated style and of the persuasive, emotive component of rhetorical discourse embedded in the discussion of the sublime. Furthermore, the markedly neoclassical style of most of the poetry produced by Alegre and other Mexican Jesuits of his generation, especially Abad and Landívar, serves to underline their positioning within the framework established principally by Boileau, as against the prior regime of *concep-tismo* and *culteranismo.*[40]

While Alegre's reflections are more strictly confined to the level of language, the problematic of the sublime is carried into the threshold between discourse and materiality in the *Rusticatio Mexicana,* in which one can simultaneously track parallels with, and divergences from, the more general trajectory of Western European thinking on the concept summarized above. Provi-sionally, I will briefly sketch out here the terms of Landívar's treatment of the related problematics of the beautiful and the sublime, prior to analyzing segments of the poem itself. First, I see in Landívar's depictions of vast natural spaces—lakes, volcanoes, and waterfalls—a concern to broaden the scope of aesthetics to accommodate objects or scenes that do not fit within the scheme of the beautiful established by neoclassicism. Second, it is my contention that the concept of the sublime acquires new degrees of intensity and ambivalence in a text whose author seeks to represent the heterogeneity and opaqueness of spaces at the fringes of colonial mapping, sites where Western epistemology encounters and seeks to incorporate a still wild and resistant materiality. Third, in the activities of the apperception and representation of such spaces, I glimpse a dynamics of the delineation and stabilization of the transcendent, overarching position of a *criollo* intellectual subject. In the experience of grandeur and boundlessness, this subject passes, alternately, through moments of instability and uncertainty, then of fixity and mastery, in a series of enactions of what Neil Hertz has called the "moment of blockage" in the literature of the sublime (40–42). In such instances the writing subject feels temporarily overwhelmed by the vastness or proliferation of the object s/he seeks to represent, but is then able to reestablish the organicity and unity of its idea of the object, and hence of his/her own self.[41] The staging of this scene is central to the mechanisms of most of the eighteenth-century literature of the sublime, although it is in Kant's third *Critique* that it receives its fullest theorization in terms of the concept of the "mathematical sublime." In Kant's formulation, reason comes to the assistance of perception and the imagination just when these faculties are overwhelmed in their attempts to calculate the dimensions of the boundless object.[42] Reason thus is seen to restore the subject's stability and the assuredness of its faculties in the face of images of vastness and grandeur, particularly the most imposing manifestations of nature (*Critique of Judgement* 108–10).[43]

Specifically, I discern, behind the organization of the material of the *Rusticatio Mexicana,* the formation of a disembodied, autonomous subject.[44] As a member of the Jesuit order, Landívar remains embedded within the institutional and discursive infrastructure of the Catholic Church. Nevertheless, that infrastructure, and the ideology that upheld it, undergoes a process of fragmentation during Landívar's lifetime. First, the changes in the curriculum of the Mexican Jesuit colleges necessarily must have introduced a certain flux or instability into the thinking of its educators and students, opening it up to the possibility that the recourse to a divine ordering principle might have to be supplemented, or possibly replaced, by a human subject as guarantor of knowledge and ethics. Second, I will argue that Landívar's poem needs to be read in the context of the sundering of the Jesuit worldview produced by the expulsions of the order's members from the territories of the most powerful Western nation-states.

It is my contention that these two factors open up Landívar's thinking to the unstable and uncertain flux that is characteristic of modernity.[45] That it is not to claim that these forces lead Landívar to embrace the new dynamic nor to acknowledge consciously the full implications of the changes taking place. However, the poem does articulate a vision of a world that is, by turns, representable and available to mathematical logic, then marked by uncertainty, instability, and violence, in the wake of the erosion or destruction of the substantive forms of authority and reason previously supplied by the institutional matrices and laws of the viceregal government and of the Society of Jesus. At the same time, in their position of estrangement, following the expulsion, Landívar and his comrades figure among the earliest Spanish American writers in exile. From such an unstable locus, Landívar will seek, over the course of the *Rusticatio Mexicana,* to delineate the outline of a theoretical subject who might restore and underwrite a new order of representation and meaning in an attempt to overcome the trauma of destabilization and estrangement.

As I will argue in the rest of this chapter, in the *Rusticatio Mexicana* I discern an articulation of the issues mentioned above. Faced with the specific problems of overcoming the very opaqueness of America for European readers and the related notions of its natural environment's wildness and its perceived inhospitability to civilization, Landívar struggles, alternately, with the discourses of the beautiful and the sublime in his efforts to represent and make sense of aspects of that environment, and of the fracturing of the institutions and discourses that had previously organized it.

Criollo Natural History: Remapping the Beautiful

Book 1 of the *Rusticatio Mexicana* is devoted to the topic of the lakes to be found in the viceroyalty. As the beginning section of the work proper, it contains three opening stanzas that synthesize the poet's motives for writing and the themes of the poem as a whole. The first of these stanzas reiterates Landívar's desire to establish a break with *conceptista* and *culterano* writing practices and convey his subject matter in clear style. The "Exordium" reads:

> Obtegat arcanis alius sua sensa figuris,
> abstrusas quarum nemo penetrare latebras
> ausit, et ingrato mentem torquere labore;
> tum sensum brutis aptet, gratasque loquelas;
> impleat et campos armis, et funere terras,
> omniaque armato debellet milite regna. (Landívar 1.1–6)

> Let another conceal the meaning in arcane figures, into whose abstruse hiding places nobody dares to penetrate, nor exert his mind in thankless labor; let him bestow reason and pleasing language upon beasts; let him fill the fields with armed men, the earth with graves, and subdue all kingdoms with armed forces.

The juxtaposition of the practice of heavy stylization with the destructive actions of war and imperialism establishes the role of letters within the range of discursive practices that serve to facilitate order and productivity within society. Landívar further develops the implicit contrast between the peaceful history of the viceroyalty and the disruptive feuding of the European nation-states already established by Eguiara. The reference to the calamitous effects of wars leads into the second stanza, where Landívar outlines the fifteen topics he will address in the poem. He introduces this synthesis with the following affirmation of patriotic feeling: "Me iuuat omnino terrae natalis amore, / usque uirescentes patrios inuisere . . ." (1.7–8; "It delights me altogether, for the love of my native land, to visit its evergreen ancestral fields").

Having introduced the individual themes of each book, he proceeds to set down more fully his reasons for writing the poem, acknowledging the role played by the nostalgic feelings provoked by the circumstances of his exile. Landívar writes:

> Debueram, fateor, maesto praecordia peplo
> induere, et lacrimis oculos suffundere amaris:

nam flores dum prata dabunt, dum sidera lucem,
usque animum, pectusque meum dolor altus habebit.
Sed tantum cogor celare in corde dolorem,
corde licet cauto rapiat suspiria luctus.
Quid tristes ergo gemitus de pectore ducam?
Ardua praecipitis conscendam culmina Pindi,
Musarumque Ducem supplex in uota uocabo;
ambit enim quandoque dolens solacia pectus. (1.18–27)

I must, I confess, wrap my heart in a gloomy peplum, and
fill my eyes with bitter tears: for as long as the fields yield
flowers, and the stars light, deep pain will hold my soul and
my breast. But I feel obliged to hide this great pain in my
heart, although the sorrow pulls sighs from my careful heart.
Why, then, will I draw these sad moans from my breast? I
will climb to the sheer tops of the steep Pindus, and hum-
bly call upon the Master of the Muses; for sometimes the
sorrowful breast solicits comfort.[46]

In this section, one witnesses the brief overt presence of
the "I" in the poem, which occasionally surfaces in spite of
Landívar's efforts to repress traces of emotionality and involvement in order to establish the fiction of an objective, scientific
description of the material space of New Spain. The voice of
the poem articulates itself at a series of intersections between
discourses and histories. It is not simply that of enlightened
reason, coldly organizing its surroundings into a controllable
ensemble of objects that are always already under its mastery.
Nor is it a voice of antagonism to reason, a proto-Romantic
subject that flees the world of artifice and industry, drawing its
creative force from "pure" nature and then spewing its presence expressionistically back onto a pastoral world.

In this emotional outpouring, one perceives the presence of
a *criollo* subject still in the process of gestation, striving to
establish some form of mastery. The poem's contradictory blend
of scientific practice and sporadic subjective outbursts signals
it as both symptom of—and response to—a situation in which
the logic of a rationalizing modernity has not been fully imposed. It is a subject who conceptualizes and imagines a *patria,*
and whose agency is forged in a symbiotic relationship with
its projection of forms of association. It seeks to constitute these
forms of association through the labor of assembling an archive,

a collection of objects that will come to be regarded as the signs binding a group together. In Landívar's poem the foundational basis of such an archive will not be artifacts, but the material context of their production: nature and agriculture.

Landívar's gaze moves across this landscape, framing its most visually stunning components, alternately, within the discourses of neoclassical beauty and of the sublime. In representing these scenes, the theorized *criollo* intellectual subject does not assume a form through the expression of awe and powerlessness in the face of transcendent natural wonders.[47] Rather, in the poem one can track a peculiar enactment of the "moment of blockage," which is ultimately resolved through the performance of the labor of empirical, scientific investigation. Specifically, Landívar engages in a dual action in which his self is apparently effaced and the unrepresentable character of sublime natural environments is overcome through the work of a gaze that breaks them down into their numerous components.

The fourth stanza of book 1 establishes the pattern according to which all the remaining cantos will be composed, offering a personal invocation of the muses, after which the poet's "I" becomes submerged in the detailed evocation of the objects of its gaze. First, a request is made:

> Tu, qui concentus plectro moderaris eburno,
> et sacras cantare doces modulamina Musas,
> tu mihi uera quidem, sed certe rara canenti
> dexter ades, gratumque melos largire uocatus. (1.28–31)

> You, who play the ivory lyre, and teach the sacred muses to sing rhythmically, be favorable to my singing of real, but certainly unusual matters, and once invoked, grant me a pleasing melody.

Having invoked the guidance of a metaphysical power to confer order and harmony on a materiality that, he acknowledges, challenges the norms of neoclassical representation, Landívar provides a brief historical background for his depiction of the poem's first set of scenes, the lakes of Mexico. The fifth stanza gives an account of how Mexico City was once ruled for many years by its indigenous population, but that it is now under Spanish rule (1.32–36). This brief, superficial version of the city's history serves as a pretext for the poet to move on to a meditation on its geographical location in an area where it is surrounded by several lakes (1.37–48). Two of the lakes, those of Chalco and Texcoco, are portrayed in minute detail, thus called because of the two towns with the same names that grew up next to them (1.49–54). First, he turns to Lake Chalco, remarking upon the powers of its waters to make the nearby lands fertile and productive (1.55–60).

Landívar emphasizes the abundance of plants that grow in the area of the lake. Thus he begins to create a picture of Mexican nature to be superimposed over the dystopian image of an unhealthy and unfriendly environment portrayed by European natural historians.[48] From this starting point, the text moves into a scientific process of piece-by-piece representation of the lake, its qualities, and the individual elements that constitute it, as the poet establishes a correlation between the rules of classical beauty and decorum that underpin the language he uses and the order of the water system depicted. The next stanza evokes the manner in which the lake derives its water supply, and affirms its tranquil character:

> Hic dulces uasto latices exaggerat alueo:
> namque per obscuros tranquilla fluenta canales
> colligit, et tenues etiam sine nomine riuos,
> puraque gramineis undantia flumina campis.
> Non rapidum Boream, non illuc Aeolus Austrum
> mittit, nec saeuis Eurus, Zephyrusque procellis
> ardua luctantes sese in certamina poscunt.
> Murmure sed posito, uentisque in claustra fugatis,
> incubuit puris tranquilla malacia lymphis. (1.61–69)

> It piles up sweet waters in its vast belly: for it gathers up tranquil streams through dark canals, and also small nameless brooks, and the clear rivers watering grassy fields. Aeolus sends neither Boreas nor Auster there, nor do Eurus and Zephyr call for fierce battle, waging war with their cruel storms. The murmur is not heard, and with the fleeing winds driven into their cells, calm lies in tranquillity over clear waters.

Landívar then focuses on the first individual component of the waters he judges to be of significance, a natural fountain.

The fountain is deemed worthy of the poet's interest because of its wildness and visually pleasing quality, for being a natural setting that is striking, but can still be accommodated within the comfortable, balanced scheme of neoclassical beauty (1.70–79). This image of the fountain is reinforced, and transposed for the European reader in the remaining lines of the stanza (1.80–87). It is elevated, and lent authority, through comparison with the details of a classical Greek myth in which the nymph Arethusa is chased by the river god Alphaeus in Peloponnesus, and is then transformed by Diana into a fountain. Nevertheless, the image is not allowed to remain as if untouched in its aura of transcendence, but is subjected painstakingly to a scientific gaze. At this point, Landívar initiates a general discussion of the origins of springs. In the subsequent stanza, he derives from the particular case a general principle, breaking down the process through which springs are formed in the following terms:

Unde tamen iugis ducatur fontis origo,
quoue reluctantes consurgant impete lymphae,
incertum. Quis enim certis se noscere signis
dicat, conclusum secretis aera fossis
in uarias cogi brumali frigore guttas
acturas exinde leues per gramina lymphas,
et largos etiam prearupto e pumice riuos.
Ni potius nigras subiens maris unda cauernas
inde per angustas quaerat spiracula rimas,
dum sale sub terris posito, prauoque sapore
irruat in campos humor, fontesque, lacusque
impleat, et grata recreet dulcedine plantas.
Aut certa irrigui ducant exordia fontes
montibus ex altis, pluuia, glacieque grauatis. (1.88–101)

However, from where the spring derives its perennial origin, or by what force the struggling waters rise up, is uncertain. There will be he who will say that he knows by sure signs that the air enclosed in underground ditches condenses in the wintry cold into many drops, which afterward will run as light waters through the meadows, and also as a bountiful brook from the steep rock. Or is it, rather, that the sea water, entering dark caves, tries to seek a vent through narrow cracks and, leaving the salt and its bitter taste under ground, the liquid rushes into the fields, fills the fountains

and lakes, and revives plants with pleasing sweetness? Or
that the fresh springs derive their beginnings from the high
mountains, heavily laden with rains and ice?

In this fashion, a natural element that appears miraculous
or inexplicable is made into something that can be compre-
hended and represented through the process of formulating and
testing experimental hypotheses about it. After describing the
different possible natural conditions that can produce springs,
Landívar comes to a conclusion about the one that exists at
Chalco, explaining that its waters are derived from the ice that
accumulates on two nearby mountains (1.102–14). He concludes
the sequence of stanzas about the spring with an evocation of
a marble cross that stands immersed in the waters of the spring
(1.115–29). Unlike the spring itself, the religious image of the
cross is allowed to retain its aura, since although it is a work
of artifice, no trace of its origin or maker remains, making it,
therefore, a sacralized cipher of cultural identity that lies beyond the scope of humanist technologies of representation
(1.122–23).

Having established this panoramic view of the lake, Landívar
initiates the process of mapping its constituent features. The
first of these are the *chinampas,* areas where plants grow on
the waters. Prior to describing them, he addresses Chloris, the
goddess of nature, requesting an explanation of how this aquatic
garden came into being (1.130–39). The dialectical movement
from objective representation of the lake to an intersubjective
dialogue between poetic voice and the classical deities of nature
is an expression of the contradictory forces present in Landívar's
project. The detailed, predominantly referential concern to
correct metropolitan perceptions of America repeatedly yields
to the impulse to will a *criollo* self that is to construct itself,
alternately, out of the experience of the beauty and sublimity
of its natural environment and the fruits of its interaction with
those surroundings. The invocation of Chloris prefaces the demystification of the unreal spectacle of plants growing not out
of the soil, but in water. First, Landívar depicts this image of
ideal beauty, then he uncovers the material processes determining its production, carefully illuminating this hidden dynamic
in great detail.[49]

The story of the watery garden is inextricably linked to that of the growth of the city of Tenochtitlan in the middle of the lake, and to its emergence as the center of a vast empire. In the following stanza, Landívar relates that one of the kings of Atzcapotzalco grew jealous and wary of the achievements of his urban subjects, and threatened to destroy the city and its people if they did not pay him a new form of tribute, in addition to those he had already cruelly levied upon them (1.140–53). The tribute required them to set out before him, in the lake, floating gardens, laden with fruit and flowers. The reader is then presented with a narrative of the achievements of a popular artisanal class in the face of a tyrannical absolutism, a tale charged with allegorical implications in a period when the Spanish Crown was trying to establish a more efficient system for extracting capital from its American territories. Although the masses ("turba") are initially moved to the kind of irrational and emotive response commonly attributed to them by *letrados* like Landívar, they soon show themselves capable of organizing themselves in such a fashion as to satisfy the unreasonable demand of their tyrannical ruler ("crudelis"; 1.154–56).

At length, the next stanza narrates the tale of how the citizens ("ciues") work together to realize this undertaking of such grand proportions. They leave their homes and the lake, and go out into the forests to gather trees for the task (1.157–60). Their activities are divided up and mapped in much the same fashion as the individual features of the aforementioned waters themselves. Landívar writes:

> Cuique suum partitur opus, sua munera cuique:
> pars lento uellit faciles e uimine ramos,
> pars onerat cymbas, pars remis ducit onustas:
> feruet opus, durosque iuuat perferre labores.
> At postquam siluae magnum congessit aceruum,
> cunctaque consilio maturo turba parauit,
> concurrit, texitque leues e fronde tapetas
> oblongae storeae similes; quos moenia propter
> expandit, textosque salo committit aperto,
> callibus hinc atque hinc multis super alta relictis.
> Ne tamen infensi spargant conamina uenti,
> aut mare surripiat pronum fugientibus undis,
> cauta trabes fundo nodoso ex robore figit,
> uimineasque ligat storeas ad tigna rudenti. (1.161–74)

137

> Everyone is assigned a labor, everyone a function; some pull
> the light branches from the languid osier, some load the boats,
> and some transport them, laden, by oar: they work energeti-
> cally, and happily endure their hard tasks. After they have
> heaped up the great piles of foliage, the crowd all together,
> with an opportune plan, prepare, join together, and weave
> light tapestries out of the foliage like long straw mats, which
> they stretch out by the city walls, and then place, once woven,
> in the open salt waters, leaving many paths here and there
> over the deep. However, lest hostile winds should scatter
> the fruits of their efforts, or the swift sea should pilfer them
> with fleeing waves, [the crowd], cautious, fasten oak posts
> to the bottom, and tie the osier mats to the posts with rope.

The representation of the first stage in this feat of agricultural engineering is striking for its depiction of a Nahuatl society
that organizes itself according to principles of rationalization
and specialization of labor. At the same time, all participate in
a collective enterprise in which the privileged form of agency
is not that of the individual, but that of the totality of the citi-
zenry. Having completed this task, the group then moves on to
the second part of the enterprise, in which they gather clods of
soil from the fields, and carry them in boats to the area that is
to be cultivated (1.175–88). The finished product proves to
satisfy the cruel ruler, and the gardens have been maintained
ever since (1.189–94). In this fashion, they have become part
of a shared heritage and, as such, merit inclusion in the com-
pendium of artifacts and topographical features that Landívar
is constructing. He observes:

> Ast alios undis hortos sibi cauta reseruat,
> qui Florae gemmis addant Cerealia dona,
> et quos assidue subigens diuturna propago
> incorrupta sui seruet monumenta laboris. (1.195–98)

> They conserve for themselves the other gardens on the wa-
> ters, where Ceres's gifts are added to Flora's buds, of which
> this ancient subject-people assiduously takes care and pre-
> serves unspoiled record through its labor.[50]

With the water garden now established as a sign of native
Mexican artifice and rational organization, the poem continues with a short stanza in which Landívar comments upon the

fact that the Indians are able to move the gardens around different parts of the lake. In this manner, they are able to avoid taking too many resources from any one area of the surrounding fields and, at the same time, protect the gardens' fruits from strong winds (1.199–202). Here the voice of the theorized *criollo* subject coalesces again and inserts itself into the discourse of the poem, addressing the reader in the second person with a comment on the scene depicted: "Hinc totidem genti ridentia floribus arua, / quot nantes placide uideas super alta tapetas" (1.203–04; "For this reason, the people have as many fields smiling with flowers as the mats which you see floating calmly on the waters").

The depiction of flora and fauna in and around the waters continues in the following three stanzas. The first lists the arboreal species that grow on the lake's bank, represented anthropomorphically here as a competitor who painfully strives to emulate the aquatic gardens, producing osiers, cherry trees, pear trees, apple trees, laurel trees, pines, cedars, oaks, and green meadows (1.205–09). The second stanza mentions the huge variety of birds that populate the surrounding wooded areas and sing on the lakeshores (1.210–15). The third stanza shifts from the position of this totalizing gaze to focus on the microscopic details of individual components of the general picture, in this case, two species of birds. Landívar evokes, first, the sparrow with its elegant red plumage and pleasant song (1.216–17). Then, he depicts in greater detail the *cenzontle* (mockingbird), a species unknown in the Old World and endowed with skills and a form of subjectivity that would appear to resemble closely those of the *criollo letrado:*

> Ludit et insignis raro discrimine uocum
> alituum Princeps, quo non uocalior alter,
> Centzontlus, prisco uolucris non cognitus orbi,
> qui uoces hominum simulat, uolucrumque, canumque,
> et modulos etiam sociantis carmine plectro.
> Nunc canit ad numerum, nunc Miluum fingit edacem,
> nunc simulat felem, litui nunc signa canori
> reddit, festiuusque latrat, lugetque, pipitque.
> Inclusus cauea gaudet uolitare canendo,
> iungereque insomnes modulis noctesque, diesque.
> Non ita compositis deflet Philomela querelis

maesta scelus, densis nemorum cum tecta sub umbris
populeas tremulis siluas concentibus implet,
lusibus ut ripas hilarat Centzontlus amoenis. (1.218–31)

The distinguished *cenzontle,* which is prince of the birds,
amuses itself with a variety of voices, [and] there is no other
better singer; unknown in the Old World, the bird imitates
the voices of men, birds, and dogs, and even music sung to
the accompaniment of the lyre. Now it sings in time, now it
pretends to be the rapacious kite, now it mimics the cat, now
it repeats the sounds of the melodious trumpet, and barks,
weeps, and chirps in lively fashion. Locked up in the cage,
it likes to flit about, singing, and continues with its melo-
dies day and night without sleeping. In composing her com-
plaints, Philomela does not mourn her misfortunes as much,
when, hidden in dense woods, she fills poplar groves with
quivering harmonies, as the *cenzontle* brightens the shores
with its pleasant playing.

Landívar's detailed evocation of the bird's skills in learning
the modes of enunciation of many species, including man, further develops the poem's interweaving narratives of natural
science and *criollo* intellectual subjectivity. At the first, referential, level, it conveys detailed information about a component of American nature that is unknown in Europe, thus
expanding the body of universal scientific knowledge and, at
the same time, inserting the bird into the scheme of the beautiful. At a second level, at once allegorical and performative,
the representation of this polyglot bird embodies a model of
experience common to the American-born man of letters. Like
the *cenzontle,* the *criollo* has become proficient in various languages and forms of knowledge, but, at the same time is unable to assume any of them individually as the exclusive basis
of an identity or essence. It is in the process of the acquisition
and the articulation of these languages that he lives his form
of subjectivity, trying out one first, then adopting another, sometimes intertwining them as he pieces together the disparate
components of his archive, mixing artifice with nature, indigenous and European cultural practices and creations. In the process of this investigation of, and experimentation with, different
languages and modes of knowledge, the poet shapes the identity of a region, organized in accordance with the coordinates
of *criollo* subjectivity.[51]

After describing the boat races and fishing activities the local natives conduct on Lake Chalco, Landívar concludes the cycle of stanzas devoted to its waters in a block of verse in which the names of great poets born in America are catalogued (1.232–66). This section takes the form of what Landívar himself refers to, in his "Monitum," as a "fiction" in which these poets are depicted as performing their art on the lakeshores (7). This picture reactivates the image of Mexico as a kind of *locus amoenus* for the cultivation of letters and learning that is presented in López's *Aprilis Dialogus*. Landívar evokes the propitiousness of the scenario for the elaboration of eloquence in the following terms:

> Ast ubi uesanus cessauit uere tumultus,
> inque urbem numerosa uadis se turba recepit,
> discurrunt placidi per amoena silentia ripa,
> queis cordi tranquilla quies, quos cura fatigat,
> et quos facundae iuuat indulgere Mineruae.
> Tunc capti tacita rigui dulcedine ruris
> litora concentu replent quandoque Poetae. (1.271–77)

> But when the furious tumult has truly finished, and the large crowd returns through shallow waters to the city, those of calm mind, those fatigued by cares, and those who delight in giving themselves over to eloquent Minerva peacefully roam around quiet and pleasant shores. Then, enticed by the tranquil silence of the fields by the lake, the poets sometimes fill the shores with harmony.

In much the same fashion as López does in his dialogue, Landívar emphasizes the tranquil, peaceful character of the geography and human population of New Spain. Significantly, the poets whom the Jesuit mentions are included for having written works on both religious and secular topics. The first poet mentioned is Juan Carnero, a cleric from Puebla who wrote a poem entitled *La pasión del señor,* as Landívar points out in a footnote (1.278–80). Diego José Abad, another Mexican Jesuit, is also the author of a religious poem, the *Luz heroica de Deo Carmina* (1.281–82).[52] Alegre, a contemporary of Landívar, and also a product of the Jesuit tradition of classical studies, translated Homer's *Iliad* and *Alexandriad* from Greek into Latin (1.283–85).[53] The author of the *Rusticatio Mexicana* celebrates all these scholars for having produced works worthy of inclusion in the universal pantheon of humanism, rather than texts that might express some sense of differentiation or rupture with respect to the models and canons of European intellectual tradition. Landívar concludes his portrayal of Mexican mastery of ordered and measured humanist poetics with eulogies for the Mexican writers Zapata, Reina, Alarcón, and Sor Juana Inés de la Cruz (1.286–97).

Amid the favorable surroundings of the lake and its shores, the poets, in turn, are held to have enhanced its pastoral order and harmony with their measured verse. Zapata is probably the lesser-known seventeenth-century lyric poet Luis Sandoval y Zapata. Miguel de Reina Ceballos, an eighteenth-century figure, wrote *La eloquencia del silencio,* a poem in honor of San Juan Nepumoceno. Juan Ruiz de Alarcón is the more famous writer of numerous plays performed at the end of the sixteenth century and the beginning of the seventeenth, during the most prolific period of the theater in early modern Spain.[54] However, it is Sor Juana Inés de la Cruz who is accorded the highest rank of all, being praised for the wit and grace of her verse. Her mastery of artifice is conveyed in the hyperbolic metaphors that attribute to her the capacity to control nature with her poetry. Landívar canonizes her unique talent by again placing Mexican cultural production within the framework of classical humanism, noting that she is commonly referred to as the "tenth Muse" in New Spain.[55]

Book 1 concludes with a briefer sequence of stanzas devoted to the representation of Lake Texcoco. In the first of these stanzas, Landívar carefully traces the course of streams that flow through the area of the city, leading into a lake that is salty as a result of the presence of asphalt in its waters (1.298–305). He then looks through the lens of the natural historian, explaining that the water's saltiness is caused by the soil of its bed (1.306–18).

The detailed analysis of the lake's saltiness reveals its negative consequences for both the waters themselves and the fields around them, and scientifically traces the cause back to the material composition of its bed. Here, the thrust toward scientific investigation and exposition overrides the impulse to depict the lake in purely utopian terms. The representation of this negative feature of Mexican nature, which impedes the vitality of natural life and the human activity of agricultural production, serves its purpose as part of a totalizing description of a space to be grasped and fashioned by *criollo* subjects. The demystification of such problems, together with the principles developed through the experience of the running of the Jesuit haciendas, offers the theoretical basis for the efficient management of that space.

The knowledge gathered and imparted in the remaining stanzas serves as the implicit basis for this future projected action. In the first of these, Landívar depicts the climatic conditions of the lake, according to which the skies above it are sunny in the mornings, but cloud over and yield storms in the afternoons (1.319–32). The following stanza relates how the lake is completely enclosed and cut off from any other water sources, such as rivers or seas (1.333–42). Having completed this mapping of the lake's key features, Landívar devotes the final section of book 1 to the depiction of the natives' duck-hunting practices. He is concerned to emphasize the ingenuity involved in this application of indigenous technical expertise to practical use:

> Nil tamen antiquus spectauit gratius orbis
> insidiis, quas turba gregi parat Inda uolanti.
> Principio fluuialis Anas, pars prima paludis,
> aethereas persaepe plagas, fluctusque secabat
> Mexiceos, nec tela uirum, fraudesue timebat.
> Quin etiam lacuum ripis errare sueta
> saepius indigenas audens ludebat inermes.
> Sed tandem audacem gentis sollertia uicit.
> Crescit enim densis uentosa cucurbita siluis,
> supremisque haeret truncorum pendula ramis
> congrua Neptuno, Bacchoque futura lagena.
> Has inter sollers maiores deligit Indus,
> et uacuas mittit uitreas innare per undas,
> maior ubi alituum collecta est turba natantum. (1.343–56)

> However, the Old World has admired nothing as pleasing as those traps which the Indian crowd prepares for the winged flock. In early times, the river duck, lord of the lake, very often flew across the Mexican skies and waters and did not fear the spears or traps of man. Moreover, usually wandering on those lakeshores, it often boldly mocked the helpless natives. However, the people's ingenuity finally conquered this boldness. For there grows among deep forests the light gourd,

> which, hanging from the highest branches, clings to the trunks,
> and was of use to Neptune, and later was Bacchus's jug. The
> skilled Indian picks the largest gourds, and, emptied, he
> places them to float across the glassy waters, where the
> greater crowd of swimming birds is gathered.

Notable here is the manner in which the Indians are able to demonstrate the application of wit ("sollertia") by having recourse to a raw material peculiar to the American environment—the gourd—in order to impose their will on the troublesome bird. Landívar then proceeds to portray what happens when the natives hollow out the fruits and place them on the waters.[56] At first, the ducks are fearful of the gourds, and take flight (1.357–58). However, little by little they return, seeing that the floating spheres pose no apparent threat to them (1.359–62). Then, the natives place more gourds over their heads and, having submerged themselves in the water up to their necks, they sneak up on the unsuspecting ducks and kill them, either by drowning them or by breaking their necks (1.363–73). This leads the poet to make the following remark in admiration of their ingenuity: "Scilicet incultae tanta est industria genti!" (1.374; "Evidently, such is the industry of an uncultivated people"). This observation brings book 1 to a conclusion that is charged with implications. First, it serves to displace the image of Americans as dull-witted, indicating the extent of the abilities of even those who have no formal education. In the second place, the exclamation looks forward to the depiction of the expanded potential of spheres of anthropocentric endeavors in New Spain, organized, theoretically, under the gaze of a subject whose knowledge is grounded in the specific agricultural, philosophical, and scientific principles developed by the Jesuits of the region.

Framing the Eruption of Sublimity: El Jorullo

Having articulated his representation of the waters of vast lakes through the register of the beautiful and the techniques of empirical science, Landívar moves on to the task of representing el Jorullo, a volcano in the province of Michoacan, and the lands around it. In the second book of the *Rusticatio Mexicana,* he expands the scope of the dialectics he has set up between the

labor of scientific representation and the project of constructing a matrix of shared Mexican experience and semiosis, moving
into a more volatile and unstable sphere. The lakes of Chalco
and Texcoco have presented a stable location for the determination of a series of images that might come to form part of a
signifying system of association for *criollos*. However, the
volcano, with its frightening capacity to destroy the stability
of such a world, and reconfigure it without concern for human
affairs, presents a more problematic and uncertain foundation
for the projection of a *criollo* utopia. Landívar opens book 2
with the following statement of its theme:

> Nunc quoque Xoruli Vulcania regna canendo
> persequar, et nigras montis penetrabo cauernas,
> qui mala tot populis, clademque minatus acerbam
> diuite florentes populauit germine campos,
> flammarumque globos, et ruptis saxa caminis
> impatiens uomuit, gelida formidine gentes
> concutiens, postrema orbis quasi fata pararet. (2.1–7)

> Now I will continue, singing of the volcanic realms of el
> Jorullo, and I will enter the dark caverns of the mountain
> which has threatened so many people with cruel ruin, pil-
> laged the blooming fields of abundant crops, and impatiently
> vomited balls of flame and broken, burning rocks, terrify-
> ing people with icy horror, as if the final doom of the world
> were being prepared.

Again, the poet's subjectivity coalesces in the prefatory section of a cycle of poems through the use of first-person verbal
forms. At one level, Landívar thus reemphasizes the notion that
his writings are the product of first-hand, empirical observation. At another level, the use of the first person signals the
formulation of the position of a lettered subject through his
representation of a geographical and social space—a *patria*—
to which he feels a bond. This subject emerges and is constituted in relation to the grandeur and sublime quality of the
objects and activities the writer represents and thereby assumes
as integral components of that space. Landívar explains his treatment of this natural wonder in a brief stanza:

> Nam quamuis animum delectent floribus horti,
> claraque fertilibus labentia flumina pratis;

sunt tamen interdum, uigili quos horrida uisu
aspectare iuuat longe, et reputare tuendo. (2.8–11)

For although blooming gardens and clear streams flowing
between fertile meadows delight the soul, there are those
who sometimes take pleasure in watching and studying
horrible sights with vigilant eyes, and reflecting.

In accordance with humanist principles, he takes pleasure
in the observation of the spectacle of the *locus amoenus* offered by the pleasant, fertile fields and waters. In fact, this
description is probably Landívar's clearest statement of the conception of pleasing beauty that is central to neoclassicism.[57]
Nevertheless, at the same time he also acknowledges the strange
fascination he feels for horrifying natural calamities, affirming
that this is a propensity common to all men.[58] Here, one glimpses
the emergence of the position of a secularized subject whose
experience of such transcendent material occurrences gradually comes to occupy the spiritual and religious vacuum created by the demystifying work of scientific experiment and
investigation over the course of the eighteenth and nineteenth
centuries. In the uncertain area where his religious formation
and his scientific education overlap, Landívar finds the basis
of a shared *criollo* symbolic and material world not only in that
which is beautiful, but also in that which is at once horrifying
and exhilarating in its power. In order to tell of the havoc
wreaked by the volcano, the poet calls upon the classical deity
Pomona to bear witness to the consequences of its eruption
(2.12–18).

The *invocatio* is followed by a series of stanzas that evoke
the different features of the nearby lands prior to the disaster.
In the first of these, Landívar depicts the Jorullo Valley, a large
area of agricultural lands containing several rivers and forests
of cork trees (2.19–23). Here, the farmer, or settler ("colonus"),
grows sugarcane on part of his land and keeps sheep on the
rest (2.24–28). The large flocks are allowed to roam around both
fields and forests, always under the watchful eyes of the shepherd and his dogs (2.29–32). In addition, the farmer raises oxen
and fast horses, which freely race across the fields and rest in
tranquil forests. The second stanza completes the picture of the
animals of the valley, offering individual portraits of the dif-

ferent species of birds found there. Most of these are species that live on the farm and are accorded significance by the poet in view of the fact that they provide an important source of sustenance for the human population (2.36–40). Among these birds, Landívar specifically mentions the duck, the goose, and the chicken (2.41–44). He also evokes the peacock, providing a detailed picture of its elegant plumage and proud demeanor (2.45–50). Finally, he creates a hyperbolic image of a flock of doves, whose members, when the birds fly into the air, block out the sky with their wings as if they together formed a large cloud (2.51–54). Represented as an organic, beautiful whole, the birds fall under the control of the farmer, who feeds them and uses them as a source of food (2.55–58). The evocation of this timeless *criollo* pastoral is completed in the following stanza.[59] Landívar depicts the working farmer's house and the church standing nearby:

> Eminet haec inter clari domus alta coloni
> antigua constructa manu, cultuque superba,
> prae foribus magna famulorum adstante caterua.
> Hanc prope surgebant parui penetralia templi,
> quod pietas olim multo lustrauerat auro,
> assiduoque frequens populus sacrauit honore. (2.59–64)

> At the center of all this, the illustrious farmer's great house stands out, built long ago in magnificent style, with a large troop of servants standing before its entrance. Next to it stood the sanctuary of a small temple, which piety once lit up with abundant gold, and which the people assiduously and frequently consecrated with worship.

The depiction of the farmer, and of the space over which his authority extends, is notable in several respects. In the first place, Landívar emphasizes the fact that the house is old and of aristocratic appearance. Through this depiction of a miniature pastoral, he develops a defense of the interests of *criollos,* asserting their long-standing control of the agricultural economy of New Spain. The passage can best be understood when seen in the context of the factional struggles between *criollos* and successive waves of peninsular immigrants. Within this dynamic, the former persistently vindicated their rights on the basis of their ability to trace their paternal origins back through a

genealogy to the first generations of *conquistadores* and settlers in the sixteenth century. Such claims derive their legitimacy from the notion that certain *criollo* families had come to
constitute a form of landed aristocracy with rights and powers
similar to those enjoyed by the nobles of feudal Europe.[60] In
the second place, this section also represents how the clergy
worked hand-in-hand with the landowners to maintain ideological control over the peasants who labored on their estates,
in areas over which the imperial state had exerted only limited
power prior to the implementation of the Bourbon monarchs'
centralizing policies in the eighteenth century.

Seen against this background, the fact that this *criollo* pastoral is undermined by the apocalyptic event of a volcanic eruption, in Landívar's narrative, acquires certain significance. The
representation of this natural disaster is laden with allegorical
resonances, prominent among which are the events surrounding the Bourbon state's confiscation of all of the Jesuits' lands
in New Spain, in its efforts to undo *criollo* monopolies over
the production and sale of certain commodities, and its policy
of diminishing the level of *criollo* participation in colonial
government.[61]

In the following stanza, the downfall of this *criollo* pastoral
is foreseen by an old stranger, who is venerable and wise in
appearance (2.65–70). The man predicts that a powerful volcano will cover the valley in fire, hurling burning rocks onto
its fields (2.71–79). The old man's portent has an immediate
effect on the indigenous population that works in the valley,
producing a sense of foreboding. However, the native laborers' fears are portrayed not as the irrational response of super-
stitious fools, but as a legitimate concern that leads many to
think of fleeing to the most remote forests (2.80–91). The episode of the portent is compared to the section of the Bible (Jonah
1.3–10) in which Jonah warns the king and the people of
Nineveh about an impending disaster (2.92–97). In fact, it is
the farmer, in the next stanza, who, in lambasting the Indians
for paying heed to a rumor spread by a stranger and question-
ing their strength of character, is made to appear foolish (2.98–
113). He has mistakenly placed too much faith in his perceived
mastery of the environment, and the words with which he calms
his workers are immediately followed by a cycle of stanzas that

depit the volcanic eruption of September 29, 1759, and the ensuing earthquake.[62]

In the first of these stanzas, the poet evokes the beginning of the disaster, a series of murmurs heard coming from underground, which prove the old man's prediction to be accurate (2.114–27). The second stanza shifts from the aural to the visual plane, and is given over to the representation of the chaotic sights brought about by the earth tremors, especially the shaking and movement of buildings (2.128–41).

Here, Landívar seeks to apply the organizational grid of natural history to the task of conveying a more dynamic visual spectacle.[63] Unfolding a panoramic gaze, he follows the chain of movement unleashed by the earthquake, observing the stumbling motion of the dazed people, the quivering of the *criollo* landowner's sumptuous home and the sturdy church, and the destruction of the Indians' huts. Terrified by the cataclysmic events, and fearful of the possibility of further disaster predicted in the skies (2.139–41), the peasants flee their lands in search of safer ground. Initially dumbstruck and absorbed in blaming the fates for their misfortune or in making promises to God, the people are calmed by the figure of the priest (2.142–49). Significantly, in spite of the latent divine implications of the disaster, the priest urges the peasants not to give themselves over to weeping, but to hurry with him to seek refuge in a safer place (2.150–58). This demonstration of ecclesiastical practicality identifies the cleric as the incarnation of the more pragmatic form of priestly agency developed by the Jesuits, particularly in their interventions in overseas contexts, faced with the more overtly material realities of life on the frontiers of European imperialism.[64] The stanza closes with a depiction of the peasants' flight from their lands, cast in terms that, at one level, are allegorically suggestive of the estrangement experienced by the Mexican Jesuits and *criollo* farmers from lands they had come to regard as their own, as a result of the policies implemented by the Bourbon state and the effects of mercantilist economics (2.159–66).

Landívar conveys the charge and import of this event to the classically educated reader by placing it within the framework of a parallel episode from Greek antiquity. In this fashion, he also elevates the stories pertaining to the history of Mexico to the status of epic, presenting the kind of setback that is, conventionally, the necessary prelude to the eventual establishment of a utopian order or republic in classical models of the genre. Therefore, the initial misfortune is closely followed by another of even greater proportions in the following three stanzas. In the first, just as the people reach a safe area, far from the site of the earthquake, the earth begins to vomit forth flames and balls of fire into the air, filling the skies with darkness (2.167–79). The second stanza represents the culmination of this violence, as a mountain is formed out of the movement of the earth and the effects of the fires. This process of destruction and mutation is broken down into a series of stages, evoked as if through the eyes of the peasants, who have fled even further in search of a safe haven (2.180–83):

> Namque flagrans intus rabidi uesania campi
> uicinas magnis urgebat motibus arces,
> totque furens taedas uasto uibrabat hiatu,
> ut magno celsas superarent impete nubes,
> purpureaque urbes implerent luce remotas.
> Quin etiam cineres liquidum per inane uolantes
> disiunctos populos passim pressere timore.
> Tot uero interea flammatae fragmina rupis
> impatiens ructat monstris fecunda uorago,
> ut saxum saxis, ac rupes rupibus addens
> ingentem mediis montem glomerauerit agris. (2.184–94)

> For such was the insanity that raged within that mad plain that it beset the nearby towns with great tremors, and so many were the sparks which it furiously hurled from a huge opening that with great force they rose above the high clouds, and filled remote cities with a crimson glow. Ashes also, flying through open space, even randomly afflicted distant towns with fear. Meanwhile, the monstrous abyss petulantly belched forth so many fragments of molten rock that, heaping rock upon rock, boulder upon boulder, it has made a huge mountain in the middle of the valley.

In this passage, Landívar gives what has come to be regarded as a largely factual account of the eruption (Kerson, "The Heroic Mode" 151). He bolsters the scientific effect of his depiction of events through the use of three footnotes. The first of these refers to the fact that the town of Páztcuaro, forty miles away, was lit up by the volcano's flames. The second relates that ashes fell in the city of Querétaro, at a distance of one hundred and fifty miles. The third footnote informs the reader that the newly formed mountain grew to a height of three miles (34nn2–4). The depiction of the immediate events of the eruption is concluded in the subsequent stanza, where details are given of how the volcanic activity expanded as four more craters opened up, each of them adding to the damage already wreaked on the land (2.195–201). Only after relating all of these elements in predominantly referential language does Landívar reintroduce a metaphorical dimension into the canto, claiming that the violence and extent of the eruptions surpassed similar effects produced by Mounts Vesuvius and Etna, with which he compares the actions of el Jorullo (2.202–06).

After conveying the key events of the earthquake and eruptions, Landívar analyzes, in a sequence of five stanzas, the short- and long-term consequences of the disaster for the area that constitutes the Jorullo Valley. In the first of these, he maps the effects on the agricultural lands and architecture of the lowland areas. The trees are blackened and stripped of their foliage, the grass pastures and fruit have been burned, and most of the area's cattle were killed (2.207–13). Neither have the products of human artifice been spared, since even where the *criollo* farmers' old houses and the elegantly decorated church once stood, there is now only rubble (2.214–19). The image of the ruin and decay of the products of anthropocentric agency is completed in the second stanza of the cycle, where wild animals are depicted as moving out of the forests and into the damaged towns and villages (2.220–24). Among these animals, Landívar identifies the bear, the lion, the coyote, and the tiger, all of whom reclaim the urban spaces back from man (2.225–28). This situation is interpreted by the poet as an inverted mirror-image of the world as it should be, a dystopian scene where humanist order is turned on its head:

> Ceu cum postremus mundi post tempora finis
> concutiet terrore feras; hominesque trementes
> motibus insolitis, flammisque uorantibus orbem
> tuta in speluncis atris habitacula quaerent,
> inque uicem uacuas errabunt bruta per urbes:
> haud secus exterret uallem Vulcania pestis. (2.229–34)

151

> Just as at the end of time, the final hour of the world will
> strike wild animals with fear; and unusual tremors will make
> men shake, and with the world in hungry flames, they will
> seek safe dwelling in dark caves, and the beast, in turn,
> will wander through empty cities: in like manner the ruin
> wrought by Vulcan threw the valley into terror.

In the third stanza of this sequence, Landívar depicts one consequence of the disaster that appears to have persisted for a period after the initial event of the eruption. After some time passes and a few sheepherders overcome their fears, they head back to their lands with their flocks, only to find that a black cloud, filled with sulfur fumes has gathered around el Jorullo (2.235–43). Without making the sounds of thunder customarily associated with storms, the cloud unleashes innumerable bolts of lightning down onto the valley (2.244–56). They split oaks, strike cedars, and kill many sheep on the spot, inducing young bulls to run into the hills and the rest of the surviving cattle to flee into the woods (2.257–61). It is observed that the volcano causes problems periodically, either covering the fields in flames or striking the towns with lightning bolts (2.262–66).

Landívar continues his analysis of the space of the volcano and its surroundings in the fourth stanza of the cycle dealing with its effects. Here, it is noted that the normally cool waters of a river running through the valley rise in temperature because of the heat that emanates from underground as a result of the eruptions (2.267–78). The fact of the changes wreaked in the condition of the waters leads Landívar to reiterate how the volcano brings about an inversion of the general natural order. It is related that at night the temperature of the waters rises to the point that they can scald human skin, but that during the day, even under the heat of the sun, they cool down (2.279–82). The stanza concludes with a comparison that helps lend greater weight and authority to the account. This apparently disordered and unnatural feature of American reality is not represented, and made legible, through the medium of a tale from classical mythology. Rather, it is compared, in a footnote, to a spring in Africa, which the natural historian, Regnauld, declares to be cold by day and hot at night (2.283–87). Thus, in accordance with the principles of scientific investigation, it is the supporting empirical data that serves to reinforce the verisimilitude of the effects described.

The tone on which this cycle of stanzas ends is not that of helpless horror in the face of destruction, but is, instead, optimistic. The final segment describes how the volcano contributes favorably to the workings of the valley's ecosystem. In the fifth stanza, the changes that the volcano's activity brings about in the area's climate and soil are related:

> Accedunt nec parua tamen solacia tantis
> excidiis; sua nam campis sua gratia maior.
> Vallis enim primum nimio feruentior aestu,
> repleuit postquam Xorulus cuncta ruinis,
> graminaque infensus maculauit caede cruenta,
> nec Libyco eneruat languentia membra calore,
> frigore nec Scythico torpent ad munia palmae;
> aere sed gaudent populus, pecudesque benigno.
> Sic laetos quamquam spoliauit germine campos,
> terraque per lustrum nullis fuit apta ferendis
> fructibus, at uero ex illo tot tempore fetus,
> antiquum ut uincant praesentia commoda damnum. (2.288–99)

> However, by no means small consolation accompanies such destruction; since after [the destruction] the fields acquire greater charm. For, too hot in its earlier state, the valley, after el Jorullo filled it all over with ruins, and angrily defiled the meadows with gory slaughter, does not weaken faint limbs with Libyan heat, nor make hands too numb for work with Scythian cold, but men and beasts alike enjoy a favorable climate. And although the rich fields were despoiled of their crops, and for one lustrum the land produced no seed nor fruit, in fact, from then on it produced so much that the new gains surpassed the prior loss.

Landívar thus does not dwell on the damage done to men's plans and endeavors by a transcendent force of nature. Rather, the sublime negative energy of the volcano is rewritten as a power that is not irrational, but that can reconstitute an environment, making it more fertile and more productive than before. The images of ruin and darkness recede with the passage of five years ("lustrum"), and the farmer, the shepherd, and the indigenous workers are able to return to their labors. The volcano cannot be mastered and controlled by man. Nevertheless, its violence and chaos can now be represented, or rendered comprehensible, as the poet has done through the process of tracking and mapping the individual elements that come together to produce the experience of its sublimity. Having attained knowledge of the volcano's dynamics and effects, both positive and negative, the region's citizens can adapt their plans and practices around its actions. Thus, Landívar has staged an instance of the "moment of blockage," as the experience of the indeterminacy or failure of the attempted representation of sublimity, and the resulting "anxiety" and uncertainty of the representing subject are ultimately overcome through the reestablishment of its coherence and stability in the face of the seemingly overwhelming boundlessness of the object.[65] Specifically, Landívar's enactment of this drama sets in motion a process in which a form of mastery and stability coalesces in the position of a subject who demystifies and grasps the workings of the volcano through the unfolding of reason in its thought. In this fashion, the position of this subject is posited as the ordering center of the poem, and of the representation of Mexican space.

The second book of the *Rusticatio Mexicana* concludes with a sequence of three stanzas devoted to the earthquakes of Bologna, the city in which Landívar spent much of the period of his exile. Here, the drama of the encounter with the indeterminate, disorienting moment of the sublime, with the subsequent stabilization of the understanding through reason, is replayed, as if to revisit the productive potentialities of that drama and, thereby, reinforce the position of the subject established in the face of el Jorullo. Landívar remarks that just as he has been trying to forget his worldly cares by writing these verses, he is shaken out of his labors by the sight of Bologna's river overflowing, the sounds of beams creaking, and the feeling that the earth is moving (2.300–05). The feeling of terror he shares with the other inhabitants of the city is inextricably bound up with the process of the articulation of the analytical discourse of the natural scientist: "Corda pauent, gelidosque quatit tremor horridus artus. / Excessere omnes domibus, consistere contra / nec possunt, tota passim discurritur urbe" (2.306–08; "Hearts

were terrified and awful fear shook chilled limbs. Everybody
fled from their houses, and could not withstand the danger, but
ran haphazardly throughout the entire city").

Vesuvius is portrayed, in the following stanza, as a voracious
force that has damaged the city of Parthenope and nearby agricultural lands, but feels aggrieved to see the walls and towers
of Bologna still standing (2.309–12). Enraged, Vulcan once
again breaks free from the subterranean prison that briefly con-
strains him, hurling forth fire and causing tremors in Bologna
(2.313–28). Significantly, at this point Landívar shifts tack once
more in order to identify a final feature of the volcanic activity in the area of el Jorullo. He notes that in similar fashion to
Vesuvius, el Colima, another volcano close to el Jorullo, has
erupted at unexpected moments, in periods when the latter has
been dormant and people have returned to their lands, assuming that things are safe again (2.329–37). Landívar then directs
a question at his readers that establishes that natural forces
hostile to man are just as prevalent in the Old World as they
are in the New. He inquires:

> Quis uero infernus cum rumor fertur ad aures,
> aut fremit horribili tellus conterrita motu,
> ingenti subito mentem formidine pressus
> non pariter nobis (terris auertite nostris
> o Superi monstrum) Xorulia fata timebit? (2.338–42)

> But who, when the subterranean noise is carried to their ears,
> or the earth roars and trembles violently, will not suddenly
> suffer great fear and, like us (O Gods, avert the monster from
> our lands), will not fear the fate of el Jorullo.

In this fashion, Landívar establishes the universality of the
experience of sublimity as experienced specifically in the face
of the destabilizing force of volcanoes. The implicit comparison with the better-known Italian volcano serves to render the
radical otherness of its Mexican counterpart intelligible to European readers. Landívar then concludes book 2 with an expression of religious faith in the protection the Virgin Mother will
afford the citizens of Bologna against the volcano. The poet
notes that the city should have nothing to fear as long as it pays
tribute at the Holy Virgin's altars (2.343–49). He intercedes on

behalf of its inhabitants, calling upon the Virgin Mother to place them under her protection in return for the homage they will always pay her so long as the volcano is active (2.350–55).

The appeal for divine protection against the volcanic forces of Vesuvius serves to underline the potential fragility of human artifice and of the position of the subject stabilized earlier. At the same time, the representation of sublimity in a European context may be seen as serving to validate the rearticulation of the field of aesthetics to incorporate the more anomalous and unruly components of American nature under the concept of the sublime. Nevertheless, at this stage the dual labor of establishing an ordering *criollo* subject-position and expanding the scope of aesthetics remains incomplete. It is, by its very nature, overflowing, polysemic, a force of signification, the power and sense of which will now be conveyed through the spectacles afforded by the waterfalls of the region of Guatemala.[66]

Cataractae Guatimalenses: Channeling Sublimity

As if to quell the flames of the volcanoes, the poem returns, in book 3, to the topic of water, focusing now on the waterfalls of Guatemala. In concentrating his attention on this aspect of geography, Landívar confronts the misleading images portrayed by European natural historians, who had tended to depict America as a continent in which human activity was severely restricted, in part, because of a predominance of marsh lands (Buffon 20: 316–23). Here, as before, an instance of the unruliness of American nature is mapped in such a manner as to establish *criollo* mastery of even the most difficult geography.

The third book opens with a proposition of the theme, followed by an invocation to the classical gods associated with that theme. Having declared that he is now going to return from the mountain to the rivers (3.1–4), Landívar asks the deities to speak to him about the waters of Guatemala (3.5–10). The first piece of information the water deities provide, in the third stanza, concerns the destruction of Antigua, as it stood when the Spanish arrived. It narrates how the city was built by its pre-Hispanic founders in a favorable setting, on the side of a mountain, amid dense forests and fertile lands, which yield fruit without requiring much human intervention (3.11–19). Between the crags of the mountain, a fountain spouts forth waters that quench the thirst of the young Indians and irrigate fruit groves (3.20–23). However, in Landívar's account the pastoral calm of this setting and way of life is brought to an end with the arrival of the Spanish *conquistadores* and the almost simultaneous destruction of the city by a flood of water that poured down from the mountain on September 10, 1541 (3.24–29). Symbolically, the waters engulf the city's temples and deities just at the time when the European invaders are imposing their new laws on the indigenous inhabitants of the region.

Faced with the absence of a center from which to administer the newly conquered territory, the Spanish move the remains of the city to the middle of a valley surrounded by high mountains and green fields, possessing favorable waters and a pleasant climate (3.29–33). The rebuilt city is evoked as an elegant and well-planned urban space, with beautiful churches, façades, meadows, and fountains (3.34–46). Nevertheless, in spite of the care with which the new city is constructed, it too falls victim to a natural disaster, the earthquake of July 29, 1773, depicted in the following stanza. The earthquake tremors cause buildings to collapse, and the fallen stone renders the system of roads impassable (3.47–51). The order and beauty of the city are disrupted even further when a huge cloud unleashes a deluge of water over it, burying its treasures ("gazas") in mud and leaving its remaining inhabitants to mourn the loss of their relatives (3.52–60). In the face of this aquatic force, Landívar stages another performance of the drama of sublimity. At first held rapt by its power, he then reasserts the position of a rational subject, analyzing its constituent parts and demystifying its force.

At this point, the frame of the poem switches from tragedy back to the register of natural history, as Landívar looks at the processes through which powerful masses of water are formed and affect their surroundings. This investigation is the topic of the subsequent two sections of book 3. The first of these begins with a stanza that depicts a very high mountain. It is represented, first, as an overwhelming, bellicose shape that rises so far that it challenges the sky itself (3.61–76). Then, piece by piece, the various individual aspects of the mountain's position within a broader natural scenario are delineated. The process begins in the second stanza of this section, which describes how the waters begin as small streams on the highest parts of the mountain, and then are transformed into powerful flowing rivers by the time they have descended to its foot (3.77–80). This is followed by a sequence of stanzas evoking the positive features of the mountain, all of which are made possible by the natural supply of water. The third stanza portrays the forests that cover the hillside and are filled with happy, singing birds (3.81–84). The fourth illustrates how the peasants plow the land at the foot of the mountain in order to grow fruit and grain (3.85–88).

The focus of the fifth stanza is the various species of flowers that grow in the fields around the mountain. There, one finds violets, marigolds, lilies, and nards, the last of which are celebrated for the characteristic that they bloom all year round (3.89–94). The sixth stanza of the section lists some of the types of fruit trees that flourish at the foot of the mountain, thanks to the constant moisture in the soil, providing melons, plums, citrons, and nuts for the skilled Indian pickers (3.95–101). In the seventh stanza, Landívar conveys the workings of natural ditches that carry water down from the mountain to irrigate the agricultural lands below (3.102–07).

Continuing with the topic of the movement of water, the following two stanzas contain a study of the clouds that constantly form out of the moisture at the upper reaches of the mountain. The eighth evokes the manner in which a cloud takes shape, from the end of the morning onward, around the mountain, at a point about halfway from the summit (3.108–12). Slowly, the cloud encircles the forests, and then rises up the slopes toward the constellations of the Great Bear and the Little Bear ("septem [. . .] trioni"), carrying its moisture with it (3.113–24). In the ninth stanza, the scrutinization of cloud formation and movement is completed, as the poet tracks how the cloud, after reaching the mountaintop, splits up into two separate bands, one of which is blown back down the mountain slopes toward the west, the other toward the east (3.125–30).

The last stanza of the cycle devoted to the mountain and its ecological system serves to mark the transition to the final section of book 3. It is noted that a village named Pedro Mártir stands on the lower part of the southern slopes of the mountain. Located in a spot beset constantly by a fierce sun and intolerable temperatures, it is plagued by gnats, flies, and harmful spiders (3.131–35). However, the village is most noted for its proximity to another natural spectacle of breathtaking proportions, a huge gorge with falling waters, which is depicted in the first stanza of the concluding section of the book:

> Propter enim pagum longo se scindit hiatu
> et rimam tellus aperit rescissa profundam,
> qua saliens amnis scopulis illiditur altis,
> ac praerupta cauas effingunt saxa cauernas.
> Haec autem sapiens latebris natura recondit;
> nec potis est ullus miros penetrare recessus,
> ni scalis lapsus uallem ducatur ad imam. (3.136–42)

> For near the village the earth splits wide open, and, torn apart, it reveals a deep crack, through which the stream leaps, crashing against high rocks, and steep cliffs form hollow caverns. However, wise nature conceals those marvelous recesses, and nobody can enter them, unless one descends to the bottom of the valley by means of ladders.

The first element of this hidden wonder is a kind of natural portico in the rock, which is evoked in the next stanza. It is notable that the poet chooses to focus upon this image of solidity and endurance, in contrast to the depictions of inhospitable marshlands fostered by the architects of European natural history, converting it metonymically into another component of the foundation for his reinterpretation and re-presentation of American reality. It is introduced in the following terms:

> Ast ubi planta solum patuli compressit hiatus,
> consistit subita stupefactus imagine rerum
> obtutuque animus perstat suspensus in uno.
> Namque statim, dextram fluuii labentis ad oram,
> obiectat se oculis ingens sub rupe cauata
> porticus aequa iugo, multasque extensa per ulnas,
> naturae constructa manu, saxoque rigenti
> sculpta olim. Tenues fastigia lata per auras
> diffugiunt muros nullis innixa columnis;
> sed scopulo nodata rudi compagibus artis
> pendula tecta uolant bis dena ab moenibus ulna. (3.143–53)

> But when one's feet press upon the bottom of the wide chasm,
> the mind becomes suddenly stunned by the unexpected sight,
> and remains transfixed, staring at one thing. For, immedi-
> ately, on the right bank of the stream, there stands up, huge
> before one's eyes, hollowed out of the rock, a portico which
> is like a mountain, and many cubits wide, built and carved
> long ago by the hand of nature out of the hard rock. The
> wide ceiling extends from the walls in different directions
> into the thin air, without the support of any columns; but
> fastened to the rough cliff by tight joints, it hangs twenty
> cubits above the walls.

The portico is presented as another component of the archive of transcendent natural spectacles in the region, a huge pres- ence that escapes the observer's comprehension because of its vastness and complex structures, all produced without human intervention. In the face of this bewildering sight, Landívar adopts, alternately, the subject positions of the scientist, with his transparent lens, and of the individual, with his heavy emo- tional investment in his homeland and who conceptualizes a network of images that might bind together the members of a *patria criolla*. Significantly, the image of the timeless rock struc- ture serves to introduce stability into the larger tableau, freez- ing and constraining the violent force of the waters and, at the same time, restabilizing the position of the subject ordering the representation.

The reconstruction of the panoramic vision of this natural scenario continues in the following stanza, which portrays, in minute detail, the constituent elements of the hill that stands opposite the portico. Here, the text shifts back into the realm of the beautiful in nature, as Landívar further develops his at- tempt to expand the range of the discourses of both aesthetics and natural history to incorporate American species. It is noted that the hillside is adorned with myrtles, oak trees, and an ar- ray of birds that bring it to life with their songs and bright col- ors (3.170–75). Among the birds, the poet focuses on the macaw, which he singles out for closer inspection in view of the beau- tiful variety of colors to be found in its wings (3.177–84). In a footnote, Landívar acknowledges the problems of rendering such unusual species in Latin, explaining his use of the word *pica* (magpie) to refer to the macaw (*guacamaya*) in terms of the close resemblance between the two birds (49n3). The translation of this American bird into European semiosis is completed through the comparison of the spectacle of its wings, as they open, to the action of the Roman goddess Thaumantias, also known as Iris, in fanning cloudy skies with rainbows (3.184–90).

The metonymical identification of the macaw with the visual image of the rainbow leads the reader back into the representation of a waterfall in the subsequent stanza. Here, the depiction of the final components of the landscape, in addition to the mountain and the gorge, is initiated. The falling waters are evoked in the following terms:

> Haec inter, lustrum dextra, collemque sinistra,
> uoluitur in praeceps undanti flumine riuus,
> inque imam uallem scopulo descendit ab alto:
> at tanto fluuius cumulo se uoluit aquarum,
> ut rauco uallis resonet concussa fragore,
> ingentique nemus strepitu, lustrumque reclament.
> Vox aures refugit, nec fas est uerba profari,
> ni leuibus placeat uoces committere uentis. (3.191–98)

> Between the cave, on the right, and the hill, on the left, the stream pours out swiftly, in billowing streams, which descend from a high precipice into a deep valley; but, the stream carries forth such a mass of water that the valley resounds and shakes with a thundering din. The sound of the voice escapes the ear, and it is not possible to say a word, unless one is happy to address oneself to thin air.

This stanza continues the process of the construction of a landscape comprising images of a magnitude that transcends the scope of the delimited norms of neoclassical representation. The waters are depicted as a powerful force, set against a rocky backdrop of great visual impact that it tests the poet's ability to convey the scene linguistically. The difficulty of the ecphrastic task is exacerbated by the aural dimension of the landscape, which provokes Landívar to complain, in these lines, that the noise made by the cascades as they hit the bottom of the cavern is so deafening that it prevents him from formulating any comprehensible discourse. The indeterminate character of the experience of sublimity is thus rendered here in terms of an inadequacy of discourse, which is unable to contain such a force within the representational bounds of neoclassical language.

Nevertheless, it is in the very process of his encounter with this sublime landscape that Landívar projects and reconstitutes a position of subjectivity, in the very attempt to render its seemingly transcendent reality intelligible to the European component of his implied readership. This undertaking is achieved again through an act of metonymic translation as the Guatemalan waterfall is compared, in its visual and aural excess, to a similarly violent and noisy waterfall that forms part of the Nile, in the more familiar territory of Egypt (3.199–207). Although its violence and the representational overload it effects strike fear ("timendum") into the poet, he is able to encapsulate its presence through reference to an object that already forms part of a body of knowledge.

The struggle between the will to representation and mastery, and these unruly objects is conveyed through the dialectic of control and chaos that characterizes the course of the waters. The following stanza maps their movement after their descent from the cliffs to the bottom of the valley, where they are forced between the more constraining boundaries of a river's banks, depicted metonymically as a prison ("carcere"), and over a rocky bed that they erode and shape into a form of canal (3.208–15). In this fashion, the torrent runs through a passageway between rocks until once again it breaks loose and insanely ("demens") hurls itself through an opening into the air (3.216–24). It thus creates another, even bigger, waterfall, which eludes the constraints of the rocks and returns the poet to the problematics of representing an almost supernatural force. He addresses this task in the subsequent stanza, first depicting the eddies that the exiting waters produce in a chasm located among the higher parts of the rocks (3.225–36). This area is overshadowed by the presence of a very high cliff, from which the waters once again hurl themselves downward at great speed (3.237–40). This process is depicted in a long, detailed series of lines:

> Tunc latices fluuius tumulo delapsus ab alto
> distrahit in minimas uenti spiramine guttas
> inque leuem totus casu dissoluitur imbrem.
> Vndique lympha uolat, ceu nubes cana, per auras.

Plena tamen gelida, terret quae subter, abyssus
perstrepit horrendum, circum spumante barathro,
undaque curuatas ripas corrodit auara
absorbens torto disiunctas gurgite cautes.
Ceu mare, cum ualidi permiscent aequora uenti,
nunc undas tumidum faciles iaculatur in astra,
ut caelum credas iamiam contingere pontum;
nunc fundum retegit, dissectis fluctibus, imum
tartareas ardens sonitu terrere cauernas:
tunc rabido cautes caedit, murosque furore,
absorbetque cauas sinuoso uortice pinus:
non aliter uallo saxi praecincta cuati
unda ferit crudas, deglutitque anxia rupes. (3.241–57)

Then, the waters, having slipped down from the high preci-
pice, are scattered by the force of the wind into very small
drops which, as they fall, dissolve into light mist. On every
side, water flies through the air like a white cloud. In the
same fashion, the abyss, filled with icy waters, brings terror to the regions below, and the foam-covered pit makes a
horrible roar. Its greedy waves eat away the curved banks,
devouring the rocks torn loose by the whirlpools. Just as
the sea, when the powerful winds agitate its surface, now
quickly lifts its swelling waves toward the stars, until you
might think its waters to be about to touch the sky, and then
parts its waves and uncovers the ocean's floor, eager to
frighten the caves of Tartarus with noise, and then, with
uncontrolled fury, breaks down cliffs and walls, and swal-
lows up boats in its swirling eddy, so the surging waters,
confined by the walls of the rocky depression, anxiously
strike the rough rocks and swallow them up.

In this fashion, Guatemalan nature is portrayed as a dynamic
space, the components of which are unstable and subject to
shifting processes of large-scale destruction and reconversion
into new formations. The waterfall is a powerful force that is
simultaneously able to project itself into the sky and crash down
onto the rocks below, reshaping them at every moment. At the
bottom of the valley, the waters form a whirlpool that erodes
the cliffs around it and drags rock fragments down into its vortex.
Through a series of parallel movements, the poet's gaze wan-
ders over the waters' course and effects, struggling with the
demands they place on his representational skills and seeking
to trap them within the linguistic framework of the stanza.

From these images of violence, the canto moves on to the more tranquil visual spectacles that complete the picture of this landscape of rock and water. The first of these is the sight of the rainbows that frequently arise as a result of the interaction of the falling waters with the sun's rays. In the subsequent stanza, this process is conveyed through the medium of classical mythology, as Iris, the Greek deity who stands for the rainbow, is depicted as descending and sitting in the waters under Phoebus's rays of sunshine, which split the light up into the individual components of the color spectrum (3.258–66). In this fashion, sublimity gives way to beauty in a dynamic that conveys the variety and malleability of both American nature and Landívar's techniques of representation.

The following stanza depicts the course taken by the waters after they have left the area of the gorge. Now they have been dispersed into smaller, weaker streams that run quietly, and in more controlled fashion, down a canal (3.267–70). They barely make a murmur as they flow further along into the Pacific Ocean, where their sweet waters are mixed with, and subdued by, the harsher brine ("mordaci [. . .] lymphae") of the sea (3.271–76).

Book 3 concludes with two stanzas that return the reader to the sublime, reiterating the grandeur of the image of the rocky portico portrayed earlier, now firmly installed as a symbol of *criollo* patrimony through the representation of a ceremony that is performed by Guatemala's "nobility" annually. The first of these stanzas reads as follows:

Nobilis huc properat Guatimala tota quotannis
tempore quo rigidis torpent Aquilonibus artus,
brumaque immiti tabescunt gramina campi.
Pensilibus scalis ad saxea tecta relati
ponte domant fluuium, donec sub rupe recepti
concaua suspenso perlustrent lumine saxa.
Omnia mirantur, montemque, amnemque, specusque.
Ore tamen presso nutus, et signa sequuntur,
siue salutatum pubes exoptet amicum,
seu uelit ad tectum prono iam Sole reuerti. (3.277–86)

To this place, all of noble Guatemala hastens every year, at the time when the stiff north winds numb the body and the grass is withered in the field by the harsh winter. Having let themselves down to the stone roof by means of hanging

ladders, they cross the river by bridge and, entering the rocky
cavern, they scan the vaulted chamber with astonished eyes.
They marvel at everything: the mountain, the river, and the
cavern. With a hushed voice, they communicate only with
nods and signs, whether one anxiously longs to greet a friend,
or wishes to return home at sunset.

Here, a mode of association is derived from the physical entry
into, and observation of, this natural landscape.[67] The stanza
evokes a ritual, according to which the inhabitants of Antigua
gather and descend into the chasm at the beginning of every
winter. Observing the breathtaking sight of the mountain, the
waters, and the cavern, the citizens are united by a common
feeling of awe, which draws them into a form of experience
that transcends the individual. Of significance is the fact that
the noise of the torrents drowns out any attempt at linguistic
communication between these spectators. Nevertheless, the
citizens are able to understand one another through the performance and reception of visual signs, by moving their hands
or nodding their heads. Their verbal silence points also beyond
the problem of the noise of the waterfall to the articulation of
something that exists still outside of the scope of linguistic
representation, to an unexplainable feeling of attachment or
association, the basis of which is constituted by the shared affect
felt in the presence of the natural wonders of the region. The
perception of the landscape transmits something that has not
yet been fully articulated linguistically, a bond that unites a
disparate group of individuals into the imagined form of a
republic in the process of gestation.

The valley's status as transcendent signifier is consolidated
in the final stanza. Landívar declares that the Egyptians should
keep silent about the green fields irrigated by the Nile and that
the ancient world should cease to boast of its seven wonders,
for the valley surpasses them in beauty, offering shade to nymphs
in spaces enhanced by the sweet fragrances of the mountain
and the singing of the birds (3.288–95). In this fashion, sublimity is transmuted again into beauty, affording the incorporation of the represented images of American nature into the
framework of neoclassical aesthetic norms.[68] Transformed into
a sign ("portentum") by Landívar, the valley now assumes a
discursive existence over and above its immediate material

presence, similar to that which has been conferred on the seven wonders by fame ("fama").[69]

The staging of successive enactments of the experience of sublimity has facilitated a demonstration of the productive possibilities of Mexico's material and aesthetic riches. First, these enactments have served to mobilize a protean form of intellectual subjectivity that can oversee and order the heterogeneity of American space. The coordinates of this subjectivity shift and move over the course of the dialectic Landívar unfolds with sublimity, finally becoming fixed at the moment of the silent association of the young Guatemalans as they contemplate the huge gorge from a position deep inside it. Second, the process of signification is also restabilized in the closing movement from the register of the sublime to that of beauty, manifested in the final, panoramic view of the valley, now reinserted into the organic, tranquil framework ordained by neoclassical poetics.[70]

Having explored American sublimity and having produced, out of its tensions, a stable basis for the elaboration of images and meaning, Landívar can now move on to the second stage of his project. In this second phase, which comprises books 4 through 11, he will depict the interaction of American humanity with that natural environment, a dynamic of labor and representation that will reshape it into an organized system of agricultural, economic, and cultural production.

After the Sublime
The Rationalization of Colonial Space

In the *Rusticatio Mexicana* the sublime serves as a medium for thinking through the problem of mapping that which is not easily grasped and incorporated into Western semiosis. At the same time, it stages a drama through which the position of a *criollo* subject of literary discourse and knowledge is stabilized. Nevertheless, Landívar's labor does not conclude with the establishment of an irreducible, natural force as the metaphysical core of a *criollo* patriotism. Rather, over the course of the next eight books of the *Rusticatio Mexicana,* he attempts to chart a variety of spheres of human activity in which the inhabitants of New Spain have developed modes of knowledge that enable them to intervene upon and assert authority over parts of their environment. In this section, they are depicted as having developed a prosperous and self-sufficient mode of existence, in accordance with sets of principles that have emerged out of the process of their interaction with American nature. The description of agricultural and industrial forms of economy in the viceroyalty serves to develop a narrative of *criollo* agency. In the sections that follow, I will discuss certain of the models of production and social organization that Landívar represents and analyzes in books 4 through 11 of the *Rusticatio Mexicana,* namely, purple dye, a beaver community, precious metals, and cattle raising.[1]

Dye Making: Landívar's Demystification of the Marks of Distinction and Imperial Power

The rewriting of the history of the development of solutions to the problem of how to render an unruly or unrepresentable space

167

meaningful and productive begins in books 4 and 5 with the depiction of dye manufacturing in Guatemala.² The opening quartet of book 4 incorporates the reader into the work of the text, reiterating the course of the journey so far in the first person, and pointing toward the next step:

> Postquam Neptuni uitreos inuisimus agros,
> regnaque Vulcani tremulis armata fauillis,
> uisere fert animus roseum cum Murice Coccum,
> ac totum fixis oculis lustrare laborem. (Landívar 4.1–4)

> Now that we have looked into Neptune's glassy territories
> and Vulcan's fiery kingdoms armed with quivering embers,
> I am inclined to view the cochineal with the murex, and to
> examine all of their processing with attentive eyes.

With these words Landívar begins to insert a narrative of production into the representation of a space most commonly depicted as resistant to human attempts to fit it into a framework of rationalization and manufacture. In this fashion, he initiates an attempt to show that while America may offer a natural environment filled with enormous and overwhelming features, it is not the empty space bereft of signs of human activity depicted by Buffon and Cornelius de Pauw. In place of such an image, Landívar endeavors to render visible the traces of American subjects' interventions on their material surroundings. Significantly, the first commodity he considers is one through which colonial subjects have made a lasting impression not only on their local geography, but also on the map of human history. Landívar represents the contribution of American labor to a universalist schema with the following invocation:

> Tu, quae puniceo, Tritonia Virgo, colore
> intextos auro Regum perfundis amictus,
> et Lydam laetaris acu uicisse puellam;
> dic mihi, quae dederit regio tibi prouida fucos,
> atque orbem Cocco, tyrioque impleuerit Ostro;
> quis legat haec campis, quae mittant semina terrae,
> et quo nascantur regalia germina cultu. (4.5–11)

> You, virgin Tritonia, who dyes with purple the robes of kings,
> embroidered with gold, and rejoices, having surpassed the
> Lydian maiden with the needle, tell me which region gave

you dyes, and supplied the globe with cochineal and Tyrian
purple, who gathers these in the fields, which lands provide
the seeds, and by what tilling the royal shoots spring forth.

Having set up a fictional intersubjective dialogue with the
Roman deities Lydia and Tritonia (Athena), Landívar starts to
recount a story in which the process of the production and in-
scription of purple dye as the universal sign of social ranking
on clothing is to be traced back to an American origin. With
the formulation of this rhetorical request to Tritonia, he is able
to integrate the account of the dye's elaboration into the order
of universal knowledge and value derived from classical antiquity. It begins with a sequence of stanzas that give specific
details of one of the geographical sites where dye is manufactured in New Spain. In the first of these, information is provided about the town around which the dye-making labors take
place, Antequera, or Oaxaca, as it is more commonly called,
because of its location in the valley of the same name (Landívar
4.12–15). A large population, sumptuous houses, high-quality
goods, and magnificent churches are singled out as the key
features of this town. Landívar extols the fertility of the soil of
the plains around the town and the favorableness of the climate,
which allows for cattle raising and yields blossoming flowers
and healthy trees all year round (4.16–27). The evocation of
this pastoral scene serves as a familiarizing ground onto which
Landívar can graft the scientific representation of the cactus, a
plant largely unknown to European readers. It is introduced in
the following terms:

> Hos inter diues gemmat Nopalis in aruis
> edita sex ulnas terra, suffultaque trunco
> imbelli, quem nulla comis frons mobilis ornat,
> ardentem pecudi Phoebum neque submouet umbra.
> Carnosas uero Nopalis uiuida frondes
> induit intextas duro subtemine fibrae,
> munitasque rubis canis, ac pelle uirenti
> obductas, ouum referunt quae saepe figura.
> At frondes quamuis fortis compago coartet,
> interiora tamen replet circumfluus umor
> coccineis quondam pascendis uermibus aptus.
> Nec tamen hoc uideas folium pubescere ramis;
> sed frondes frondis natas mirabere limbo,

169

altera ut alterius culmen radice coronet.
Quin et luteolis uestitur floribus arbor
e folio exortis patulo, limboque sub ipso;
quos subit armatus densata cuspide fructus
deformem celso tollens in uertice florem. (4.28–45)

Among these [trees], the bountiful nopal sprouts in the fields, rising six cubits out of the ground, and supported by a weak trunk; not even do flexible leaves adorn its tops, or provide shade to protect the cattle from Phoebus's blazing rays. However, the vigorous nopal dresses itself with fleshy foliage, interwoven with firm strands of fibers, protected by white thorns, and covered with green skin. These often have the form of an egg. Although the branches are solidly constructed, nevertheless, a flowing liquid fills its interior, suitable to feed the cochineal worm some day. Neither will you see leaves growing on the branches; but you will wonder at [new] leaves growing out of the edge of branches, since one crowns the top of another with its roots. In fact, the tree is adorned with yellowish flowers, which grow out of the very fringe of the flat branches, under which a prickly fruit grows, holding the misshapen flower on its highest end.

The cactus is depicted as a strange-looking plant, the visual appearance of which does not fit into the frame of neoclassical beauty. Landívar indicates, rather, that its visual impact derives from the very striking quality of its misshapen features. In this fashion, he shifts the established terms of the representation of American nature, and the question of its status with regards to aesthetics and knowledge. His depiction of the cactus further reformulates the articulation of that space as the estrangement or disruption of existing Western notions of beauty and order. The following stanza portrays the practices involved in the cultivation of cacti. Landívar notes that the plant has the positive value of requiring little investment of labor on the part of the farmer or peasant who wishes to cultivate it for commercial purposes. Addressing his reader in the second person, as if to give advice, he observes that if one wishes to grow cacti, one only has to scatter a few of the leaves on the ground, even if the soil is barren, dry, or rocky, and the leaves will subsequently yield new plants (4.46–52).

Landívar then switches attention to the cochineal worm for a sequence of several stanzas. The first of these deals with its behavior. It is related that the worm sucks the cactus's liquid, and lays its eggs on the plant's leaves (4.53–55). Landívar notes that the members of the species are of noble mores and seek to avoid any kind of conflict, either among themselves or with defenseless enemies (4.56–61). In addition, he reports, in the following stanza, that the species is divided into two sexes. The physical differences that distinguish the male from the female are detailed assiduously, most notably the fact that the former's back is colored red while the latter is white all over (4.62–66). Landívar then addresses the reader directly, using the second-person pronoun ("tibi"), in observing that the skin of both genders is so thin that if a person touches it, s/he will see blood (4.66–68).

The image of the cochineal worm that emerges is that of an indolent and slothful creature that devotes all its energies to the pursuit of sensual pleasure. Landívar relates that since it has no legs, it has to drag itself clumsily across the cactus leaves in order to drink their juices and inject some life into its listless body (4.69–74). Nevertheless, he then describes how, thanks to the intervention of hardworking American subjects, the sensual behavior of the cochineal worm is subjected to a discipline and turned to productive use. In early spring workers remove worms from covered baskets that they have stored in their homes (4.75–81). They carefully place the worms on the cactus leaves, ensuring that the females are mixed in with the males (4.82–84). The females busily eat away at the leaves and absorb their juice before mating with the males and laying eggs, which subsequently yield numerous offspring (4.85–90). The agency of the peasant workers thus raises the productive capacity of the worms by effecting an increase in the number of creatures engaged in the activity of imbibing the cactus's liquid. In this fashion, the workers, who are specifically identified as Indians, are able to increase their dye yield (4.91–93).

An extended metaphor is developed in which the cactus and the worms are represented as a city and its inhabitants, respectively (4.90). In this fashion, this local, peripheral phenomenon is reinserted into a universalist narrative, as the story of the worms' existence is fitted into the framework of the kind of epic poem that relates the triumphs and trials of the ancient Greek city-states. This segment constitutes a parodic component,[3] by means of which Landívar preempts the criticism that he has treated a mundane topic in an inappropriately high style. Nevertheless, it also carries on the serious project of scientific investigation, as Landívar inquires as to the identity of the natural enemies of this peace-loving species (4.94–95). The first of these is the spider, which ensnares the cochineal worms in its web and then devours their entrails (4.96–101). The worms also fall victim to chickens, to other kinds of worms, which invade the cactus leaves, and to other species of birds that swoop down from the sky and carry them off (4.102–07). The birds' attacks are compared to the actions of the wolf, which seizes young sheep and leaves the remainder of the flock bleating in anguish (4.108–12). These problems require that the cactuses be constantly overseen and maintained so that they are not destroyed by birds or insects (4.113–23).

These didactic remarks lead into a description of the human labor involved in keeping the nopal cactuses free of creatures that might be harmful to the cochineal worms. The following stanza details the techniques that the indigenous workers have developed in order to protect their livelihood from the elements. These strategies are presented in the form of advice to the reader, with the recommendation that one should plant the nopals on the side of a large hill so as to shield them from strong north winds and heavy rains, both of which can smash the worms against the ground (4.124–32). Alternatively, in case of cold weather, it is suggested that one surround the cactuses with bonfires in order to protect the worms from the destructive effects of freezing temperatures (4.133–35). Finally, Landívar notes that in case of rain or hail, it is best to follow the example of Indians experienced in this labor, who shield the plants with large mats (4.136–39). The depiction of this practice leads Landívar to express his admiration for the indigenous workers' ingenuity:

> Gens siquidem solers tignis hinc inde locatis,
> quae patulas celso Nopales uertice uincant,
> e densis amplum storeis uelamen adaptat,
> quod modo fune super ducit, modo fune reducit. (4.140–43)

These clever people, having erected on all sides beams which surpass the height of the outspread nopals, fasten to them a

large awning of thick matting, which they pull back and forth
overhead by means of a rope.

In this fashion, a narrative of indigenous artifice is incorporated into the representation of American space and, at the same
time, into the process of production that underpins the consumption and display of social and cultural rank. Having evoked the
modes of knowledge through which the Indians ensure the rationalized and efficient reproduction of the worms, Landívar
focuses his scientific gaze back onto the creatures themselves.
The techniques developed by the native laborers facilitate the
biological reproduction of the worms and thus the multiplica-
tion of their numbers. The enlarged worm population gorges
itself on the nopal leaves to the point that their bodies become
enlarged, their bellies filled with a red liquid that will yield the
dye ("regalem [. . .] colorem"; 4.144–55). At this point, the
cactus branches are broken off, either by the *criollo* farmer
("colonus"), who hangs them to dry in his warm kitchen, or
by the indigenous workers ("gens"), who place them in large
baskets in order to use them as the basis for future crops
(4.156–63).

A new stanza depicts the next stage of the manufacturing
process. Using cotton, the Indians gather the rest of the insects
from the cactuses, and then kill them by dipping them in hot
water (4.164–69). Significantly, the process through which profit
is sought as recompense for these activities is portrayed in a
negative light. An anticapitalist narrative is articulated as
Landívar describes an alternative method that can also be employed to prepare the worms for the extraction of their liquid.
He observes:

> Ni placeat niueos flammis extinguere ciues
> inmeritos, auri caeco exitialis amore.
> Tunc ingens ualido fornax accenditur igne,
> tota quoad magno rutilet flammata calore:
> fornacem pubes, semotis ignibus, intrat,
> tostaque purpuream uitam fornace relinquit.
> Aut Indus certe diffundit chortibus amplis
> Sole sub ardenti, torretque examina Sole.
> Ceu quondam Bombyx fatis cessurus iniquis
> nunc rutilis Phoebi talis substernitur alti,

nunc atris iacitur conclusus uimine flammis,
uitaque lethiferas moriens uanescit in auras. (4.170–81)

Or it may please them, in their blind lust for gold, to kill
these guiltless white citizens with deadly flames. In that
event, a large oven is heated with coals until it is red-hot
from the great heat. The fire is then removed, and the insects are put into the oven, where, having been baked, they
leave behind their purple remains. Or the Indian sometimes
spreads the swarm out on a wide patio under the blazing
sun, and bakes them. Thus, the silkworms, awaiting their
harsh destiny, sometimes are spread out under the bright rays
of the noonday sun, and sometimes, having been placed in
baskets, are thrown into the consuming flames, and their life
passes away into the deadly air.

This manifestation of indigenous technology is dissected with
evident ambivalence, as a sense of anguish over the violence
and pain involved in the dynamics of capitalism and knowledge is expressed. This conflicted attitude is reaffirmed in the
following stanza, where it is observed that the cruel death that
the cochineal worms suffer by the hand of the "barbarous Indian" ("barbara [. . .] Inda") is what enables the extraction of
the scarlet dye that will be used by the peoples of the entire
world, most specifically, of France, Holland, Italy, Spain,
England, Russia, and Belgium (4.182–87). Through this reference to some of the major European nations, a narrative of
peripheral agency is introduced into the articulation of metropolitan power. In this fashion, Landívar foregrounds the position of colonial space and economy in the material praxis
through which one of the key signifiers of the semiotics of power
is configured, thereby demystifying the aura of that power.

Significantly, the cycle of stanzas devoted to the analysis of
the production and harvesting of the cochineal worms for dye
concludes with a final stanza in which this industry is identified
as the specific domain of the native population of Guatemala,
as an activity that cannot be successfully exploited for profit
by whites. Landívar warns the reader in the following terms:

Ne tamen haec lucri quemquam deludat imago,
nouerit hoc Indis caelum seruasse colonis.
Saepe etenim ciues quaestus ingentis amore
coccineos aliqui magno conamine gnatos

frondibus aspersos auidi excepere colendos.
Ipse tamen dulces pastus porcellio frondes,
aut magnam passus uentorum murmure cladem,
aut propriam renuens foliis educere prolem,
elusit domini misero tentamina casu
desidia gazas consumens pauus inerti.
Indica gens autem duros edocta labores
perferre, algentes nec mollis pallet ad imbres,
nec rubram metuit quassantem lampada Phoebum.
Hinc omnes tolerat casus tranquilla uerendos,
et Lunam, et Solem, pluuiamque, et frigus, et aestum,
inuigilatque diu Cocco noctesque diesque,
uermibus infestos abigens candentibus hostes.
Improba cura quidem, sed tanto debita lucro! (4.188–205)

However, lest the vision of profit should deceive anyone,
let him realize that heaven reserved this [industry] for the
Indian farmers. For often certain greedy citizens, for love
of profit, have, with great effort, worked to cultivate the
young cochineal insects which lie scattered over the branches.
However, the swine, having fed itself on the sweet leaves,
either suffered great losses from the roaring winds or, re-
fusing to produce their young on the leaves, mocked their
master's efforts, causing him distressing losses and per-
versely wasting his riches by their idleness and sloth. The
Indian people, on the other hand, taught to endure hard labors, are not easily daunted by the cold rains, nor do they
fear Phoebus when he brandishes his bright red lamp. Thus
calm, they bear all things which might be feared—the moon
and sun, the rains, cold, and heat—and day and night they
maintain a long vigil over the white cochineal worms, driving
away dangerous enemies. It is indeed a troublesome task,
but it is required for such great profits.[4]

The analysis next moves on to the study and representation
of the circumstances through which another raw material, a
mollusk, is also exploited, in Guatemala, as a source of purple
dye. The first stanza of this cycle identifies this creature with
the murex (4.206–10). Landívar supports his identification of
the mollusk with this European species by means of a footnote,
in which he quotes from the journal of a French traveler, who
confirms having found a mollusk similar to the murex, on the
south coast of Guatemala in 1712 (62). The second stanza of
this sequence describes the region in which this species is found,

a province close to the sea, noted for its warm temperatures, springs, evergreen fields, and abundant supply of fruit (4.211–18). Called Nicoya by the ancient Indians, it has since acquired fame on account of the purple dye it produces (4.219–20).[5] With this general geographical panorama established, the focus shifts, in the third stanza of the sequence, to the immediate physical environment of the creature. Landívar relates that on this region's shores a small shellfish can commonly be found, notable for the purple liquid it contains (4.221–27). Indians search among the rocks by the sea, and collect these creatures in water-filled containers (4.228–31).

The study returns, in the following stanza, to the level of generalization, as Landívar presents information about the factors that determine when one should pick the mollusks from the rocks. It is observed that the degree to which the fluid inside this shell turns purple depends upon the intensity of the moonlight to which it is exposed. Consequently, it is recommended that one only gather the mollusks around the time of month when the moon is at its brightest, in its fourth quarter (4.232–40). It is noted that the Indians always consult the sky before proceeding to collect the creatures (4.241–46). Landívar then recounts the process through which they extract the dye and use it to color cotton and silk (4.247–60). The segment also depicts how the mollusks' contents are processed exclusively for local usage, in contrast to the cochineal dye, much of which is exported to Europe. Notably, the dye produced is of such quality that the clothes to which it is applied retain their coloring almost indefinitely. This characteristic of endurance makes it particularly suitable to be recycled as part of the material and symbolic matrix of the *criollo* archive, standing as an immutable component of the organic order that is being constructed over the course of the poem.

Landívar concludes his account of these dye-making procedures in a final stanza that links it to a point of origin in classical mythology. He recounts a story according to which a dog's mouth was once seen to turn scarlet when it carried a mollusk out of the waters of the Tyrian Sea (4.261–65). Thinking that he was bleeding, his owners tried to clean his lips, and their hands became covered in purple in the process. Intrigued, they prized the shellfish from the dog's jaws and examined its internal coloring, thus giving rise to the practice of utilizing the purple substance to dye fabrics (4.266–75). The reference to this anecdote serves to reinforce the incorporation of native American knowledge and artifice into the frame of Western letters and signification.

Through his exposition of the mechanics of the production of purple dye, Landívar displaces the image of America as wild, unmanageable materiality. Native labor is depicted as the agency that reduces that materiality into commodity form and shapes it into a sign that can be fitted into the classical symbolic system for the demarcation of social rank and order. At the same time, the portrayal of the production process serves to demystify the aura of that commodity that denotes and guarantees the hierarchies integral to the structure of empire.

Managing the Flow of Signification

Book 6 of the *Rusticatio Mexicana* develops, more fully than the earlier parts of the poem, the vision of American space not as indomitable wilderness, but as both context and product of a dialectic of artifice and nature. In the first quatrain, Landívar signals his intention to analyze the beaver in the following terms:

> Quid moror astutos telis inuadere Fibros,
> ac uarios animo gentis uersare labores,
> ingeniumque sagax, atque altis oppida muris,
> delicias nemorum, ripaeque undantis honorem? (6.1–4)

> Shall I not now rush upon the clever beavers with the spear,
> and consider their various labors, their sharpness of mind,
> and study their high-walled towns, the delights of the woods
> and the glory of the river bank?

Landívar thus opens the canto by making explicit the engagement of his studies and text with the material context from which he is extracting knowledge. The invocation of the hunting metaphor goes beyond the immediate level of hyperbolic rhetoric, establishing the use of the spear to capture the beaver as a cipher for the act of studying the species, and representing it through the action of pen on paper. Landívar develops the image still further in the following stanza, where he beseeches Diana, who is portrayed as hunting the animal with

177

arrows in the forest, to assist him in his quest for knowledge about its activities, skills, and body (6.5–10).

The third stanza of canto 6 determines the geographical regions inhabited by the beaver, establishing it as one of many wild animals that lurk in the forests of New Spain (6.11–13).[6] It is identified as a wary ("sortitum") and exceptional ("praestantique") animal that conceals great gifts underneath its furry exterior (6.14–15). Then Landívar launches into a detailed study of its physical features, capturing it linguistically through the work of his metaphorical pen-spear. He observes, first, that it possesses a double layer of smooth fur, the inner one being of such quality that it is used to make hats destined for the heads of kings ("vertice Regum") since it is almost as soft to the touch as silk (6.16–21). Second, its head is notable for its small eyes, almost perfectly round ears, and huge teeth (6.22–26). Third, it is observed that the animal has hooked toes and claws, and that, even though the webbing between the digits makes them look misshapen ("deformes"), it enables the beaver to move in water as well as on land (6.27–32). Fourth, the reader is informed that the beaver's strange-looking and scale-covered tail is protected from dampness and lubricated by an oil that the animal secretes and guards in a pouch underneath its belly (6.33–38).

In the fourth stanza of the canto, Landívar seeks to construct a psychological portrait of the animal. He stresses that the beaver possesses noble customs ("ingenuos [. . .] mores"), in spite of being endowed with an ungainly appearance that does not conform to neoclassical norms of beauty (6.39–40). It is noted that the beaver does not attack its natural enemies with its teeth, does not hunger and search greedily for more than it requires to fulfill its minimum bodily needs, nor allow itself to be driven by desires for revenge against assailants (6.41–48). Only when it is captured and imprisoned does it become agitated, always seeking to gnaw its way out of its cage, in order to escape back to its home in the forest (6.49–54). However, the characteristics upon which most attention is focused are the industriousness and ingenuity that the beaver shows in its daily activities. These are depicted in the subsequent stanza, which opens with the following expression of admiration for the beaver's activities:

Hunc etiam placuisse Fibris mirabere morem,
quod uigil ingenium, sollersque industria ripis
hospitium populo, fluuiisque repagula condat,
ingentemque urbem tranquilla pace gubernet.
Vix etenim Phoebus, rapto in sublimia curru,
lampade succendit fulgenti Sidera Cancri,
cum subito pecudes, siluarum pube coacta,
conueniunt, urbisque parant attollere molem,
perfugium sociis, et propugnacula bello.
Explorant saltus, fluuiosque, et amoena paludis
littora, ubi tacitae frondescant arbore ripae.
Area tranquilli non raro ad fluminis undas
deligitur; gaudetque amnes habitare iuuentus.
Ne tamen alluuies aedes inopina reuellat,
concutiat socios, urbemque a culmine uertat,
ante domos ripis ponat quam callida turba,
obiicit e truncis densata repagula riuis
illuuiem ut frenent, aequataque flumina ducant. (6.55–72)

Also to be wondered at is that habit which has pleased the
beavers, because of their alert mind and skilled diligence,
to build dwellings for their people along the river banks,
dikes across the streams, and to rule their great city in tranquil peace. Scarcely does Phoebus, as he mounts the heavens in his carriage, brighten Cancer's constellation with his
blazing torch, when suddenly herds [of beavers], having
gathered their members from the woods, come together and
prepare to build their city, a refuge for their fellows and a
defense against war. They search the woods, the streams,
and the pleasant lakes, whose quiet banks are lined by leafy
trees. It is not unusual for them to choose an area by a gently
flowing river; and their young enjoy living by the waters.
However, lest a sudden flood should uproot their homes,
frighten their members, and overturn the city, the shrewd
mass places thick barriers of tree trunks across the streams
in order to stem and control the flow, before they build their
homes along the banks.

What is striking here is the depiction of the beavers as a mass
group ("turba") that is able to show ingenuity and diligence in
the pursuit of rational goals. In the unfolding of this representation, there emerges an allegorical narrative about the organization of American societies as productive and rational
entities.[7] Such an image is presented in the form of a utopia,

framed within a scientific analysis. The beavers appear as appropriate subject matter for such a narrative because of their unique positioning at an intermediate point between the conventionally separated poles of artifice and nature. In the same fashion as American humanity, the beaver is a creature that is perceived as a part of a disordered, unfriendly natural space, but that, on closer inspection, reveals itself to be engaged in complex and noble actions. It is an animal that projects itself out of the imagined sphere of a purely "natural" wilderness constructed by European thought, and into the realm of rationalized, collective social organization and manufacturing.

In the following stanza, the tools of natural history are employed in a step-by-step analysis of how beavers construct their dams and homes. It is noted that the animals initiate their task by gnawing through the trunk of a tall willow, standing close by a stream, causing it to fall in such a fashion that it stretches, like a bridge, from one bank to the other (6.73–78). When this trunk, the height of which is evoked in terms of transcendence ("truncum / uertice sublimem"), is brought down to earth, it produces a loud, crashing sound that echoes around the waters' banks (6.79–80). Undaunted by the noise, the beavers immediately set about lopping the branches off the fallen tree with their teeth (6.81–88).

The next stanza depicts the variety of tasks in which the beavers then engage as they start building their dam in order to control the flow of the river. First, the "busy cohort" ("cohors operosa") divides into groups, each cutting up different kinds of trunks and branches according to the specific skills of the members, and then they carry the finished products to the edge of the stream in order to prepare for the labor of construction (6.89–96). The beavers in one group carry branches, others, stakes ("sudes"), and those in a third carry clay on their tails (6.97–98). While the rest of the workers swim to and fro, carrying building supplies (6.99–101), a special group labors around the area of the fallen willow. Some members of this group dig trenches in the river bed below, some sink heavy oak stakes down into the trenches once they are ready, and others pack sand around the bottom of the stakes in order to make them hold (6.102–11). In this fashion, they place an entire line of stakes vertically between the fallen willow and the river bed in order to block the flow of the water (6.112–17). Finally, they connect the stakes by filling up the spaces between them with branches, clay, and a gluelike substance. Together, those elements prevent any water from flowing through (6.118–22).

The description of the feat of the dike's initial construction is followed, in the next stanza, by a study of its key engineering features. It is noted that the dam ("moles") stands three cubits on the side where it stems the flow of the water, and ten cubits on the other side (6.123–29). In addition, the workers make passageways within the dam, which they close if the stream is low and open when its surface is rising in order to regulate the flow of water. Landívar indicates that the system functions just as effectively as a breakwater that a wealthy people ("gens praediues") might build next to a harbor (6.130–39). In the event that the waters break through the barrier, or a hunter damages it, a team of beavers is always ready to repair it with fresh branches (6.140–42).

The subsequent sequence of stanzas is devoted to the representation of the process through which the beavers then construct their dwellings over and around the dam, building a large structure that is referred to metaphorically as a "city" ("urbs"). Here, Landívar further develops the representation of American space not solely as natural wilderness, but as a more complex space, also marked by works of elaborate artifice. As in the case of the dam, the beavers are depicted as realizing this undertaking through a division of labor. Landívar relates how different members of the community devote themselves to their specific tasks, gathering clay, branches, and pieces of rock from the bank. They purposefully construct their homes next to streams, so as to afford themselves access to a constant supply of water (6.143–50). Although they build dwellings of different shapes, they all take care to provide their homes with solid, long-lasting foundations, combining clay, rocks, and short sticks, and can make the walls as thick as three cubits (6.151–57). From the depiction of the external architecture of individual homes, Landívar then moves on to offer a detailed picture of the internal features of the living quarters. It is noted that each contains several compartments for various beavers, and separate storerooms for food (6.158–62). Their "extraordinary palaces" ("insueta palatia") usually have two doors, one overlooking the stream, the other facing the woods, and a window, also on the side facing the waters (6.163–71).

The final stanza of the sequence devoted to the beavers' homes relates the diligence the animals show in trying to make them look beautiful and clean. It is observed that they gather up earth, knead it, daub it onto the homes with their tails, and then polish it once it is dry. As a result, Landívar observes, the walls gleam like those an artisan might create in the mansions of a wealthy family (6.172–78). He adds, however, that this is less a manifestation of disinterested aestheticism than it is of the refined manners ("nitido [. . .] cultu") for which the beaver is noted, and which form part of its practical concern for hygiene (6.179–82). The animal takes great care to maintain the cleanliness of its living quarters, covering the interiors daily with layers of leaves and branches (6.183–89). Thus, in spite of its ungainly appearance, the beaver is represented as elaborating objects that simultaneously conform to the neoclassical standard of beauty and are functional.

In the next sequence of stanzas, Landívar pulls back the gaze of the natural historian from the private lives of the members of the species, in order to focus on the areas in which the individual beavers participate in forms of communitarian experience. In the first, it is observed that if some of the young beavers become tired from these labors, the rest of the herd ("agmina") rush to the aid their comrades ("sociis") and signal them to stop and take a rest (6.190–94). The second of these stanzas is devoted to the analysis of what the species does in order to ensure its survival through the cold winter. It is related that each individual beaver is inclined to suspend its individual concerns in order to further the good of the community as a whole: "Ut uero finem tectis posuere superbis, / priuatae studio uitae nudata caterua / tota sodalitio rursus se prompta resignat" (6.195–97; "Now when they have completed their magnificent houses, the entire crowd gives up its enthusiasm for private life, and readily devotes itself again to communal existence").

Equipped with the knowledge that the winter covers the ground with frost, makes the rivers freeze, and strips the trees of leaves, the beavers search in anticipation for food to store for the cold period (6.198–206), "lest the entire republic should be destroyed by a terrible fate" ("Hinc ne tota ruat misero respublica casu"; 6.204). Again it is observed that they split up, all going in different directions, and dedicate themselves each to specific tasks, some tearing branches from oaks, others stripping bark. Then, they carry the fruits of their labors back to their houses (6.207–13). Like the farmer who assiduously stores his harvest, the beavers pile the pieces of wood in ordered rows so that their fellows can more easily get to them in the future (6.214–23).

With such labors completed by dint of great effort, the animals then calmly retire to their dwellings ("penates"), each of which can accommodate at least four, and as many as twenty, "citizens" ("ciues"; 6.224–27). The young show deference to the older and infirm animals, ceding the upper rooms to them, and occupying the lower ones themselves (6.228–30). Thus, the "forest tribe" ("Natio nemorosa") rests, eats, lives in harmony, and engages in sexual reproduction, free from acts of violence and thievery (6.231–37). In this fashion, the beavers are portrayed as offering an image of a utopian society that interacts with its environment and other species in a peaceable fashion.

The possible implications of this portrait with respect to human society in Spanish America are complex. In using the word *natio* to refer to this society, Landívar is not necessarily thinking of the space of the emergent nation-state, and its necessary framework of mercantilism and economic competition. Rather, he might also be read as articulating a vision overdetermined by Jesuit ideology, and specifically the notion of the concept of a "people" or "tribe," inhabiting an idealized world free of the boundaries and restrictions set up by states and their institutional matrixes.[8]

The focus of canto 6 then turns, over the course of the next series of stanzas, to the secondary aspects of the beavers' existence. First, Landívar relates that the beavers have their own system of law, in accordance with which it is understood that any member of their community caught stealing or dirtying another's quarters is banished from the city, and forced to live as an outcast in the forests (6.238–43). The second stanza of this segment studies how the animals rest from their labors by hanging from the windows of their dwellings to enjoy light breezes, and dipping the lower part of their bodies in the water

(6.244–51). The third stanza deals with the circumstances pertaining to the reproductive behavior of the beavers. It is observed that they mate during the time they spend indoors during winter, and that the female gives birth to twins, and sometimes triplets, after a four-month period of gestation (6.252–57). The mother then sees to the initial education of the offspring in her quarters, until they are sufficiently grown to follow her into the outdoors (6.258–60). In the following stanza, Landívar describes how the mother takes her young to live in the forest and feed on tree bark while the "cruel father" ("genitor [. . .] crudelis") abandons them all and goes off on his own (6.261–66). The creatures do not return to their homes until the time of the autumnal equinox (6.267–68).

In the next stanza, information is provided about how some beavers come to live on their own, in open fields and around forests, having been sent into exile for having committed any of the aforementioned crimes (6.269–71). In addition, others, having been forced to leave their dwellings by hunters, do not go back to building dams and homes over rivers, but dig holes along the banks, where they can live and enjoy a constant, gently flowing supply of water (6.272–83). The depiction of the existence of those who live outside the norms and framework of the beaver cities leads back into the discussion of other animal species that pose a threat to the integrity of their communities. These include the wolf, the marten, the carcajou, and the bear, all of which are depicted as barbarous and irrational creatures that prey on the beaver (6.284–90). Significantly, the difference between the species is cast in terms of class hierarchy. The words *ciuis* and *plebs* are used to refer, respectively, to the beaver and the other species, which are given to violence.

Nevertheless, it is man who presents the most serious threat of all to the beaver, as is described in the next cycle of stanzas. The first analyzes the cunning ("astutia") that the animals show in evading the hunters' darts and trickery (6.291–92). Some beavers constantly stand on the lookout, listening for their foes. On hearing any sound, they immediately pass on the news to the rest by flapping their tails in the water and making a strange noise (6.293–97). At first, the citizens of the beaver city flee in a cowardly panic (6.298–301). Nevertheless, soon they compose themselves and intelligently escape by watching to see from which direction their assailant is approaching (6.302–06). If the hunters place nets on the side of the forest, the beavers make their getaway by swimming under water. Alternatively, if the hunters approach the city via the river, they escape into the forest and hide, only returning when the men have left (6.307–15).

Having studied the cunning ruses of the beaver itself, Landívar gives information on the techniques American hunters use to outfox them in the following three stanzas. The first option is to attack their dwellings in the middle of winter, when the ground is covered in snow and the rivers are frozen over (6.316–18). On sensing the hunters' presence, the beavers try to flee through the water, under the surface of the ice (6.319–22). However, when they try to climb onto the river banks, through holes the men have dug in the ice, they are caught and killed (6.323–32). A second, alternative, hunting strategy requires stretching out nets in the woods and luring the beavers into them by tempting them with the kinds of bark they like to suck and gnaw on (6.333–39). Fooled in this fashion, they become entangled in the traps, and the men cut their throats with knives (6.340–52). A third and simpler method involves the use of dogs, which are deployed to seek out and encircle the beavers, making them easy targets for the men to wound with spears or darts (6.353–60).

The final stanza of book 6 details the different uses man makes of the slain beavers. First, castor is extracted from the animals' pouches in order to exploit it for medicinal purposes (6.361–64). Then, the hunters remove the pelts, and make them into hats, boots, or other warm clothing (6.361–69). In this fashion, the investigation of the existence of the species is brought to a conclusion with the spectacle of its capture and insertion into human economy. Notably, it does not end simply with the depiction of the beavers' utopian model of social and productive organization, which might, in view of the species' ungainly appearance and apparently underestimated capacities, be construed as a metaphor for the experience of the heterogeneous subjects of the New World. Rather, following the totalizing and practical imperatives of natural history, Landívar adds to his study the information required for the successful human mastery over, and exploitation of, the species, since the very act of capturing the beaver, both literally and figuratively signals the possibility and realization of his projection of a form of modernity. In the first place, the reconfiguration of this anomalous creature, which does not conform to neoclassical standards of beauty and order, as the agent of a highly rationalized social structure serves to further Landívar's labor of reconceiving the representation of space and subjects. Second, Landívar's encapsulation of this most rationalized component of nature through the dual work of scientific organization and poetic depiction, further establishes the credentials of the *criollo* intellectual as a subject invested with the authority to represent and make sense of American materiality.

Wealth Unearthed: Landívar's Representation of Mining in New Spain

The sign that sets in motion a great segment of Spanish imperial praxis in the Americas is that of the precious metal. Gold and silver constitute the basis of a colonial metaphysics that draws ambitious Spaniards across the Atlantic during the sixteenth century. The lives of innumerable indigenous subjects were sacrificed in the arduous quest for what became, over time, ever more elusive substances. The consequences for Spain would also be double-edged. The initial easy accessibility of the precious metals fueled both Spanish inflation and the mythical image of a New World laden with readily available riches. In spite of the decline in the yield of gold and silver over the course of the sixteenth and seventeenth centuries, the image of the viceroyalties as a source of easy income lived on, especially in the policies of the Spanish state, ever anxious to extract the maximum revenues from the lowest possible investment.[9]

In books 7 and 8 of the *Rusticatio Mexicana*, Landívar looks beyond the sublime image of colonial surplus value in order to analyze the material conditions of the extraction of precious metals from the colonial natural environment. He comments specifically on this kind of transition at the beginning of book 7. In the first stanza, he emphasizes the dramatic, transcendent character of the topics he has treated thus far in a brief recap of the first six books (7.1–5). He uses the first person to stress

his empirical involvement in these images and then to introduce the next task into which he is to throw himself, writing:

> nunc caelum linquo, nunc terrae lapsus ad ima
> aggredior cantu, Plutonis regna, fodinas:
> regna refulgenti semper radiata metallo,
> et quae diuitiis complerunt prodiga mundum. (7.6–9)

> [N]ow I leave the sky, now I descend into the depths of the
> earth, and I undertake to sing of the mines, Pluto's realm, a
> realm ever glittering with shining metal, and which abun-
> dantly supplies the world with riches.

Having stated his intent, Landívar addresses Pluto himself
in the second person, requesting that the god of the underworld
guide him with his torch so that he might more closely examine the dark world underground, and the precious metals hidden therein (7.10–14). He then proceeds, in the third stanza,
to portray the large-scale geographical context of his topic.
Continuing his dialectical negotiation with vast or abundant
images of nature, he evokes the western range of the Sierra
Madre in all its magnitude. He notes that it stretches far from
the southern coast of New Spain to the very north of the region, comprising innumerable high mountains, beautiful forests, cliffs, and volcanoes (7.15–23). On each side it is flanked
by wide valleys abounding in springs, streams, and orchards
(7.24–32). However, it is underneath this pastoral scene that one
finds the greatest source of wealth, the precious metals that
can only be extracted by means of arduous labor (7.33–34).

From the very outset, the transcendent signs of gold and silver
are demystified, recast in the language of difficulty, as the genealogy of their discovery and production is retraced. In the
fourth stanza, Landívar offers information about how to find
out where to dig, addressing the reader in the second person
("tibi"). It is recommended that one not begin boring into the
ground until one has discerned which veins ("uenas") promise
to yield silver or gold rather than just lead (7.35–39). The veins
descend into the earth, dividing up into branches and hiding
traces of gold and silver amid layers of sand and lead (7.40–
50). Sometimes, when excavated, the rock containing the precious metal is so hard that it can only be made to yield its riches
through the use of fire or mercury, processes that require

187

substantial economic investment (7.50–58). However, if the rock can be broken apart with steel tools, then riches soon flood into the nearest town (7.59–60).

It is noted that individuals with specialized knowledge ("periti") are employed to determine the location of the richest veins. Once these experts have found traces of a precious metal, the workers set about digging tunnels into the earth using steel tools (7.61–62). Landívar relates that they merely discard the surface rocks because they tend not to yield much silver (7.63–68). The text emphasizes that the best deposits are only to be found by those who are willing to work the hardest, and to bore the deepest into the earth (7.69–70). Assuming a muted critical tone, Landívar observes that the desire for profit drives the most dedicated of these laborers: "Hinc omnes ferro certant penetrare profunda, / thesauros donec reddat cum faenore tellus" (7.71–72; "Therefore, all strive to penetrate the depths with pick until the earth gives up its treasures, with interest"). The following stanza depicts one of the key problems involved in this labor, the darkness that makes it hard to walk and work in the tunnels (7.73–78). In order to see through the dark and soot, the workers use torches to light their way (7.79–85). The reflection upon these terrible working conditions leads Landívar to intervene, posing a rhetorical question about the motivating power of the desire for wealth. Nevertheless, he does not appear to allow himself the indulgence of drawing any moral conclusions. Maintaining a neutral, scientific attitude, he depicts the workers' actions as signs of dedication to hard work and to the painstaking task of hewing the metals out of the rock. He asks:

> Quid uero non cogat opum uesana cupido?
> Insistunt operi, facibusque hinc inde locatis
> nigrantes penetrant aditus, murosque fodinae
> ictibus abrumpunt crebris, impressa secuti
> antra per et rupes nitidae uestigia uenae. (7.86–90)

> But to what does the insane passion for riches not drive men? They keep at their work, and with torches placed here and there, they enter the dark recesses, and break away the walls of the mine with repeated blows, pursuing the imprinted traces of the shiny vein through crevices and rocks.

Here, the observation of this form of moral weakness does not acquire a condemnatory tone. Rather, it is only given a small presence within the unfolding scientific narrative as one component within a totalizing portrait of a huge sphere of activity. The revelation to the reader of the means and conditions of production, which are usually shielded from his/her eyes by the gleam of the supreme commodity of the precious metal, then continues with the depiction of other technological features of American mining. First, it is related that the workmen erect oak pillars and place arches under the ceilings of the tunnels in order to prevent them from caving in (7.91–97). Landívar observes that since the veins sometimes descend almost vertically, the workmen have to dig directly downward and use ladders to follow their course (7.98–105). For this reason, the mines often take on the appearance of large buildings, possessing successive levels of compartments ("lares") supported by columns skillfully wrought from the rock itself (7.106–11).

The following stanza depicts what the workmen do when they discover a particularly rich deposit. It details how they dig a very large tunnel, bolstering it with large pillars (7.112–15). Then, the foreman, or boss ("Magister"), divides his men up to undertake specialized tasks: some hold torches, some dig into the walls with picks, and others, through the application of skilled judgment ("recto discrimine") garnered from experience, separate the valuable ore from the rest of the fallen rock (7.116–20). The subsequent section details the techniques the workmen use to break the rock. First, they attempt to break the ore open with hammers while young boys hold lanterns in order to provide them with light (7.121–27). If the rock proves too hard to be chipped away in this fashion, the child laborers draw water into their mouths and spit it onto the stone in jets. This practice serves to soften the rock so that the miner can then break pieces from the wall (7.128–35). Unfortunately, this procedure also poses a safety hazard to the workers. Sometimes, Landívar notes in the next stanza, this opens up cracks through which pockets of dangerous gases seep into the tunnels, often killing the miners (7.136–50).

The study of different techniques used to break open the harder areas of rocks is developed over the next series of stanzas.

The scrutiny of these practices serves to bring into view the material dynamics that yield the finished products of gold and silver, but tend to be obscured, hidden from view by the dazzle of these commodities. In the first of these stanzas, it is related that the miners sometimes hammer a hole into the rock face with a sharp steel point, or chisel, all the while continuing to apply water to the surface (7.151–57). Having created an opening, they then fill it with a mixture of powdered sulfur and sharp-edged sand, into which they insert a fuse (7.158–65). They then light the taper, and quickly retreat to a safe distance before a loud explosion shatters the rock into many pieces (7.166–70). The second stanza of this sequence portrays an alternative method: the miners pile wood under the more unyielding areas of rock, and set fire to it with the idea that the heat thus produced will separate the precious metals from it (7.171–78). Landívar addresses the reader directly, in order to warn of the danger this practice can pose to the workers. He observes that the miners must wait until the black smoke caused by the fire abates. Even then they must proceed with care because some fumes often linger, trapped against the roof of the shaft, suffocating anyone who enters too soon after the fire has ceased (7.179–90).

When all is clear, certain laborers carry the yield of gold and silver ore up from the mine, sometimes climbing up and down ladders, at other times conveying it in sacks attached to pulleys (7.191–96). In order to facilitate this work, it is also necessary to make other openings in the side of the mountain containing the mine. First, a hole is bored into the mountain and is made to connect with the mine shafts, so that the men can be provided with a source of fresh air, and a rope can be lowered down to pull up pieces of rock as they are excavated (7.197–206). Then, the workers above ground construct a winch, supporting it with stone pillars and thick wooden beams. To it they attach long, thick ropes, bearing leather bags at intervals. As a wheel is driven round and round by donkeys, some of the bags are lowered into the cavern to be filled while others rise to the surface so the workers can remove the ore from them (7.207–17).

Landívar conveys this piece of technology in great detail, indicating a fascination with the mechanics of industry. Nevertheless, at the same time he continues to analyze the material

problems in which this activity is embedded. It is noted that
the openings tend to let in not only air, but also water, which
all too often pours through them, down into the work areas,
flooding them (7.218–25). Landívar recommends that, in such
instances, it is advisable to close up the mines with piles of
rock, since a continuation of mining activities would lead to
severe loss of life and increased cost for the investor (7.226–
27). Notable here is the concern that such decisions should be
made not just on moral grounds, but also in accordance with
the criterion of economic efficiency. Such a stance, with its
apparent location of financial concerns on the same plane as
humanitarian ones, might appear to go against the grain of the
priorities of the moral code of the Jesuit order. I would argue
here, however, that it is indicative of the emergence of a secularizing, pragmatic line of thought in Landívar's writing, one
in which value and legitimacy come to be based on a principle
of effectiveness that is believed to be compatible with ethical
concerns.[10]

The preoccupation with practical feasibility continues in
another sequence of stanzas, which study attempts to overcome
the obstacles posed by a mountain containing multiple pockets of water. In the first of these stanzas it is related that some
entrepreneurs go to the expense of boring passages to the center of the hills, and then mine inward, until water is encountered (7.228–35). Then, deep holes are dug underneath vertical
shafts, so that the water can be drained away from the areas to
be mined and loaded into buckets, which are pulled out by means
of a winch system (7.236–46). Should this strategy not work,
alternatively they use another machine ("machina"), which is
installed in a lower passageway inside the mountain itself, and
is powered by the motion of mules (7.247–54).

The subsequent stanza portrays what happens once the water has all been removed from the mountain. The miners set to
work with fire and iron picks, chipping ore out of the rock. Other
men carry the fragments to the shaft entrance, where a guard
("custos") tirelessly stands watch (7.255–60). He collects the
pieces of rock, setting aside some for the Church and others
for the poor, as charity (7.261–65). Then, he hands the rest over
to other workers, who shatter them with mallets. When the
precious stones have been separated from the worthless ones,

they are transported on mules (7.266–68) to "an expert in the art of extracting precious metals from the veins" ("eruat ut uenis thesauros arte peritus"; 7.269).

Following the representation of this dynamics of large-scale capitalistic enterprise, book 7 concludes with a sequence of stanzas in which attention is turned to the margins of such undertakings, namely, the strategies through which the miners themselves seek to supplement their incomes. In the following stanza, it is noted that when they have finished their day's work, the laborers go into the mines and extract for themselves large piles of stones (7.270–73). This extra labor allows each worker to accumulate a limited amount of capital for himself, since he is allowed to keep one half of his yield after the guard has set aside the other half for the boss ("domino"; 7.274–78).[11] In similar fashion, young boys sometimes sneak into the tunnels and gather rocks that the workers have missed (7.279–81). However, they too have to show their haul to the guard, who again claims half for the mine owner before handing the remainder back to the boys (7.282–86).

The subsequent stanza contains some general observations about the practice of petty theft. It is observed that the light-bearers, child laborers, diggers, and bag carriers alike all attempt to sneak rocks out of the mine, even though they are required to undress before they can exit the shaft (7.287–92). Although the guard carefully examines them, they are often able to spirit pieces out by hiding them in their underwear, in self-inflicted wounds, or in their hair (7.293–98). Whatever the guard finds, he retains for the mine owner, but if the thief is able to sneak something past the search, he can keep his booty for himself, and the boss has no legal recourse through which to recover the stolen rocks (7.299–301). In this fashion, economic accumulation, on the part of the popular classes is framed within a discourse of criminality and moral degradation.

Such a description reaffirms Landívar's simultaneous commitment to the values of private property and efficiency, which appear to overdetermine heavily notions of the moral responsibilities of private enterprise and Jesuit institutions to the region's inhabitants. In the concluding stanza of book 7, Landívar's gaze turns to the character of those who work in the mines. They are portrayed as rebellious elements who are unwilling to submit to authority, and as criminals who have managed to escape punishment for their offences by blending, undetected, into the dirty, opaque mass of a nascent proletariat to whose members the possibility of individuation is negated (7.302–10). The space of the mine affords them protection from justice, since no representative of the Crown is prepared to attempt to enforce the law in an area where the threat of violence hangs so heavy. Landívar concludes:

> Est scelus in tuto, gestit sine uindice crimen,
> nec loca Praetor adit poena exercere nocentes,
> ni uelit ingentem turbam, Martemque ciere,
> ac uitam saeua campis effundere pugna.
> Haec circum taetras habitat scelerata fodinas,
> diuitiasque parat congestis turba metallis;
> quae subito ad fossae nigrantia limina uendit,
> seu merces fuerint proprii condigna laboris,
> seu potius foedis nuper sublata rapinis. (7.311–19)

> Wickedness is sheltered, crime goes unpunished, nor does a magistrate go to these places to prosecute the guilty unless he wishes to incite the vast mob to war, and to give up his life on the savage field of battle. These criminal hordes live near the gloomy mines and get their wealth by gathering metals, which they immediately sell at the entrances to the dark pit, either as worthy reward for their own labors, or rather, as booty recently taken by vile thievery.

Within the scheme of organized economy idealized in book 7, such activity becomes marked as transgressive and unproductive. It hinders the efficiency of mining and the process of the accumulation of wealth by *criollo* entrepreneurs. The representation of an unfettered market as leading to unruly and criminal behavior implicitly posits the desirability of a model of managed capitalism, overseen by a private *criollo* elite and/or by the institutional matrix offered by the Jesuits. Significantly, the consideration of this barbarous, unregulated commerce is wound up abruptly at this point.

In book 8, the investigation into metal mining continues with a study of the techniques used to process the ore into pure gold and silver. The first stanza not only proposes the topic for the canto, but also furthers the dialectical relationship between

Landívar's poetic labor and the material space that he scrutinizes and represents through the act of writing. He thereby establishes a parallel between the task of representing this world and the physical dynamics of mining that goes beyond the level of poetic license. Rather, Landívar here reformulates the continuing complex positioning of his work within a broader framework of human intervention upon, and interaction with, a specific natural environment. He declares:

> Post sectas dudum magno sudore fodinas
> protinus aduectas opulenta in praedia cautes
> comminuam, saxisque uigil conabor auaris
> eruere argenti pretiosum pondus et auri,
> ac totum partis orbem complere talentis. (8.1–5)

> Now, having worked the mines with much toil, I shall forthwith crush the stones which have been carried to the opulent estates, attentively seeking to draw out precious masses of silver and gold from the avaricious rocks, and fill the whole world with the riches obtained.

Reaffirming his personal engagement with the narrative by using the first-person verb, Landívar draws an analogy between the labor of transforming ore into precious metal and that of hewing a fitting literary representation out of words. In a simple metaphor, the act of fashioning elevated poetic language out of the raw material of the topics at hand is equated with the work of extracting surplus value from the rocks mined. This metaphor is developed further in the second stanza, where Landívar invokes the rhetorical figure of Fortune, addressing it in the second person, and requesting that it take account of the weary state that afflicts his body as a result of the long and arduous efforts he has endured in trying to represent the mining and processing of gold and silver (8.6–9). He beseeches Fortune to extract the treasures from the rocks so that he might convey them more convincingly in his poem, thereby presenting the success of the mimetic operation as depending not solely on human agency, but as an endeavor achieved with the aid of transcendent force of inspiration (8.10–13).

Having established the terms of the mimetic exercise, Landívar shifts his attention to the next stage in the production of gold and silver in New Spain. Over the course of the next two brief stanzas, he depicts the locales in which the ore is processed. Some distance from the mines there are prosperous estates ("florentes [. . .] fundi") with spacious grounds, fresh waters, wide colonnades, storehouses, and great halls (8.14–16). Each contains large furnaces, a powerful mill, and an iron machine that grinds the ore brought from the mountain (8.17–19). It is carried there on mules, and is then broken up with hammers before being processed into even finer pieces in the grinder (8.20–23).

The next set of stanzas presents a detailed study of the apparatus used to turn the rock into small granules. It consists of a heavy iron basin and shiny brass grinders powered by the swift motion of mules or by the power of falling water (8.24–28). Young boys ("impubes") shovel the ore under the grinders so that it can be steadily pulverized into fine dust. This dust is caught in boxes that are firmly attached to the machine and covered with very tight-woven copper gauze (8.29–38). At this point, Landívar interrupts his portrayal of the production process to indicate another hazard it poses to workers. In the second stanza of this segment, he notes that many of the boys who perform the aforementioned task die after a period of time because of the cumulative effects of the dust emitted by the machine on their brains and lungs (8.39–43). Significantly, Landívar is unable to propose a form of technology that might protect the workers from this occupational hazard. He merely observes that the boys must be offered high wages for risking their lives in this fashion.

Landívar then turns his attention back to the technology used to pulverize the ore. The subsequent stanza relates that the harder pieces of rock are placed in a mill, which quickly grinds them down into small particles (8.46–50). These float in the air for a while before coming to rest on the large boards placed around the machines. There, workers form them into piles, adding water in order to produce a mudlike substance, which they then sprinkle with salt (8.51–55). The following day, they tread the mud, adding more salt to the mixture after a fixed amount of time (8.56–58).

Landívar tracks how the work then becomes more technical, requiring the intervention of individuals specialized in the art ("arte peritus") of extracting the precious metal from the ore. In the following stanza, he initiates a portrayal of these procedures, depicting the process of purification in medical terms. The choice of technique depends on the type of illness ("languores"; "morbis")—either "chills" ("gelidis") or a "feverish plague" ("pestis febrilis")—that is believed to afflict the "mud" ("limi"; 8.59–62). Landívar acknowledges in a footnote that the pathological metaphors are not the fruit of his own intellect, but are, rather, derived from the terminology utilized by the metallurgists themselves (110n1). He relates that a skilled expert dissolves the substance in a bowl of mercury, then adds water, and gently rotates it (8.63–65). If the metal assumes a leadlike appearance, it means that the mud is suffering from "chills"; but if it becomes milky and turns the water white, then a "fever" is the problem (8.66–70). Nevertheless, the expert can cure both of these conditions with "medicine" (8.71).

If the mud is afflicted with the chills, a metallurgist, or "physician" ("Machaon") well-versed in Apollo's art ("doctus Apollinea [. . .] arte"), places crushed rocks of copper in very salty water and heats the mixture at high temperature until it yields a puslike substance that turns the water murky (8.72–77). Then, he exposes the gold or silver ore to the sun, and sprinkles the copper over it so that it removes the "disease" ("morbum"; 8.78–79). In the following stanza, Landívar relates that the problem of excessive cold takes longer to treat (8.80). When faced with this pathology, the expert packs mercury in a closely woven net and pushes it through the mesh onto the muddy residue (8.81–88). In this manner, the technician, or "wise doctor" ("sapiens medicus"), is shown to be skilled in diagnosing and resolving the problem (8.89–90).

Landívar relates how the specialist then has the workers reprise their labors, mixing chemical agents into the mudlike mixture and trampling it for ten days, much as peasants tread grapes in order to make wine (8.91–98). Once this stage is completed, each man fashions a portion of the mass into the shape of a cone and marks on a piece of paper the weight of the mercury, copper, and salt added (8.99–102). Then, after a few days, the boss ("magister") tests the quality of the mixture by taking a sample, and mixing it with a pan of water (8.103–06). Quickly, the most valuable grains sink to the bottom, leaving a scum that is carefully drained away (8.106–08).

With a trained eye, the expert gently rotates the pan until a fringe of silver appears on the edge of the sandy residue (8.109–12). He then lightly presses the silver with his thumb to see whether it secretes any mercury (8.112–15). If it does not, more mercury must then be poured over the metal, and the mixture must be compressed again; but if it does, then the muddy amalgam is sent to a storeroom, where it is rinsed with spring water (8.116–22).

The description of the process of purification is continued in the following stanza. The next stage requires the use of a tank, which is encircled by iron rings and which has at its center a wheel fitted with twisted wooden paddles (8.123–26). This device is powered by water or by an animal running swiftly in circles (8.127–28). The muddy residue is poured into the tank, mixed with water, and then powerfully spun around by a spindle ("turbo"; 8.129–33). Then, when the spindle is brought to a stop, the purified metal sinks to the bottom of the tub while a form of scum floats to the surface of the water and is removed by a young man who opens a siphon (8.134–38). The process is repeated over and over again, until all the metal has sunk to the bottom, having been purified (8.138–41). Even after it has gone through this many purification stages, the white substance is still submitted to one more cleaning by workers who wash it with water in wooden troughs (8.142–48).

The next sequence of stanzas analyzes the steps that are taken to separate the silver from the mercury. First, the remaining deposits are removed from the wooden troughs and placed in cone-shaped linen bags, which are hung from a high beam. The bags are made of a texture that enables them to retain the purified silver while the mercury drains away (8.149–55). The second stanza of this segment depicts how the workers remove the silver from the bags and mould it playfully into different shapes, in the image of a calf, a vase, a small box, or a steep mountain. Here, Landívar reassumes the position of an overarching subject, surveying the workers' actions and portraying them as uncouth folk who play with the malleable silver like children (8.156–65). Nevertheless, this moment of transgression and unproductive activity is soon foreclosed. The workers are then made to shape the silver into heavy plates and small round balls so that they can more effectively serve their employer's interests

(8.166–67). Finally, the soft pieces of metal are placed on a tight-woven screen, covered with a metal sheet, and heated over a fire (8.168–71). As the temperature rises, any remaining mercury is deposited into pots while the silver comes to rest, pure and solidified, on top of the screen (8.172–75).

Over the course of the final group of stanzas in book 8, Landívar depicts some alternative methods of purification of precious metals also used in New Spain. In the first stanza of this sequence, it is observed that sometimes the "prudent mass" ("turba [. . .] prouida") of workers apply a different strategy once they have completed the work of treading the muddy residue left after the initial pulverization of the ore. Knowing that leaving the substance to bake in the sun often reduces the value of the metal produced, they instead place the crushed ore in tanks of boiling water (8.176–89). At the same time, the specialist, or skilled worker ("opifex"), tests the mixture in a pan in order to judge whether it is necessary to add mercury (8.190–93). After repeatedly examining the boiling liquid to see if the mud has deposited its metal component at the bottom, the specialist scoops the valuable materials out of the tank using a large spoon (8.194–203). Having placed the materials in a nearby trough, he rinses away the rest of the mud with more water, and then purifies the silver in a hot crucible (8.204–05).

In the following stanza Landívar turns to the procedures followed in processing the kinds of metal ores that need to be smelted in furnaces. Landívar advises that when working with such ores, one construct two separate furnaces and connect them together with a long duct (8.206–08). After bringing the ore up from the mine, one should crush it into small pieces. These must then be mixed with lead and buried under a layer of soft grains of clay (8.209–13). The small rocks should then be heated in one of the furnaces until the pieces of soft stone melt and flow in a stream through the duct, into the other furnace (8.214–21). The melted ore sinks to the bottom of the furnace while the technician draws off impurities with a hook (8.222–27). For a considerable time the liquid mixture swirls and lashes violently against the furnace walls like a rough sea, as the impurities are extracted or evaporate into the air (8.228–34). However, once these unwanted components have disappeared, the remaining metal settles to the bottom. Then, the workers are able to let the fire cool and, after some time, remove a sheet of silver from the furnace (8.235–40).

At this point, Landívar develops, in the subsequent stanza, a reflection on the techniques used in processing gold ore. This segment opens with a reference to gold's position of supremacy among all metals, as the one that is used to adorn palaces and the heads of monarchs (8.241–45). In keeping with the rationalizing and pragmatic scheme of the *Rusticatio Mexicana,* its value is discussed primarily in scientific terms: "Prae reliquis Aurum mortalia pectora raptat, / quod dominum citius ditet, parcatque labori" (8.246–47; "More than all other things, gold grabs the hearts of mortals, because it more quickly enriches its owner and frees him from work"). Landívar notes that after the ore has been crushed, it is a relatively quick process to mix the resultant dust with mercury, run it through a mill, wash it with water, squeeze it through bags, and then purify it in a crucible (8.248–55). Through the development of an involved simile, he compares the relative ease with which, using this method, the gold can be processed to that with which a group of armed men can rob a lone noble (8.256–64). Alternatively, Landívar observes, analyzing the procedures in terms of efficiency and cost effectiveness, the gold is sometimes refined using the aforementioned system of dual furnaces, arranged in such a fashion as to reduce the owner's ("domino") costs and increase his profits ("quaestum"; 8.265–67).

The final three stanzas of book 8 examine the last stage of the manufacturing of gold and silver, addressing the question of its insertion into the dynamics of monetary exchange. This segment depicts the Spanish state's administration of the industry, representing, in the first of these stanzas, the process through which an official of the Crown ("Praepositus," or "prefect") examines the precious metals in order to determine their quality and to gauge how much gold the silver has absorbed and retained (8.268–75). This official is allowed to keep a small amount as payment for his labors, and also sets aside the fifth part of the precious metals for the Crown (8.276–77). Once the pieces of gold and silver have been given the royal seal, the owner then stores them in a safe place (8.278–79).

The following stanza analyzes the practice of using the precious metals to make coins. For this purpose the silver must first be separated from the gold using scientific techniques and fire (8.280–83). The presence of the Spanish state is made explicit here for the first time in the poem. Landívar notes that this labor can only be carried out by ministers whom the king himself has appointed to the task (8.284–86). The final stanza of book 8 details how those employed to do this work are divided up in order to undertake different, specialized jobs within the process of separating gold from silver. Some men stoke a fire with wood, others bring glass beakers, and others handle the acid that is to be used for the task (8.287–90). The workers place bars of silver and the acid in the beakers and place them over a fire. As the liquid heats up, it causes the silver to disintegrate and form a solution, which then flows in a stream along the inside of the glass container (8.291–97). Then, the technician, or "prudent hand" ("Prouida [. . .] dextra"), inserts a copper rod into the neck of the beaker, until it touches the hot contents. In this fashion, he cools the contents a little and causes the gold to settle to the bottom, leaving the silver just above it, while the other components remain at the top of beaker (8.298–305). Finally, after the fire has been extinguished and the glass has been allowed to cool more, the workers are left with separate layers of the different substances and are able to extract the separated gold and silver, which will be used to make coins (8.306–07).

In this fashion, the investigation delves into the material conditions and manufacturing processes that the icons of gold and silver tend to obscure behind their shiny veneer as commodities and exchange media. In demystifying the aura of these transcendent cultural symbols, the text institutes, in their place, the dynamic of industrial technology, and the spectacle of human agency transforming raw materials into commodities.

Corralling the Wilds: Landívar's Vision of Mexican Cattle Raising

The final component in Landívar's projection of New Spain as a sphere of human enterprise is livestock farming, which is depicted in cantos 10 and 11 of the *Rusticatio Mexicana*. These cantos, the first of which deals with larger animals, the second with smaller ones, complete the representation of Mexican nature, conceived not as a vacant, wild space, but as a realm that is administered and ordered by *criollo* subjects for the purpose of agricultural production.

Landívar establishes the terms of the literary and agricultural management of the larger types of cattle in the first stanza of canto 9, outlining the topic that he intends to portray:

> Pinguia uernantes late diffusa per agros
> angustis armenta iuuat concludere saeptis.
> Nunc opus infracto, natoque ad dura bubulco,
> agmina qui pecudum cogat palantia campis,
> montanosque bobes regnis detrudat auitis. (10.1–5)

> It is pleasing to enclose, within the confines of corrals, the fat herds that roam far out over the blooming fields. Now there is need of a cowherd, strong and naturally suited to hardship, to bring together the herds of cattle which range over the fields, and to dislodge the mountain cattle from their ancestral realms.

He then returns, in the second stanza, to the convention of invoking the assistance of mythical figures in the realization of the task of capturing and representing the different kinds of cattle. He requests that they help him to corral those animals that are too rebellious and live in places so remote that he and his compatriots ("nobis") are unable to do so themselves (10.6–11). In exchange for this favor, he declares that he will erect a temple on Mount Parnassus in their honor, working as a "loyal companion" ("fidus comes") of "distinguished youth" ("iuuenum primis"; 10.12–13). Here, Landívar evokes the figure of a *patria criolla,* conceived as a youthful and vigorous form of agency.

The planned space of this cattle raising matrix is constituted not by small farms, but by large estates ("praedia"), many possessing a circumference as large as thirty leagues (10.14–19). It is noted that the owners grow crops on much of these lands, but also leave meadows, woods, and streams untouched so that herds of cattle can roam around them (10.20–25). The first animal placed within this environment, and identified as being preeminent amongst all others, is the white horse (10.26–27). The reader is informed that these animals usually move around in groups of twenty-four, lead by one male, although some herds can number between forty and eighty (10.28–33). By means of cries or by biting, the lead horse keeps the members of his herd together, taking them to graze in fresh pastures, drink at streams, and rest in shady places (10.34–45). They travel around these open spaces for six months of the year, enjoying the temperate climate that keeps them supplied with green vegetation and fresh water (10.46–53).

Nevertheless, Landívar relates that the freedom the horses enjoy is limited, to the extent that cowherds seek to capture and tame them. Aided by several companions, the cowherd ("bubulcus") captures the horse of his choice and encloses it in a corral next to the farm buildings (10.54–58). Next, he throws a lasso around the animal's neck and holds it until his helpers can put a knotted halter over its mouth (10.59–63). After a saddle has been fastened to the horse's back, the experienced horseman then mounts and rides it while it gallops around and tries to throw him off (10.64–69). Here, Landívar intervenes to provide more practical information for the reader, observing that the horse tamer ("domitor") grips the animal's back with his knees, repeatedly turns him around by pulling the reins, and frequently digs his spurs into its sides until he has broken it in and taught it to trot across the meadows with a measured gait (10.70–75).

The depiction of the dynamics involved in horse raising continues over the course of the next few stanzas. In the first of these, it is observed that when the cowherds mix the different groups of horses together, enclosed in the corral, the males become aggressive, eager to demonstrate to one another that they have patriarchal domain over the females in their herds (10.76–80). They bare their teeth, bite each other, and rear up on their hind legs in order to threaten and kick one another (10.81–96). The second stanza of this sequence relates that the rancher periodically opens the corral gates, and lets the horses out to graze in pastures (10.97–98). Landívar notes that the male head of each herd leads the female horses to a discrete area, where he watches over them as they feed (10.99–103). If any female should stray, he forces her back into the fold by kicking and biting her (10.104–11). Significantly, this narrative is cast in the taxonomy of class hierarchy, according to which the male is identified with the soldier of noble blood (10.94) while

the female subjects are grouped under the rubric of a proletariat ("plebe"; 10.110).

After depicting the specific details of horse raising, Landívar
turns his attention, in the third sequence of stanzas of canto
10, to bulls and cows (10.112–47). First, he observes that these
animals are left to graze freely in the woods and fields during
the day, but are brought back to be cared for in corrals and stables
at night (10.148–52). The second stanza relates how the cowherds constantly go out into the forests to look for any calves
the cows attempt to hide under cover of trees (10.153–60). As
a result of these labors, the ranchers are able to gather together
one hundred or more calves in each pen and, at the same time,
can exploit the mothers' milk for human needs. In cases where
a cow tries to remain in the woods and nurse her young there,
large groups of cowherds are sent out in order to drag and coax
them back to their enclosure (10.161–72).

The third stanza of this section analyzes the practices involved
in the business of milk production. Periodically, they allow the
hungry calves out of their pens to seek sustenance from their
mothers (10.173–80). However, as soon as each young animal
puts its lips to its mother's teats, the cowherd pulls it away, taking
care to tie it to her legs, since the cow will withhold its milk
unless its young is in sight (10.181–88). Then, the cowherd
squeezes the animal's teats so that the white liquid falls into a
bucket, to be used later to make butter and cheese (10.189–94).
Nevertheless, the prudent cowherd always leaves one teat untouched, so that there is some milk left for the calf to drink.
When the milking is completed, the cows are allowed back into
the fields to graze, while a young boy leads the calves to eat
grass in a secluded spot where they are unable to gain access
to their mothers' milk (10.195–202).

Over the course of the next few stanzas, Landívar's gaze turns
more closely to the different procedures followed in raising the
male calves. The first stanza portrays the manner in which the
cowherds brand the young animals with a hot iron after about
one year of growth (10.203–07). They tie each calf's legs together with rope, hold it down, and mark it with the symbol of
the estate ("fundi"), thereby incorporating him into the semiosis
of large-scale capitalist agriculture (10.208–11). If the animal
manages to free itself and resists its insertion into this system

of organization, the cowherds gradually wear down its energies and resistance by repeatedly goading it with cruel blows,
and then running away (10.212–17).

The poetic performance of a will to power over Mexican fauna
continues in the next stanza, where the skills used by the
cowherds to capture fully grown bulls are studied. Landívar prefaces his depiction of these arts by remarking upon the sense
of wonder that the spectacle of their realization produces in
the viewer: "Interdum rabidos etiam mirabere tauros / submitti,
facilesque globum concurrere in unum" (10.218–19; "Sometimes one will also admire how the furious bulls are subdued
and willingly gathered together in one herd"). Early in the mornings, the cowhands ride into the forests and fields and gather
the animals together, some forcing them out of the woods, some
bringing them down from the mountains, and others watching
over the herd as it assembles (10.220–28). Should a bull try to
escape, one of the men chases after it on horseback, forces it
to the ground, and brings it back to the herd (10.229–34). Finally,
the men separate the fatter animals for the slaughterhouse, and
pick out the stronger ones to work with the plough, releasing
the rest back into the pasture lands (10.235–38).

The subsequent stanza portrays the techniques used to tame
the stronger bulls so they can be used to pull ploughs. First,
the animals are castrated, then they are hooked up to a plough
with oxen that have already been broken in, and made to work
alongside them until they too have lost their rebelliousness
(10.239–43). It is related that the farmer ("arator") places the
bull between two tame oxen and harnesses them all to the same
yoke so that the trained animals hold their new companion in
check until he also is tamed, and can then can be tied up to the
plough itself (10.244–59).

The final two stanzas of canto 10 depict the strategies used
against the wildest of bulls, which avoid the open meadows and
seek to hide away from humans in the darkness of the forests
(10.260–63). In the first of these stanzas, it is pointed out that
these animals can only be caught at night, when thirst forces
them to venture out into the open where the cowherds can
ambush them (10.264–68). Mounted on the fastest horses, the
men approach the task through a division of responsibilities,
some brandishing spears, some wielding a crescent-shaped

bronze weapon, and others tying ropes to the tails of their horses with which to drag along the bulls, once they are bound and wounded (10.269–74). The final stanza evokes in more detail the different tasks involved in the enterprise. First, during the night, they spread out and hide throughout the areas the bulls cross in order to gain access to water, while sentries wait near the woods to give advance warning of the animals' approach (10.275–82). Then, once the bulls reach the open spaces, the men chase after them, some wounding them with spears, others with curved knives (10.283–88). Landívar focuses most admiringly on the technique whereby the horsemen lasso a bull, and drag it along on a rope tied to their steed's tail. In a footnote he indicates that this is the method that is most commonly used by the cowherds of the region of Guatemala (145n). Although the bulls attempt to get close to the rider, the skilled man stuns them with a heavy blow, and his comrades then wound it with their weapons (10.289–96). Finally, the men skin the animals and cut away the breast and the ribs, which they take home for food (10.297–300).[12]

Having encapsulated the images of the horse, the mule, and the bull, and harnessed them within a program of organized economy, Landívar moves on, in book 11, to the study of smaller species of cattle. In proposing to capture the sheep, the goat, and the pig, in the first stanza of this book, he notes that he needs neither arrows nor traps, but only requires the assistance of "expert herdsmen" ("Expertis [. . .] pastoribus") and hounds ("molossis") to realize the undertaking (11.1–9). For further guidance he invokes, in the second stanza, the figure of Pan, asking the deity to "urge [the herdsmen] to instruct him about the manifold nature of the flocks" ("naturam pecorum uariam compelle docere") of smaller animals raised on Mexican estates (11.10–17). In this fashion, Landívar continues to encode in this literary conceit the work he himself appears to have carried out in learning about these forms of agricultural observation through observation and interrogation of the farmworkers themselves.[13]

In the third stanza of book 11, the description proper of these spheres of cattle raising opens with the observation that specialization is a key feature of farming in New Spain. It is noted that while some farmers enjoy dealing with the larger animals, there are others who prefer to rear sheep, goats, and pigs (11.18–24). From this statement the text moves first into a sequence of stanzas that portrays the procedures involved in American sheep farming. First, it is related that these animals are raised by "wealthy landowners" ("diues erus") on "estates" ("Praedia") surrounded by green pastures and abundant natural supplies of water (11.25–29). The large pastures, where the sheep roam freely, contain shady wooded areas, to which shepherds guide them, assisted by dogs, whenever the sun becomes too fierce or it starts to rain (11.30–38). Aided by three assistants and by his dogs, each shepherd moves his flock day and night across the vast tracts of land that constitute each estate (11.39–41). A footnote informs the reader that a Mexican ranch typically sustains at least twenty-five flocks, each of which contains 2,000 sheep (150n).

The following stanza conveys information about the practice of transhumance in New Spain. As soon as the sheep have been shorn of their fleeces, the shepherd takes them on a long journey to warmer pastures (11.42–47). Here, the device of the footnote is utilized to establish that this journey, which is undertaken during fall, is usually as long as two or three hundred miles (151n). The reader is also informed that the rams, ewes, and lambs are divided up into distinct groups, each of which is driven in a separate direction by different shepherds, making all the fields appear to turn white in the process (11.48–55). The herdsmen strike the animals whenever necessary in order to keep them moving, but also allow them to stop and take shade under any available trees if the sun becomes too hot (11.56–62). If there is no cover at hand, the shepherd forms his flock into a tight circle in such a fashion that the animals are alternately able to offer cover to each other with their bodies (11.63–69).[14] Landívar adds, in the next stanza, that only at night does the herdsman stop to permit himself, his sheep, and his dogs to rest, having fed the latter first (11.70–88). Should a thief or wild animal attack the sheep under the cover of darkness, the dogs awaken and bark until their masters stir from their slumber (11.89–93). Then, the shepherds walk around their flock carrying torches and beat the bushes until they are sure that the predators have been chased away (11.94–99).

Over the course of the journey, the shepherds bring the largest and strongest rams together with the ewes so that they mate repeatedly until the females are impregnated (11.100–08). Finally, the shepherds call a halt to the animals' trek when they reach a winter pasture, where they fatten themselves up eating lush grass under a warm sky (11.109–14). The pastoral scene portrayed here is not, however, a scene of idealized, platonic love, but the location in which the very material act of birth occurs. An exhaustive account of the physical developments involved in this act is provided in the subsequent stanza. It is noted that once each ewe's udder becomes swollen with milk, it gives birth to weak-looking creatures, which at first stumble about the meadows, apparently on the verge of death (11.115–23). Nevertheless, after the mother licks the bodies of her young, they gradually become able to stand on their legs in order to drink her milk and, after some time has passed, begin to jump and frolic about in the fields (11.124–33). In cases where the mother dies as a result of the strain of the birth, the shepherd, his wife, and his children gather up her offspring, and carry them along until they are strong enough to walk on their own behind another of the ewes (11.134–40).

Continuing with the theme of health and reproduction, details are provided, in the next two stanzas, of the medical care the shepherds give to sick animals. First, it is noted, a herdsman isolates the unhealthy sheep in a pen, where he cleans and bandages wounds, and nurses them with herbal remedies (11.141–50). The second stanza relates how, in situations where a mother's milk is unhealthy or where she cannot provide any at all, the shepherd entrusts her young to another ewe, which acts as a "wet nurse" ("nutrix") for the lambs (11.151–59).

The next series of stanzas portrays the circumstances involved in the return of the flocks to their owners' estates. First, when spring arrives, the shepherd guides his animals back to the hacienda lands (11.160–66). Once the flock has arrived at the estate, the "very rich proprietor" ("praediues erus") orders that the sheep be counted. After the animals have been incorporated into the realm of accounting, the *señor* pays a tithe of ten percent ("dena [. . .] parte") to the Church and sets aside a tenth of the lambs for the foreman ("uillicus"), as compensation for his labors (11.167–73). Next, each shepherd locks his animals up in enclosures, again at the orders of the hacienda owner, and has a group of young men tie up each sheep, hold it down, and cut off its fleece (11.174–78). The men roll the fleeces into bundles and closely guard them before handing them over to the rancher, who pays them according to the number each shearer gives him (11.179–81). The following stanza relates how, while they are waiting to be sheared in the tight enclosures, the rams often become angry, lower their heads, and run at one another with their horns (11.182–94). However, these brief manifestations of excess and unruliness are soon curtailed by the farmhands, who pull the aggressive animals out of the enclosures and immediately cut away their wool, thereby controlling their wildness and inserting them again into the scheme of large-scale rationalized agriculture (11.195–96). Finally, in the last stanza of the segment devoted to sheep, it is related that when the work of shearing is done, the herdsmen gather to one side a large number of male lambs that have earlier been castrated. The shepherd sends the fattest of them to be slaughtered and sold at the meat market ("macello"; 11.197–201).

   After discussing the practices involved in goat raising (11.202–322), Landívar switches focus, over the course of the final eleven stanzas of the canto, to the practices involved in the raising of pigs. It is remarked in a footnote that there can be up to 10–12,000 pigs in a herd (160n). The first step a ranch owner takes is to build a high wall around an open field near his farmhouses and set up two corrals within the enclosed area, strategically located so they afford access to a stream of water (11.323–32). One of the corrals contains small buildings in which the impregnated sows can rest (11.333–34). In the other, the rest of the females sleep in large huts after they return from the fields (11.335–37). The males are kept in other fields, where they are provided with food, water, and shelter (11.338–41).

   Once a general picture of the managed environment constructed for the pigs has been sketched out, more specific details are offered about the key elements involved in raising them, beginning with feeding and the animals' behavior. Early in the morning, the swineherd scatters barley on the field for the pigs (11.342–47). Once they have eaten their fill, boys take them out into open pastures, where they eat and frolic about, while the herdsman stands ready to control them with a whip (11.348–53). When the sun reaches its highest point, the swineherd gathers the animals together and takes them back to the corral, where the pigs cool themselves down in a stream (11.354–63). Then, the herdsman spreads a mixture of earth over the floor of the pen, feeds salt to the pigs, and moves them into the buildings, where they can take shade from the sun (11.364–67). Once the sun has started to go down, he takes the herd out to graze in open pasture once more before finally returning the animals to the enclosure, where they rest after being fed another ration of barley (11.368–78).

The next stanza depicts how the swineherds carefully manage the reproduction of their animals. Periodically, they choose the best of the males, and place them together with the sows for a period of ten days (11.379–87). Once the females have been impregnated, the swineherd waits until the stomachs of the sows become fully swollen, and their teats stretch down to the ground (11.388–89). Then they are all confined to small pens during the period of the birth and early life of their young (11.390–98). The farmworkers make these hardships more bearable by constantly providing the mother and her piglets with supplies of grain and fresh water (11.399–403).

The following stanza relates how the process is further systematized by the foreman, who examines the litter as soon as a sow has given birth. Any piglet he judges to be too weak or too small is swiftly removed and killed. In general, he leaves the mother with between three and five of her young to suckle (11.404–09). Subsequently, after twenty days have passed, the young piglets are allowed out of their huts. From this point on they are allowed to indulge themselves in a carefree life, alternately playing around in the pens, covering themselves with mud, and then returning to their mother's sty in order to drink her milk (11.410–18). When four lunar months have gone by, the young are divided up into separate herds, with the males being sent out into the fields to graze with their fathers while the females are left to share quarters with their mothers (11.419–26). At this point, the foreman decides the terms of the animals' insertion into the mechanisms of capitalism, having all sterilized, marking the large numbers that are to be fattened on grain, and signaling out which of the young males are to be used to father future generations of the herd (11.427–30).

In the penultimate stanza of book 11, it is noted that the animals that are to be fattened are no longer allowed to roam and graze in open pastures, but are kept in their pens where their movement is restricted and they do little more than eat beans and barley for three months (11.431–35). The combined effect of the constant feeding and the lack of exercise is to render the animals heavy and slothful (11.436–41). The final stanza depicts how they are slaughtered. It is observed that one man cuts their throats, another pours the animal's lard into pots, or grinds the meat to make sausages, while the rest of the workers gather up its now clotted blood (11.442–47). The final fruit of all this intense hard work is the variety of pork products that the butcher makes out of the different parts of the slaughtered animals. Significantly, emphasis is placed on the fact that the trade and elaboration of these commodities will yield a profit ("faenore") for the "wealthy ranch owner" ("opulentus erus"; 11.448–49).

With this representation of large-scale capitalist ranching, Landívar concludes his portrayal of New Spain and Guatemala as spheres of organized human endeavor. American nature, cast in books 1 through 3 as a sublime force that escapes the scope of the rationalizing gaze and hand, is now stabilized as a manageable, fertile space that offers its inhabitants the materials to fulfill their necessities and to trade with their European counterparts. Landívar's representation of this space of organized and specialized labor not only portrays the image of the region's self-sufficiency, but also comes to embody such an ideal, through its incorporation of disparate spheres of activity into a totalizing, utopian vision of coordinated production. Having constructed this landscape of rationalized economy, Landívar now returns, in the last four books and the appendix of the *Rusticatio Mexicana,* to the depiction of the areas that fall beyond the bounds of that framework. These areas constitute a space of surplus that requires the writer once more to expand the scope and character of his projection of America as a locus of power and rationality.

Chapter Six

Framing American Heterogeneity

In the final four books of the *Rusticatio Mexicana,* and in an appendix,[1] Landívar shifts his focus away from the depiction of a diversified and rationalized economy founded on the calculated exploitation of American materiality. The subject installed through the dynamic of the natural sublime, and who has been posited as the agent of the economic order of the various regions of Mexico and Guatemala following the removal of the discursive and institutional matrix of the Jesuit order, will now be deployed in the task of further shaping the heterogeneity of American nature and cultures into a new totality. Books 12 through 14 deal with natural objects that are grouped, respectively, within the classes of springs, birds, and wild animals. The final book and the appendix treat cultural topics more explicitly, the first portraying the different sports played in the viceroyalty, the second giving details of the symbol of a grassy mound that forms the shape of a cross near the small town of Tepic, and of the significance it holds for the inhabitants of New Spain. In these parts of the poem, Landívar combines the techniques of natural history with the discourse of the beautiful in his efforts to frame objects of study that are often anomalous and appear resistant to representation.

As was noted in chapter 4, the beautiful tends to be expressed in terms that are counterposed to those of the sublime, although there is often slippage between the two signs in many eighteenth-century discussions of aesthetics. The beautiful is usually configured as small, regular, and ordered, affording the viewer or reader pleasure by virtue of its unthreatening charm. Its effect derives from its smallness and proportion, which do not represent a threat to the security and stability of the viewing subject.[2]

In the final cantos of Landívar's poem, I will argue, the representation of certain natural features and cultural practices—most specifically, his depictions of birds, sports, and the cross of Tepic—comes to be framed in terms of natural history and the aesthetics of the beautiful. In my analysis of these sections, it will be my concern to propose that Landívar uses the well-known register of the beautiful in order to render familiar to Western European readers species and practices that appear to fall outside the archive of their knowledge. At the same time, the poetic representation of the heterogeneity and natural abundance of American space, not as chaotic and threatening but as available for domestication and visual pleasure, serves to complete the process of the construction of the ideal reader and subject of Landívar's poem, that is, a *criollo* subject who is master of the codes of Western European aesthetics and natural history and who, through their use, will become the ordering center of Mexican and Guatemalan economy and society.

Classifying the Beautiful: The Birds of Mesoamerica

In book 13 Landívar engages in the depiction of the more unusual birds to be found in Mesoamerica. By virtue of their heterogeneous appearance, they serve as markers of American otherness. In this canto he negotiates the material discursive terrain that had traditionally been covered by the superimposed bestiary developed by European imaginations through the textual production of early modern European humanism. Fictional images clustered around American wildlife as a result of Spanish travelers' projections of the mythical creatures of classical mythology onto the animals they encountered on their expeditions. Such images had acquired a more scientific status and had a greater basis in empirical observation by the time Buffon was compiling his *Histoire naturelle*. Nevertheless, the representation of America's animals as, alternately, too weak or too wild, constituted an important part of the continuing discursive construction of images that marked the continent as not conducive to the development of civilization and rationalized economy. In book 13 Landívar sets out to provide nuanced pictures of Mexican birds, with a view to fitting such representations into a totalizing vision of a world organized into complex, rationalized activity by *criollo* subjects of knowledge.

Landívar opens canto 13 by dividing the birds of Mesoamerica into four kinds, the order of which reflects the rationale articulated by Buffon in affirming that the natural historian should always begin by observing those species that are most useful and pertinent to the existence of humans.[3] The groups that Landívar treats are as follows: poultry, birds known for their bright colors or harmonious singing, and birds of prey (13.1–6).

Having invoked the assistance of mythical wood nymphs in garnering knowledge about the birds' habits, character, and songs (13.7–10), Landívar proceeds, in the third stanza of book 13, to portray the kinds of fowl grown for food on farms. In a brief passage, he notes that although America possesses many species that are native to the continent, chicken has become the most common source of poultry meat in the cities, on the ranches, in the hamlets, and in the huts of the poor, ever since the birds were imported by the Spanish (13.11–22). Noting that a French Jesuit has already written extensively on the topic of the most common species of poultry, the *criollo* declares that he will not go into any further detail himself (13.23–25).[4] In a brief stanza, he then states that he will dedicate himself to portraying the wild species that are native to America's forests, reiterating the sense of his first-hand involvement with the world he is representing in the following terms: "Chortibus hinc tutis, et chortis gente relicta, / in nigras siluae tacitus decedo latebras / fallere siluestres laqueo uiscoque uolantes" (13.26–28; "Having left the sheltered poultry yard, with its flocks, I silently depart into the dark recesses of the forest to trap the wild birds with snare and lime").

Landívar thus signals his intentions by means of a metaphor that identifies the procedures involved in trapping with those involved in studying and representing a species, recalling his earlier treatment of the beaver (6.1–10). The first bird he analyzes is the peacock, noting that the peafowl raised in farmyards are descended from this more elegant creature (13.29–36). Landívar provides information about its mores and appearance, relating that it cannot fly very far but runs swiftly, and that the females carefully build nests in order to protect their young from the sun (13.37–41). However, he goes into the most detail in depicting the symbolic gestures that serve to demarcate the terms of the patriarchal order of the species. Specifically, he relates how the male arches its neck and opens its impressive plumage in the signifying rituals by means of which it leads its flock to drinking waters and communicates its desire to mate (13.42–54).

As in the study of the beaver, the treatment of the species proceeds from the classification of its distinguishing physical features to the portrayal of the techniques that can be used to hunt and capture it.[5] In the second stanza devoted to the peacock, he addresses the reader in the second person singular, observing that one hunting method involves beating the bushes the birds inhabit with sticks, making them run into the open (13.55–62). Once they have been driven out into the fields, the sticks are used to break their legs, rendering them helpless (13.63–66). In the third stanza of this segment, he describes an alternative strategy, to be used at night when the peacocks are asleep in the trees (13.67–69). In such instances, the hunter attaches a noose to a stick and stuns the birds by making loud noises and flashing a torch into their faces (13.70–76). While the peacocks stare into the light, dazed, one man climbs the tree and throws the noose around their necks, one by one, and lowers them down to a companion (13.77–91).[6]

Landívar implements here the discourse of natural history, moving dialectically between relations of similarity and difference.[7] This discourse affords a mechanism for the representation of divergences from European norms in American species in terms that conceive of those species, no matter how anomalous in appearance, as having their own specific rationality, bestowed on them by nature.[8] Landívar next considers the pheasant, a species that is closely related to the peacock, with some small differences. It is noted that it is similar in size, in its inability to fly long distances, and in its swiftness of foot, which enables it to outrun dogs. In addition, it is differentiated from the other species in its class by a tall crest that rises above its head and in the color of its plumage, which can be a yellowish copper or jet black (13.92–107). Having related the details of the bird's abilities and appearance, Landívar again offers advice on how to catch it, either with snares or with lead darts

(13.108–09). He also explains the benefits the animal can provide: its meat provides excellent-tasting food, its bones can be used to make poison, or it can be reared as a continuous source of poultry meat in the farmyard (13.110–17).

The process of the construction of a relational system of difference and similitude continues in Landívar's descriptions of the *chacalaca* and the *pava,* two birds with which the pheasant tends to associate. The *chacalaca* is depicted as small, with lead-colored feathers, and noisy, while the *pava* is portrayed as slightly larger, having dark plumage, and as quieter (13.118–25). Although the *chacalaca* is easier for the hunter to catch, careful measures must be taken in preparing both birds for eating once they have been killed. If one does not hang them to cool slowly in the open air, the reader is advised, their meat will be too hard for anyone to chew, no matter how long it is cooked (13.126–37).

The study maintains its focus on related species in the next stanza, where the partridge and the quail are analyzed. Like the birds mentioned above, neither of these is very adept at flying. Instead, each hops around, dwells near ground level, and hides its young in nests under bushes (13.138–46). Landívar records that the meat of these birds is a choice dish at the tables of monarchs. He indicates that they can be caught either with nets or by surprising them during the night (13.147–50). The final species placed in this grouping are the thrush and the dove, both of which are described as "associated" ("sociatus") with those already depicted (13.151–54).

Here, Landívar concludes his treatment of the species notable for their utility as food sources. Next, he shifts register, supplementing the rhetoric and logic of natural history with the language of the aesthetic mode of the beautiful. He declares, at this point, that he prefers to turn his attention to those species that please the senses with their songs or beautiful colors (13.155–58). These qualities serve to familiarize the reader with birds that would appear, initially, to fall outside the order of Western knowledge and the norms of beauty established by neoclassical aesthetics. At the same time, to the extent that they can be shown to reproduce the qualities associated with the beautiful—they are small, charming, unthreatening—they serve to develop further the picture of American nature as a space the heterogeneity of which can be ordered and administered by rational subjects. Significantly, Landívar reiterates the dialectical, intersubjective terms of his depiction of these creatures, affirming that he himself derives great joy from them: "Me iuuat alituum cantus haurire sonoros / auribus, atque oculos uario recreare colore" (13.157–58; "I take joy in listening to the melodious songs of birds and in refreshing my eyes with their varied colors").

Individual stanzas are devoted to the depiction of several of the species in this group, the first of which is the *yulqueo.* The elegance of its golden plumage is emphasized, and it is described as being more beautiful and larger than the sparrow (13.159–64). As for its character, it is related that it can be easily tamed and will entertain people by singing greetings, hopping on their shoulders, and playing (13.165–68). The second bird portrayed is the cardinal, in whose red plumage, prominent neck, bright eyes, and melodious song the poet delights (13.169–76). As the focus shifts to the *calandria,* the technique of detailed observation is applied carefully through the delimitation of the different colors of ash, white, and yellow (13.177–82). In the fourth stanza, the green woodpecker (*pito*) is portrayed, its most salient feature being its harmonious singing (13.183–90). Similarity in color enables Landívar to group this bird with another, which he describes in the following stanza. He notes that this bird—the *guarda barrancas*—is only differentiated by a tinge of yellow, and by the fact that its natural habitats are deep ravines and forests. Straining to find the metonymical analogy to capture the sound it makes and to maintain it within the terms of the beautiful, he compares its repetitive ringing call to the noise of beating cymbals (13.191–98).

The text proceeds through the logic of differentiation over the next few stanzas, beginning with a study of the black sparrow, or the *cenzontle.* Landívar comments on the effect produced by the bird, noting that its song, while sweet, tends to induce gloom in the listener with its somber tones (13.199–204).[9] He relates, in the subsequent stanza, by contrast, that the *rise,* which is blue, sings in a manner that brings cheer, even when it is kept in a cage as a pet (13.205–10). This bird is then associated with the sparrow, in view of its size and pleasing song. At the same time, the sparrow is identified in terms of the combination of purple, violet, blue, and emerald in its plumage, that is, the features that differentiate it from the *rise* (13.211–16). The logic of differentiation continues in the following stanza, where Landívar's gaze fixes on the hummingbird, which, the reader is informed in a footnote, is called *colibrí* in South America and *chupa-mirto* in the northern regions (192n3). It is noted first that it does not sing, is small, wears bright green plumage speckled with bright colors, and has a sharp beak that is almost as long as its body (13.217–24). Then Landívar describes the species' striking physical abilities. He observes that it flies very fast, making a humming sound with its wings, and is able to hang in the air as it beats them in order to suck nectar out of flowers through its beak (13.225–34). Finally, he relates that when winter comes, the hummingbird leaves the forests and gardens and takes shelter in mountain caves (13.235–42).

In the following stanza, the focus turns to another songbird, the canary. Having observed that it is a species that was first brought over from Spain, Landívar proclaims its capacity to produce a variety of musical sounds (13.243–47). He relates that it is common for these birds to be kept in cages and indicates that it is great fun to offer them food on the end of one's finger. In addition, he notes that the canary cleans itself assiduously and that the females take great pains to build safe, comfortable nests for their young, using twigs, soft cotton, and feathers from the breasts of the males (13.248–61).

From the canary, Landívar's account of the birds jumps again, through the logic of contrast and differentiation, to the study of the buzzard, or *zopilote*. Landívar remarks upon his own close observation of this species: "Dum moror, et uigili contemplor lumine nidos" (13.262; "As I linger, and observe the nests with a keen eye"). In particular, he focuses on the fact that one bird tends to rule over an entire flock, as if a king. He notes that in contrast to the aforementioned birds, it has a raucous call. It is added that, as its distinguishing features, it has an elegant forehead encircled with a fleshy diadem, a white neck with a scarlet collar, and is comparable in size to the eagle, and more beautiful (13.263–67). As for the species' social customs, it is observed that the leader of each flock resides in the most secret parts of the forest and that he is so respected by his fellows that they will not eat the carcass of any animal until he has touched it first (13.268–74).

Landívar's ornithological study returns to the common feature of multicolored plumage in the following stanza, where attention is turned to the *tzacua*. He identifies this bird's principal distinguishing feature as its social nature. Each member of a flock always looks out for the others (13.275–78). Not only do the *tzacuas* build their nests carefully in high trees, but they also take turns acting as sentinels and call to their fellows to warn them of the approach of predators such as humans (13.279–92). Landívar's gaze then shifts to the parrot, the last of the birds identified primarily according to their calls and the color of their plumage. Landívar relates that its plumage is mostly green, save for its yellow neck and forehead. He focuses most attention on its intelligence, its ability to imitate the human voice, sing, and cause mischief, especially when it has been tamed and made to live in a cage, surrounded by people (13.293–303).

At this point, Landívar concludes his classification of the birds grouped in accordance with their color and songs. Next, he seeks to establish a framework for several species that come to constitute part of the supplement, or excess, beyond the grid of the existing body of knowledge produced by the discipline of natural history. They are fitted into a body of information that renders them more familiar and facilitates the production of a sphere of specifically *criollo* knowledge. Here Landívar has to construct a modified framework in which to house and order these species. This segment of the *criollo* natural archive is completed in the final series of stanzas of the book, where Landívar's gaze shifts to various species of birds of prey. This switch is effected by means of a transitional stanza, which conveys the conflictual relationships between the different classes of birds. In this stanza, a scene is depicted in which a parrot, absorbed in its chatter, is attacked and torn apart by a bird of prey (13.304–06).

The first of this class is the eagle, identified as the queen of all birds (13.307–09). Landívar indicates, in a footnote (195n5), that he has chosen to represent the royal eagle, since it is one of the most renowned types of this bird. First, its physical appearance is outlined. It is noted that it has a wing span of six cubits, has black-and-white plumage, and possesses long, curved claws (13.310–13). The second stage of his study describes its habitat, relating that it lives in forests and remote fields. Third, details of its mores are provided, with the observation that it descends at great speed from the skies and carries off its prey, before tearing it apart with its claws and eating it (13.314–22).

By means of comparison, the study moves, in the second stanza of this sequence, to the subject of the falcon, which is said to fly even faster than the eagle (13.323–24). The most notable of its physical features are its yellow feathers, its purple-speckled neck, and its size, roughly equal to that of a rooster. The portrayal of the falcon concludes with the remark that it is so quick that it is able to capture and kill doves in midair (13.325–35). Continuing with the exploration of the criterion of speed, the poet turns his attention, in the following stanza, to the sparrow hawk. It is characterized as being less swift than the falcon, and unattractive because of its shape and drab color (13.336–37). In contrast to the more illustrious members of its genus, it waits close to nests for its prey, and then carries chicks away to the cover of the forest, where it devours them (13.338–43).

The treatment of Mexico's birds of prey concludes with a study of the hawk, which is associated with the sparrow hawk because of the similarity of its appearance. Landívar relates that although it is smaller than the sparrow hawk, it shares with that species similar features and a black plumage (13.344–45). It hangs in the air by maintaining its wings outstretched, and swoops down upon poultry yards, carrying off any chick that strays away from its fellows. Then it tears the infant bird apart in an act of furious violence (13.345–55).

Having completed his account of America's birds of prey, Landívar declares, in a transitional stanza, that he will report upon one last bird, which stands apart from all the others on account of its strange appearance and unusual qualities. This final piece of information is presented as another instance of local knowledge and technology that he deems to constitute a valuable contribution to humanity in general:

> Nunc uero postquam siluae spectacula nostrae
> grata dedi, subito uolucrum mirabile monstrum
> saltibus abducam densis, circumque per orbem
> ipse feram, morbis laturum forte medelam. (13.356–59)

> Now that I have presented the pleasing spectacles of our
> forests, I shall suddenly bring forth from the dense woods
> an extraordinary monster of a bird and shall convey it my-
> self around the world so that I may, perhaps, bring healing
> to the sick.

The final stanza of book 13 portrays the *cucharón,* a species of spoonbill that is said to reside in the deepest recesses
of the forests. He describes its appearance in much greater detail
than any of the aforementioned species, noting that it is small
and slender, although its thick and predominantly black plumage makes it look bigger (13.360–63). In addition, it has a short
tail, long legs, and large patches of red and white on its back
and breast, respectively. However, its primary distinguishing
feature is its enormous, shell-shaped, and multicolored beak,
which is larger and heavier than the rest of its body (13.364–
72). In spite of this freakish aspect, however, its tongue contains healing properties. Landívar relates that sick people can
often be cured if they are made to drink water that the bird has
first sucked up into its beak (13.373–80). Thus, while the bird
does not conform to the conventional terms of the aesthetics
of the beautiful, it is shown to have been bestowed by nature
with a utility peculiar to it alone, a utility that is rendered comprehensible once the apparently anomalous species is fitted into
the rationalized system of classification and difference drawn
up by Landívar.

Criollo Modernity and the Organization of Leisure: Mexican Sports

A second sphere that exists in an ambiguous position with respect to the rationalization of viceregal space is that of leisure.
This is an area of activity that is conceived as enjoying a relative autonomy with respect to economic production. At the same
time, however, it exists in a relationship of complementarity
to agriculture and manufacturing, insofar as the staging of dis-
traction or diversion and the experience of disinterested play
offer the respite necessary to maintain and facilitate the worker's
acceptance of the intensified character of labor under the more
calculated order portrayed in the *Rusticatio Mexicana.* Play

exists through the management of a contradiction, to the extent that it is experienced as a sphere separate from organized relations of production and the exploitation of labor, but, at the same time, is conceived by the *criollo* subject as an integral part of that regime. This dynamic is projected in Landívar's representation of sports and games in canto 15.

This system of relations is articulated in the first stanza of the book, in a turn of phrase that appears as a convention of rhetoric, but, in fact, enacts, or performs this dialectical relationship of work and play. Landívar writes:

> Lustra uenanatis postquam montana sagittis
> horrentesque canum turbaui murmure saltus,
> fert animus prauum ludis miscere laborem,
> et uires blanda fractas reuocare quiete. (15.1–4)

> Now that I have disturbed the mountain haunts with deadly arrows and the dreadful forests with the barking of dogs, I am inclined to mix games with the difficult labor, and to revive weak strengths with pleasant relaxation.

In the quest for knowledge of such activities, Landívar invokes the assistance of the mythical sons of Tyndarus, so that he might be informed of the "spectacles" ("spectacula") that are put on by young men in "festive games" ("festis [. . .] ludis") in the "west" ("occiduis"), the term he uses here to refer to America (15.5–9). It is notable that Landívar should use such a vocabulary to denote these practices, since it firmly situates them within a modern framework of mass leisure and social control.[10] The emphasis Landívar places on leisure oriented around the staging of events of great visual impact, performed by the most physically vigorous members of the population, indicates the importance of such activities in disciplining and managing the operations of the social body, not just at work, but also in its leisure.

Landívar does not represent the different kinds of sports and spectacles as barbarous, as irreducibly other, but as important features of a harmonious social order. They are portrayed as having their own rationalized systems of norms and procedures in keeping with the principles of civilized society. Just as the images of the beautiful stand as icons whose aesthetic qualities all viewers recognize, so also do the games and entertainments serve as means of association, binding together the inhabitants of the New World into social bodies through the experiences of play and spectatorship.

Significantly, the first kind of game depicted is one that presents a display of orchestrated violence: cockfighting. In the evocation of this sport, the poem returns to the dialectical play in which a nascent subject of reason engages his powers of representation with an object of knowledge that resists efforts at classification and calls into question the integrity of his desired rationality. The observation of the cruelty and violence involved in the practices of which this sphere of activity is composed induces in the writing subject a mixture of admiration and horror, reminiscent of the sublime sentiments aroused in the portrayals of lakes and volcanoes. The position of centrality that events of such controlled transgression of the terms of good taste and order come to occupy in the constitution of the position of a *criollo* subject of reason is indicated by the opening lines of this segment, in which Landívar, in the first-person-singular form, projects himself once again onto the literary and material landscapes of the poem: "Protinus armatos generosa in proelia Gallos / ipse sequar. Nec enim fas est obducere pugnas, / quae noua lymphati recludunt monstra furoris" (15.10–12; "Immediately I myself will turn to the roosters armed for noble battles. For it is not right to cover up fights which reveal new marvels of wild rage").

These activities are introduced because of their quality of excess and transgressive violence. Of particular importance here are the words "noua [. . .] monstra," which reiterate the preoccupation with depicting events and objects that appear to fall outside the purview of an epistemology based on the ordering principles of beauty and reason. At the same time, the labor of the representation is precisely one of capturing, of encapsulating such things, a task that can never be successfully completed, as is indicated by the complex and contradictory semantics of the word "monstra."[11] In this segment, the related concepts of novelty and monstrosity become bound up with the task of integrating that which seems anomalous or barbarous into a systematized rational order.[12]

The reader is presented with a narrative about the process through which the roosters come to be used for entertainment. Notable for its haughty demeanor and the manner in which it attacks its fellows in the yard, the bird is, in part, the author of its own fate, insofar as, by its nature, it signals to men that it might have a purpose beyond the realm of the farm (15.13–15). Landívar attempts to explain what leads men to single out some cocks, and tie them with a rope in a small cage. He lays the blame on humanity's susceptibility to "the insane passion for sport or cruel pleasure" ("cum ludi uesanus amor, cum saeua voluptas"), which draws individuals outside of the regime of labor that Landívar, in his vision of the social order, projects for them (15.16–18). At first the birds are unhappy, but then they adjust to the regimen the men impose upon them. Their owners feed them well, remove some of their primary distinguishing features—their claws, combs, and wattles—and attach a sharp blade to one of their spurs, in preparation for their fight (15.19–36).

Having conveyed the bird's physical appearance and the process through which it is reared for combat, Landívar then depicts the specific circumstances of the fights themselves. In the second stanza of the sequence devoted to this topic, an image of the arena in which the contests are staged is constructed. Its identifying signs are a small area of level ground always stained with blood and the surrounding wooden benches in which the crowd ("turbae") of spectators sit and place bets on the outcome (15.37–42). The arena serves as a space of association that brings individuals together as they share in the spectacle.

The third stanza depicts the typical actions of the fights. Landívar, assuming a detached, reasoned perspective, notes that they are played out in front of a plebeian crowd, which he identifies in terms of its low social class ("uulgus") and the unruly noise ("clamosum") it makes (15.43–45). Nevertheless, Landívar's evocation of the mortal struggle itself involves a level of detailed description that suggests close personal observation of such events. He relates that the birds, though filled with accumulated rage, observe each other's movements for some time before they actually engage in battle with their feet and spurs. They never stop fighting until one falls to the earth, blood streaming from its breast (15.46–58). Landívar points out that the surviving rooster is proclaimed the winner, unless it becomes frightened by the death throes of its opponent, in which case the victory is awarded to the dying bird in view of the cowardice of the survivor (15.59–76). He notes, in conclusion, that the crowd ("uulgus") stages numerous fights in one day, only calling a halt to their leisure at nightfall (15.77–79).

The second variety of sport depicted in book 15 is horse racing, which is treated over the course of the next three stanzas. In the first of these, Landívar relates the procedures involved in the selection and preparation of horses, noting that such events are put on whenever the turf is in suitable condition, thus affording people another opportunity to indulge their taste for gambling once they become tired of cockfighting (15.80–82). The most experienced horsemen choose horses according to their beauty, the leanness of their bodies, and the length of their legs. Then they remove the horses' iron shoes and appoint young men to ride them, arming them with osier branches for whips (15.83–92).

The second stanza of this series describes how the horses are slowly ridden over to a starting point in a field, where their impatience and nerves are calmed by the soothing hands of their jockeys (15.93–101). The third stanza offers a representation of the races themselves, relating that they usually involve two horses and are started at the sound of a trumpet blast. At the end, the winner is crowned with laurels (15.102–18).

The third form of sport studied in book 15 is that of bullfighting, which receives the lengthiest and most detailed treatment of all. In the first stanza of this section, Landívar remarks that this is the sport that is most popular of all among the youth of Mexico. He draws a picture of the typical form of the arena where the events are staged, noting that it is one of the kinds of forums that bind the population together into a social body:

> Nil tamen occiduis pubes ardentius oris
> optat, quam circo tauros agitare feroces.
> Area lata patet duro circumdata uallo,
> plurima quae fusae praebet subsellia turbae
> pulchra coloratis, uariisque ornata tapetis. (15.119–23)

> But the youth of the Western world love nothing better than
> to torment the fierce bull in the ring. There is a wide open
> area, surrounded by a solid wall which provides a great many
> seats for the thronging crowd and is beautifully decked with
> many-colored awnings.

Specifically, it is the experience of viewing the matadors achieve artful mastery over wild nature, manifested in the bulls, that unites the spectators as a group. The dominant performers are described as men skilled in the techniques required to dupe the bulls, either on foot or on horseback (15.125–26). The second stanza of the segment sets a narrative of shared cultural tradition in motion. Landívar relates that an angry bull is allowed out into the ring "when these things have been arranged in accordance with the ancient customs of the people" ("[h]is ita longaeuo gentis de more paratis"; 15.127–32). At this point, the bullfighter starts to goad the animal at close range by waving a white cloth (15.133–34).

The third stanza of this section focuses specifically on the procedures involved in the contests where the matador is on foot. It relates how a pattern develops in which the bull runs repeatedly at the man, who, in turn, always dances out of its path at the last moment. After some time, when the animal becomes increasingly angry and weary, the matador pierces its back with a short spear as it passes his side, inducing it to roar out in pain (15.135–48). When the bull then seeks to remove the weapon from its back and relieve its pain by running, the matador continues the contest on horseback. This initiates a new series of maneuvers that are narrated in the following stanza (15.149–53). As the bull repeatedly charges at the horse, the rider pulls his steed to one side and pushes the assailant away with a spear (15.154–65). At the end of these interchanges, when the animal has become severely weakened as a result of its wounds, a judge ("praeses") rules whether it should be killed. If so, an athlete ("athleta") with a sword or a horseman ("eques") with a spear goads the bull into charging him. When the animal responds, the athlete plunges his sword into its flesh or the horseman delivers the mortal blow, driving his spear between the bull's horns, uniting the spectators in the pleasure derived from a victory achieved by means of skill and artistry (15.166–79).

Continuing his analysis of bullfighting, Landívar notes that sometimes a matador ("gladiator") is gored by a bull and dies in the arena. He describes the feeling of horror this provokes in the spectators. Landívar also relates that the contests continue one after the other, in multiple formats with a view to providing more varied entertainment for the crowd (15.180–86). These different kinds of displays are described over the course of the remaining stanzas of this section. First, Landívar describes a spectacle in which a boy fastens a saddle to a bull's back and rides it while it runs at other young men around the arena. The animal tries to throw off its rider and jump up into the stands, thereby frightening the crowd (15.187–210). In the second type of spectacle that Landívar depicts, a boy rides on the back of the bull while carrying a long pointed rod, which he uses to goad another bull that has been let into the ring. After a while, the second animal becomes enraged and locks horns with its saddled counterpart, leading to a contest that comes to a conclusion when the animals are too weary to continue (15.211–22). Landívar also evokes a third form of bullring spectacle, one in which a young man comes into the arena standing on two horses, with one foot on the back of each, controlling their movements with the reins and making them run in circles (15.223–33).

In the subsequent two stanzas, Landívar scrutinizes a fourth kind of spectacle that brings together the inhabitants of New Spain: a kind of flying acrobatics realized by indigenous performers. In the first stanza, Landívar focuses on the apparatus ("machina") from which the acrobats suspend themselves and swing around. It is noted that a tall pine trunk is erected, and a revolving square frame is placed at the top, around which coils of rope are wrapped in such a fashion that they can be subsequently unraveled. Leather girdles are attached to the pole all the way from the bottom to the top so that the young men who participate in this activity can climb up to the frame (15.234–61). The problems of representation that this spectacle poses are addressed and the description made more explicit by the writer as he supplements his linguistic depiction with a drawing of the spectacle, abrogating for himself again the role of mediator of objects and practices that fall outside the parameters of European knowledge (232). In a footnote, he proclaims, in the first person, his own experience of eyewitnessing this kind of spectacle. Additionally, he emphasizes that it represents a mutated form of a similar spectacle that was performed by members of pre-Hispanic Mexican society. Nevertheless, in marking this difference he simultaneously reaffirms its relationship to that non-European past and its place within a historical matrix characterized by the effects of transculturation in indigenous practices as a result of the clash with European forces and practices (227n2).

In the second stanza, the dynamics of the sport itself are conveyed. After climbing up to the frame, four young men fasten the ends of the ropes around their waists and jump into the air. Then they swing around and around, weaving and swaying in order to avoid crashing into one another, as the ropes unwind, until they finally come back to the ground. The effect of the spectacle is heightened by the fact that the participants wear masks, kick at the air with their feet, and shake tambourines as they circle and descend, drawing loud applause from those who watch the entertainment (15.262–77).[13]

The fifth sphere of leisure depicted in book 15 is the greased pole, the description of which serves as a vehicle for further exploration of the unifying role of spectacle and play within Mexican society. The first of the two stanzas devoted to this sport relates how an artisan ("sollers") strips a pine log, polishes it, and smears it all over with grease. The pole is then placed upright in the middle of a ring ("circo"), and a bowl filled with coins is placed on top of it, the goal of the activity being to successfully scale the log and retrieve the money (15.278–89). The second stanza provides details of the contest itself, relating the techniques that the participants use in attempting to maintain a grip on the pole, in order to scale it. However, even those who attach ropes to their limbs or carry spikes in their hands usually only manage to climb a short distance before they slip back to the ground (15.290–300). Although the crowd bursts into laughter at the sight of this, the spectators also urge the tired young men on, until one of them finally manages to reach the top and claim the bowl of money. At this point the spectators join together in applauding the victor, singing his name and praising him (15.301–12).

The final sport depicted in book 15 is a ball game ("pila"), invented and played by native Mexicans, specifically, the Nayarit and the Tarahumara peoples living in the northern regions of the viceroyalty of New Spain (231n4). Maintaining that it is the most fantastic spectacle of all, Landívar, assuming the perspective of the enthralled spectator, relates that the Indians gather up quantities of a thick, elastic gum from trees and roll the material into a ball that can bounce high into the air (15.313–16). Then he relates the organized system of rules of the game itself:

> atque pilam uario magnam glomeramine format,
> quae tenues superet geminatis saltibus auras.
> Tunc manus ingentem fingit sinuata coronam,
> primus ubi grandem sursum iacit impetus orbem,
> quin ulli manibus liceat contingere iactum. (15.317–21)
>
> The crowd then forms a large circle in which the large ball is tossed, and it is not permitted for anyone to touch it with his hand when once it has been thrown, but rather he must hit it with his hips, or elbows, or with his shoulders or knees.

The fact that the participants acknowledge and conform to these rules demonstrates that the game stands as another custom that ties individuals together in a rationalized social order. Landívar observes that the participants can only touch the ball with their hands when throwing it into play at the beginning. Once play has started, they can only make contact with their hips, elbows, shoulders, knees, and heads. Moreover, when the ball lands on the ground, it must be cast back into the air by lifting it between the elbows or knees. If someone touches the ball with his hands once it is in play, that person loses the game automatically (15.319–36). In this fashion the game is shown to have its own internal logic, a shared system of conventions that binds its participants together in a rational social order.

Blessing the *Criollo* Archive: The Cross of Tepic

As a supplement to his project of totalizing representation, Landívar adds an appendix, in which he switches from his ethnographic studies of organized human activity, be it labor or play, and returns to nature in order to extract from it a final symbol that might synthesize the components of Mexican social and cultural space within the domain of *criollo* knowledge and power. In this addendum, he focuses upon the image of a cross that grows naturally in the grass of a hill near the village of Tepic.[14] In the first stanza of the appendix, Landívar, having recapped the contents of the fifteen books of the poem (A.1–8), introduces this space in the following terms: "His autem, mutata mente, remotis, / nunc tibi sacra cano mundi monumenta redempti, / quae nostris natura sagax excudit in agris" (A.8–10; "But now, with these subjects far removed, I change my purpose and sing to you of the sacred memories of the redeemed world which wise nature forged in our fields").

At this point, Landívar invokes the assistance of divine agency in the execution of his task. Importantly, for this final, transcendent symbol, he dismisses the pagan deities of classical antiquity and requests the intervention of the most exalted wisdom of the Christian God—"Tu sola Omnipotens summi Sapientia Patria"—described now in the deistic terms of a being who is present in the material world itself, overseeing all events that occur in it (A.11–20). Addressing this being in the second person, Landívar reactivates the process by which intellectual subjectivity is articulated through the performance of the task of cataloguing the reservoir of material and cultural symbols that constitute the archive of Mexican *criollo* ideology.

This process begins with an evocation of the vastness of America, portrayed again as a sphere of overwhelming sublimity, as in the first three books of the poem. From the description of the mountain ranges that reach high into the heavens and stretch all the way down toward the Arctic, the text then descends into the Tepic Valley, a large area of lush green vegetation that extends between these peaks and is itself intersected by a clear river (A.21–32). In the middle of this valley is situated the small town of Tepic.

Landívar's description serves to complete the reconfiguration of rural space, seen not as a sensuous pastoral of leisure, but as a simple, unadorned sphere of productive labor. The town does not have grandiose country houses, nor elegant columns, nor ancient churches, nor precious stones and metals. Rather, it is signaled as being notable for the modest style of its houses, the diligence its inhabitants show in frequenting its churches, and the agricultural riches that nature has bestowed upon it (A.33–42).

Nevertheless, the feature that makes the region significant is a miracle of nature ("prodigio natura"; A.43). It is a patch of land composed of two natural mounds of earth that rise out of the grass in a field on the edge of the town and intersect with one another to make the form of a cross (A.44–55). The observation of this spectacle moves the poem into the exploration of the miraculous, of a phenomenon that cannot be submitted to the mechanisms of scientific analysis and rationalized economy. In the next stanza, Landívar notes that the cross-shaped mound always stands out from its surroundings. When the grass around it withers during the winter, it remains lush and green; conversely, when rain causes the rest of the grass to flourish, the grass forming the cross fades to a sickly yellow (A.56–73).

In the subsequent two stanzas, Landívar relates that the cross constantly emits a stream of reddish water. Although the waters are said to have possessed healing powers at one time, legend has it that these disappeared after they were used to cure one of the sick people brought to be touched by them (A.74–89). Landívar notes also that in recognition of the symbolic importance of the cross, the devout inhabitants of the town have built a wall around the area where it lies:

> His excita diu celebris uicinia pagi
> religiosa crucem, collatis undique nummis,
> praecinxit muro semotam rure profano,
> atque frequens uotis, multaque obseruat acerra. (A.90–93)

> The religious people of this famous community remained for a long time stirred by these events, and when they had collected money from the surrounding lands, they erected a wall around the cross, separating it from the unhallowed ground, and they frequently honor it with votive offerings and the burning of much incense.

The figure of the natural cross thus serves as an icon, the appreciation of whose transcendent beauty unites the inhabitants of the region as a community. Although its appearance and ecology appear, at first sight, to be anomalous, it is shown to have been shaped by a specific form of logic, that of the miracle. Nature has produced this patch of grass so that the people of

Tepic might be bound together through the shared experience of its wonder.

The evocation of this final component of the *criollo* archive leads into the last stanza of the poem, in which Landívar addresses a specific segment of his ideal readership directly. Summarizing the contents of the stanza as an "exhortation to young Mexicans" ("Ad iuuenes Mexicanos adhortatio"), he explicitly declares that his poem is designed to be read by the potential architects of the region's projected future (A.94–101). He concludes with the following recommendations:

> Disce tuas magni felices pendere terras;
> diuitiasque agri, praestantia munera caeli,
> explorare animo, ac longum indagare tuendo.
> Alter inauratos Phoebeo lumine campos
> incautis oculis, brutorum more, sequatur,
> omniaque ignauus consumat tempora ludis.
> Tu tamen interea, magnum cui mentis acumen,
> antiquos exuta, nouos nunc indue sensus,
> et reserare sagax naturae arcana professa
> ingenii totas uestigans exsere uires,
> thesaurosque tuos grato reclude labore. (A.102–12)

> Learn to esteem your fertile lands greatly, to explore attentively and investigate with a careful eye the riches of the field, the exceptional favors of its skies. Let another, after the fashion of the beasts, survey, with inattentive eyes, the fields gilded by Phoebus's lights, and let him indolently waste all his time in play. You, however, in the meantime, with great sharpness of mind, freed from old views, now assume new ones, and, with a keen resolve to open up nature's secrets, uncover, in the search, all the powers of the mind, and uncover your treasures by dint of happy labor.

Landívar assumes a didactic position, calling upon the young people of Mexico to continue the work of making their homeland a place of intellectual endeavor that is at once enlightened and practical. Significantly, this intervention is couched in terms that synthesize the problematics of a society existing at the margins of the Western world. First, Landívar calls for the adoption and application of new ideas. One can deduce that Landívar is referring here primarily to some of the developments in eighteenth-century Western European thought, such as empiricism, the experimental method, and developments in technology. Second, however, he also takes care to recommend that his Mexican readers develop knowledge of their own environments, in order to deal more effectively and appropriately with their particular dynamics, rather than apply theories developed in other contexts clumsily to realities to which they bear little or no correspondence.

In this fashion, a shift is proposed with respect to a history in which the dominant practice had required that the region's material and cultural realities continually be shaped in accordance with the Spanish imperial model of social and economic organization. With this final exhortation, Landívar offers the *Rusticatio Mexicana* not as a static representation of an immutable world, but as part of a dynamic in which American space can be fashioned in accordance with principles developed not only outside, but also from an understanding of the specificities of the region itself. The different species of birds, the various games and spectacles, the cross of Tepic, which may often initially appear to be anomalous or irrational, have all been dissected and revealed to have their own rational systems of internal organization. The agent of this process of rationalization is projected as an ideal *criollo* subject who will achieve mastery over the different regions of New Spain and Guatemala through the performance of the labor of gathering knowledge about their natural history and the customs proper to their inhabitants.

Conclusion

This book constitutes an attempt to theorize the process of the emergence, in eighteenth-century New Spain and Guatemala, of a position of intellectual subjectivity differentiated from that established by the regime of Spanish imperial authority. My principal concern has been to trace how certain groups of *criollo* intellectuals try to construct such discourses, paradoxically, out of the framework of available European systems of knowledge and representation. In this fashion, I have sought to discern the outline of an ideological program for *criollo* political and cultural hegemony in the eighteenth century.

My analysis of this process is predicated on a conceptualization of power that does not confine the dynamics of colonial societal relations to questions of physical violence and concomitant forms of resistance. Rather, the story I have sought to relate is one in which struggles are waged in multiple loci of authority, not only in the more explicitly material conditions of haciendas and frontier spaces, but also in the discursive and institutional spheres of the viceregal bureaucracy, and in centers where the parameters for the production of knowledge are established and contested. In particular, it has been my concern to argue that certain *criollos,* seeing their possibilities of advance and success in the system of colonial government to have been curtailed in a period of centralizing Bourbon reforms, concentrate their energies in the labor of accumulating detailed knowledge about their material environment and the cultural history of its inhabitants. These *criollos* attempt to transform the sphere of knowledge production into a space from which they might exert a form of authority, establishing a certain degree of autonomy for the intellectual realm with regard to the bureaucratic infrastructure.

In an effort to account for this process of the configuration of a space of intellectual power, I have employed the concept of the *"criollo* archive." First, I have used this concept with the sense of a flexible discursive formation in order to track the protean unfolding of *criollo* ideology in New Spain and Guatemala. Through my deployment of this concept I have sought to offer insights into the connections between very different texts—the *Bibliotheca Mexicana* and the *Rusticatio Mexicana*—which, at first glance, appear to share only the common feature of having been written in Latin. What connects these two works, I have argued, is a concern to produce totalizing accounts of different aspects of life in Mesoamerica, transforming them into objects of authoritative knowledge designed to provide a legitimating ground for forms of *criollo* intellectual subjectivity and association. While texts and manuscripts constitute the raw material of that ground for Eguiara y Eguren, Landívar draws upon the features of the viceroyalty's natural and material environment, framing them primarily through the discourse of natural history and the aesthetic modes of the beautiful and the sublime. I have attempted to argue, nevertheless, that the two visions converge, to the extent that it is through their positioning within the larger dynamic of the shaping of *criollo* discourse that the significance of these works is articulated.

The second, related, problematic that the concept of the *criollo* archive addresses is that of the emergence of a mutated form of modernity in a colonial context. Through the development of this concept in relation to the study of textual representations and institutional matrixes, this investigation has unfolded beyond the scope of an initial framework derived from the teleology of European intellectual and political history, according to which the history of knowledge production in colonial Spanish America was to have been rewritten as another variation on the story of the inevitable transition from a Baroque to an Enlightenment mode. Instead, the work of the concept of the archive leads into a reappraisal of the specific conjuncture analyzed, yielding a story that does not impose the European historical model on the colonial context, but that pays closer attention to the specific dynamics of that space.

Both the *Bibliotheca Mexicana* and the *Rusticatio Mexicana* are texts that move in contradictory fashion, shifting uncertainly between different intellectual paradigms. While the first applies a totalizing and historicist focus to the study of a body of traditional, scholastic texts, the second conserves a residual structure of mediation even as it deploys an empiricist epistemology, insofar as it encloses the knowledge it produces in the code of Latin, just at the moment when that language's mediating power was being eroded by the rise of the European nation-states and the vernacular tongues. In the face of such contradictions, I have sought to place and read these texts within the conceptual framework of the *criollo* archive rather than impose upon them the logic of the aforementioned narrative of Western European history.

In effect, what emerges is not a seamless passage from Baroque to Enlightenment epistemology and aesthetics but, rather, a story of the accumulation of forms and fields of knowledge about the American world, and of the particular, uneven paradigm of modernity which that knowledge yields. This process develops in accordance with a continually self-adjusting *criollo* epistemology, one that subsumes the imputed shift from the textualism of scholasticism and Baroque poetics to empiricism and neoclassicism within its own program for the observation and reorganization of local data. This produces a body of knowledge that fashions a very particular form of modernity that conforms to neither of the models encoded in the concepts of Baroque and Enlightenment. The spheres of letters and scientific knowledge are thus projected as constituting a space that has acquired some level of autonomy with respect to the apparatuses of the viceregal bureaucracy.

Nevertheless, this form of modernity is not made present after the fashion of the "public sphere" that emerges and shapes culture in the embryonic nation-states of eighteenth-century Western Europe. Rather, this autonomy is configured as a function of the specific dynamics of the colonial situation. In the first place, it is a consequence of the division of labor, in which most positions of importance within the bureaucratic infrastructure had come, by the second half of the eighteenth century, to be reserved for Spanish-born appointees. Faced with this situation, colonial *letrados* like Eguiara y Eguren concentrated their endeavors within the spheres of pedagogy and knowledge production, in which *criollos* enjoyed greater power, since by the middle of the century they constituted the vast majority of professors and students.

The second feature of this form of modernity pertains to the social formations out of which it is articulated. As occurs in Spain, the discourse of the differentiation of *criollo* intellectual interests does not reproduce the configuration of the Western European model of critical thought and practice that emerged during the eighteenth century. It is not the work of a loose amalgam of middle-class "individuals" who assemble to debate political, social, and scientific issues in coffee houses or within the framework of agricultural and economic societies. Educated *criollos* do play an important role in the formation of an increasingly empowered civil society. However, in the absence of alternative spaces of association, the projection of a utopia outside the purview of the colonial state is realized predominantly from within preexisting institutional structures by an intelligentsia drawn from the ranks of the local economic elites. Significantly, Eguiara y Eguren is able to carry out the project of the catalogue because the wealth he and his brother inherit from their father enables them to import a printing press from Europe. In addition, the network of scholars with whom he can correspond, thanks to his position of prestige within the Real y Pontificia Universidad de México, facilitates the labor of gathering information about a wide range of institutions, authors, and works situated or produced in the various regions of the viceroyalty.

Similarly, Landívar exemplifies the subjectivity of the *criollo* intellectual to the extent that he is a product of the Jesuit pedagogic system in Guatemala and New Spain. It is specifically this mechanism, or at least its premier institutions in Mexico City, that comes to stand in place of the public sphere of the Western European nations. Moreover, the fact that this articulation of modernity is largely engineered by individuals educated within the Jesuit colleges means that it diverges further still from the liberal model of Enlightenment cultural production.

The story I have attempted to recount is that of the emergence of forms of thought and association that call into question, or seek to displace, the regime of Spanish political, legal, and cultural authority. By analyzing how two very different texts contribute to the trajectory of this discursive and material conflict, I have sought to interrogate how the process of the construction of *criollo* hegemony is one characterized by discontinuity and heterogeneity, and does not assume the form of a teleology moving inexorably and seamlessly toward a predetermined "nationalist" finitude. In this fashion, I have attempted to dismantle the narrative of protonationalism that criticism tends to impose on figures from the colonial period such as Eguiara y Eguren and Landívar. At the same time, I have, in the process, tried to shed light on a more complex genealogy through which key members of a specific racial and cultural social group theorize and articulate the projection of power in a colonial space, not exclusively in the realms of political and economic institutions but also in the spheres of the production of learned culture and knowledge.

Through my analyses of the texts considered in this book, I have tried to point toward some possible directions for future research in the field of studies on the different forms of discourse and representation that configure the cultural matrix Walter Mignolo has identified in the concept of "colonial semiosis" ("Afterword" 334–37). At a general level, I have argued for an increased attention to cultural production in Spanish America during the eighteenth century with a view to initiating discussion about the privilege prior scholarship has accorded to the role played by the texts of the period of the encounter and conquest and of the so-called Barroco de Indias in shaping the cultures of the region.

More specifically, my concern has been to call into question the assumptions that I see as guiding much criticism written about the "Barroco de Indias," particularly in the tendency to view authors such as Carlos de Sigüenza y Góngora and Sor Juana Inés de la Cruz as writing from a position of marginality with respect to the regime of economic and political power of the viceroyalty. I understand such a reading to be dependent still on a now discredited vision of the seventeenth century as a period marked by economic decline and the continuation of a political system in which the Spanish authorities exerted a quasi-absolutist power over *criollos* and other ethnic groups.[1]

If one accepts the revisionist view of the period now shared by most historians of colonial Spanish America, one is presented, instead, with the image of a society in which local elites had come, by the end of the seventeenth century, to exert considerable political influence over the *cabildos* and *audiencias,* and presided over strong, diversified regional economies (Florescano and Gil Sánchez 488–503; Hamnett 69–88; Pérez Herrero 141–44). Such a picture tends to problematize scholarship that views Sor Juana and other seventeenth-century *criollo* writers as articulating counterhegemonic discourses, or at least suggests that it is necessary to reformulate the terms of such criticism.[2] While this problem merits further attention, I have tried here to shift focus to the second half of the eighteenth century as a conjunctural moment when a breach opened between *criollo* and Spanish interests as Bourbon officials attempted to diminish the economic and political power accumulated by local elites over the course of the preceding two hundred years or so. My contention is that in the face of the Bourbon reforms, the *criollos* were pushed into a position of antagonism from which they began to question Spanish authority and conceive of an order in which they would become the hegemonic force.

In advancing such a line of analysis I have attempted to offer arguments for a renewed scholarly focus on the period of Spanish American literary history that runs from the middle of the 1700s to the early decades of the nineteenth century. I propose such a shift of emphasis with the firm belief that it will facilitate fresh and illuminating insights around certain questions pertaining to the historical trajectory of Spanish American letters. Some of these questions might be articulated as follows: What is at stake in the continuing privilege accorded to Baroque and neo-Baroque aesthetics in Spanish American literary scholarship and writing? Why, conversely, does Spanish American literary scholarship tend to neglect the eighteenth century? What might be gained from reconstructing the largely suppressed historical trajectory of the signifying system of the sublime in Spanish American literatures? Is it appropriate to continue viewing early nineteenth-century Spanish American literary production in terms of the framing concept of political independence? Or do we need to look more at the continuities of interests and philosophies between late Spanish imperialism and the nineteenth-century liberalism of *criollo* elites?

By addressing these questions, I believe that scholars can open up Spanish American literatures to the kinds of investigations that might fundamentally reshape the ways in which we conceptualize and interrogate our object of study. Such a focus will help facilitate the important task of reconstructing the complex histories of intersections between literature and other forms of discourse in insightful ways. At the same time, it will lead us to scrutinize more skeptically the assumptions that inform scholarship that continues to privilege the symbolic matrix of the Baroque while neglecting the writers and works of the eighteenth century in its accounts of the history of Spanish American literatures.

Notes

Introduction

1. I understand the term *imperialism* primarily in the sense it has acquired within Marxist historiography and theory, as a concept that denotes the globalization of the capitalist mode of production. Such an understanding of the concept is articulated by Hobsbawm (*The Age of Empire*), and in the account offered by Williams and Chrisman (2). Such a definition is, of course, inextricably linked to historical reconstructions of the trajectory of the British empire in the eighteenth and nineteenth centuries. As regards Spanish America, it is important to consider the contradictory relationship between the economic component of Spanish imperialism and the ideological program of evangelization. For a consideration of the specificities of the Spanish case, see Adorno ("Reconsidering Colonial Discourse" 140–45).

2. Differing accounts of poststructuralism can be found in the works of Dews, Smith, and Harland. The positioning of Lacan with regards to poststructuralism is discussed by Žižek (1–7; 154–99).

3. Useful summaries of Lacan's description of the subject's relationship with the world are to be found in the works of Harland (37–41), Lemaire (65–77), Ragland-Sullivan (1–63), and Smith (xxvii–xxxii; xxxiii–xxxv; 70–76).

4. This revision of the position of the subject of consciousness is articulated most forcefully in Lacan's "The subversion of the subject and the dialectic of desire in the Freudian unconscious" (Lacan 292–325).

5. On the concept of the "metaphysics of presence," see Derrida (49–50).

6. Representative of differing positions within this polemic are the works of de Man (*Allegories; Resistance*), Ryan, Smith, and Spivak ("Can the Subaltern?").

7. I rely here on the survey of these two meanings of the term *subject* offered by Smith (xxvii–xxxv).

8. Representative also is Foucault's interrogation of the character of authorship ("What Is an Author?").

9. On the concept of genealogy, see Flynn (33–37).

10. On the dates marking this periodization, see Cascardi (*The Subject of Modernity* 26). Cascardi (1–24) provides a useful and thought-provoking discussion of this conceptualization of modernity, particularly as articulated in the thought of Max Weber.

11. For a more detailed discussion of the specifics of this dynamic in Spain, and differences with regard to other Western European cases, see Cascardi ("The Subject of Control").

12. Representative of the increasingly large body of work in this area are the studies on colonial Baroque writing undertaken by Beverley (*Del "Lazarillo"* 77–97), Moraña ("Barroco"; "Para una relectura"; *Viaje al* *silencio*) and, in a very different ideological vein, González Echevarría (*Celestina's Brood*).

13. In Adorno one finds this latter narrative with regularity (*Guaman Poma*).

14. Most notable in this area are the studies of Moraña ("Barroco"; "Para una relectura"; *Viaje al silencio*), Cogdell, and Ross ("*Alboroto y motín de México*"). The term *criollo* is commonly held to designate individuals of European ethnicity born in the New World. Arrom offers a detailed analysis of the semantic changes the word has undergone over the course of its history (9–24). In many cases, it also came to denote individuals who, although ostensibly of mixed race, had come to be identified as *criollos,* as Pratt notes in her explanation of the term (112–13).

15. Among the most significant discussions of gender issues are those undertaken by Arenal and Schlau, and by Sabat-Rivers. Class is the factor that continues to remain underscrutinized. At the same time, some of the work remains heavily dependent on humanist categories and strategies, as in the case of Moraña's notion of "creole consciousness" ("Barroco").

16. Williams and Chrisman offer a useful overview of this body of criticism, particularly work carried out in the former British and French colonies (2–18). See also Bhabha (1–18; 40–65).

17. The paradigmatic example of what I take to be the dominant model of postcolonial theory is Homi Bhabha's Barthesian pyrotechnics (180–87). For critiques of Bhabha, see Ahmad (68–71), Beverley (*Against Literature* 148–49), and Larsen.

18. I take the distinction between colonial discourse analysis and postcolonial theory from Williams and Chrisman (5–8; 12–18). The issue of the articulation of postcolonial theory within Latin American contexts has been opened up by Seed and Colás.

19. The dichotomy between "substantive" and "formal" is derived from Weber (*Economy and Society* 1: 85–86; 2: 809–38; *From Max Weber* 298–99). See also Cascardi (*The Subject of Modernity* 7–12; 44–56) and Holton (42–43).

20. On these features see Gruzinski, Lienhard, and Cesareo (*Cruzados*).

21. I understand the term *conjunctural* to denote a moment in which a shift in social structures and/or thought is in the process of being articulated. For a fuller definition, see Althusser (250).

22. I derive the term *subject-in-process* from Smith (35–37; 121–26).

23. On the economic situation of the *criollos* at this time, see Burkholder (6–7).

24. Burkholder and Chandler's account of the workings and effects of this policy has been particularly useful for the purposes of this study. For an account of the conflicts caused by the Bourbon reforms, see also Brading, *The First America* (4–5; 467–91).

25. In particular, I am referring to these concerns as they are developed in Foucault, *Discipline and Punish* (195–228).

26. The problems involved in deploying Foucauldian approaches and concepts in relation to colonial situations are manifold, as Ahmad's critique of Said illustrates (159–219). Prasad offers a well-argued defense of Said and postcolonial studies (58–63).

27. Cascardi traces the workings of the fiction of the break within modernity, and the modern subject's conception of its identity (*The Subject of Modernity* 1–8).

28. In this sense I wish to set my account against narratives of protonationalism such as that reconstructed by Mignolo in a recent discussion of the *Bibliotheca Mexicana* (*The Darker Side* 163–68). Of importance here is Chatterjee's critical analysis of the deployment of nationalist discourse in colonial contexts (1–30).

29. For an account of such a dynamic in a contemporary setting, see García Canclini.

30. Gonzalbo Aizpuru develops a detailed account of the university's beginnings (*Historia de la educación en la época colonial. La educación* 57–70). In Guatemala the Real y Pontificia Universidad de San Carlos was founded in 1676, its initial purpose being to provide a forum in which priests could learn native languages (Lanning, *Eighteenth-Century* 7–10).

31. Of significance for an understanding of the earlier trajectory of humanism in the Spanish colonies are the studies by Abbott and Rama.

32. The history of humanistic learning in colonial Mexico has been traced by Méndez Plancarte (*Horacio; Humanismo; Humanistas*) and Osorio Romero (*Conquistar el eco*).

33. Di Camillo offers an interesting account of the process through which humanism, with its renewal of emphasis on eloquence and writing, comes to provide the kind of intellectual subject required to handle the complexities of the policies the Spanish state formulates as it emerges and consolidates its power, beginning in the second half of the fifteenth century (68–69; 89–94). Other important studies of the trajectory of humanism in early modern Spain are those of Rico and Lawrance. The conception of humanism articulated here derives much from the description offered by Kristeller (21–32).

34. I offer this reading as an alternative to the conception of intellectual history as a series of discrete periods that together make up a teleology culminating in modernity, a notion that is clearly underscored by the enabling fiction of the rupture. On this, see Cascardi (*The Subject of Modernity* 1–7).

35. Foucault specifically expands the meaning of the word *archive* beyond the accepted sense of a collection of books and manuscripts (*Archaeology* 169–73).

36. Durand offers a careful critique of an earlier version of González Echevarría's chapter on the Inca Garcilaso.

37. Burkholder and Chandler provide a detailed account of the goals and effects of these reforms, which were designed to reaffirm Madrid's control over affairs in the viceroyalties, diminishing the powers of local authorities and trying to make the system of taxation of *criollo* economic interests more effective (Burkholder and Chandler 89–98; 115–19; Burkholder 1–40).

38. Chevalier has produced the most comprehensive account of the emergence of the hacienda system in colonial Mexico (*Land and Society*).

39. On this, see Florescano and Gil Sánchez (473–87) and Pérez Herrero (109–11).

40. Coatsworth develops this thesis in two important essays ("Limits"; "Mexican").

41. This view of the Bourbon reforms is summarized by Hamnett (67–71; 95–101).

42. These aspects are studied by Hamnett (87–91) and Piestchmann (28–33; 64–65). Another important phenomenon is the immigration of a more aggressively entrepreneurial class of Spaniards during this period (Martínez Peláez 111–27).

43. It is my contention that the peculiar circumstances of viceregal society in the eighteenth century produce this relative autonomy and separation of civil society and the state, each organized around specific, increasingly differentiated interests. I understand civil society as a space composed primarily of various modes of association, and distinct from both economy and the state, although it is, at the same time, overdetermined by, and overdetermining of, those spheres. My discussion and investigation of these concepts here is informed by the arguments developed by Cohen and Arato (vii–xi; 1–26; 83–116).

44. On this, see Cogdell (247–50).

45. Cesareo has produced a fascinating investigation into both the utopian and paternalistic aspects of this thought (*Cruzados* 70–71; 95–96).

46. Manrique offers an interesting analysis of the *criollos'* appropriation of the pre-Hispanic cultural heritage (359–68).

47. Implicit in my discussion of these problems is a concern to critique the tendency to privilege the concept of the nation-state as the frame through which postcolonial politics should be articulated. Chatterjee has shown how this ideology tends to enclose discourses of differentiation within an inherited European model (38–43).

48. I refer to Habermas's reconstruction of the history of the public sphere. The process through which initiatives for modernization in eighteenth-century Spain tend not to be articulated from sectors within civil society, but "from above" by state officials has been well documented by Sarrailh and by Maravall (*Estudios*). The debates raised by members of the Frankfurt School (Horkheimer and Adorno), Derrida and Foucault (*Discipline and Punish*), and the discourses of postmodernism have led to a closer scrutiny of the contradictions that underpin Western modernity. For a useful synthesis of these issues, see Cascardi (*The Subject of Modernity* 1–15; 228–74).

49. I contrast the Mexican conjuncture with that outlined by Eagleton for eighteenth-century England (9–27). For more detailed accounts of this kind of dynamic in eighteenth-century Hispanic America, see Whitaker, Aldridge, and Chiaramonte.

50. Maravall offers a similar account of the articulation of Enlightenment thought and culture in Spain (*Estudios*).

51. The large corpus of works written in Latin during the viceregal period still remains relatively neglected by modern scholarship. Mignolo has remarked upon the importance of this aspect of colonial writing and the relative lack of attention it has received from critics ("La lengua" 138–39). The most significant research into writing in Latin in New Spain is that of Osorio Romero (*Conquistar el eco* 9–49).

52. For an extensive account of Eguiara y Eguren's life, see Millares Carlo (25–37).

53. One can discern here a key factor that produces the time lapses between the moments of the currency of certain styles and topics in Europe and their subsequent treatment in Spanish American literary discourse during the colonial period. Using the concept of a "retraso" or "retardo americano" ("American time lag"), Cornejo Polar (99) and Moraña (*Relecturas* 39–44) have discussed this problem in terms of the always already belated character of Latin American contributions to intellectual debates started in Europe. On a related topic, Schwarz has developed the expression "as ideias fora do lugar" ("misplaced ideas") to account for the disjunctions between the prevalent liberal ideology of the political elite and the continuation of the practice of slavery in nineteenth-century Brazil (15–16). Significant contributions to the debate on the asymmetry of Latin American literary history with the period narrative of European literary history have been made by Fernández Retamar and Losada.

54. In Western Europe one of the main targets of the new thinkers' work and polemics is, of course, the clergy, which is viewed as one of the main sources of ignorance and superstition (Cassirer 134–96; Hazard 44–110). One of the commonly identified features of modernity is the process of secularization, as part of what Weber describes as the "disenchantment" of the world. For a discussion of the state of incompleteness that always tends to characterize this process, see Cascardi (*The Subject of Modernity* 153–55).

55. As Maravall has noted for the Spanish case, I take the expression of such discourses of the particular and the national to be key elements in the emergence of forms of modernity in Mexico during the eighteenth century (*Estudios* 42–60).

56. Lacouture offers an interesting account of the broader historical context of these developments (1: 325–65; 437–77). One factor in these events is the conflict between the nationalist programs of the emergent European states and the universalist vision of the Society of Jesus. For a discussion of the international aspect of Jesuit ideology in the New World, see Batllori (*Del Descubrimiento* 77–84).

57. Batllori provides a careful analysis of the role played by the Jesuit program of studies in the development of Baroque culture (*Gracián* 101–06).

58. For fuller accounts of Jesuit education in New Spain, see J. Jacobsen, Valenzuela Rodarte (583–602), and Lanning (*The University* 15–31, 86–97). Quesada provides an overview of intellectual culture in the viceroyalties.

59. More detailed information about the regime of the Colegio Máximo and its role within the educational system of colonial Mexico is provided by Gonzalbo Aizpuru (*La educación en la época colonial. La educación* 159–72).

60. Navarro provides a fuller account of these developments (111–33).

61. For accounts of the earlier regime, and the role played within it by the Gongorine style of poetry, see Beverley (*Del "Lazarillo"* 89–96) and Concha (46). The rejection of the obscurantist style of Baroque poetry finds its most systematic expression in Boileau's *L'art poétique* of 1674, particularly in lines 143–53 of the first canto (2: 85). Significantly, this work was translated into Spanish by one of Landívar's Mexican Jesuit associates, Francisco Javier Alegre. The text is included in a collection of some of Alegre's works published by García Icazbalceta (1–132). The most important elaboration of a Spanish neoclassical aesthetics is to be found in Ignacio de Luzán's *La poética* of 1737, which contains a repudiation of Góngora and his style of poetry (145; 192–204).

62. I am contrasting this aesthetic with the various forms of *conceptista* and *culterano* poetry, which tend to be closely tied to the culture of large, but restricted, urban spaces, both formally and thematically (Vidal 101–08). The paradigmatic example is Balbuena's *Grandeza mexicana* (1604).

63. The systematic and empirical qualities of the Jesuits' knowledge of, and approach to, agricultural production are illustrated in the *Instrucciones a los Hermanos Jesuitas Administradores de Haciendas,* a manual of farming methods written at some point during the first half of the eighteenth century. A modern edition of this text has been published by Chevalier (1950).

64. In his poem Landívar seems to write for at least two groups of intended readers. On the one hand, the use of Latin and the frequent didactic sections about species unknown in the Old World suggest that he hoped to reach educated European readers, particularly with a view to offering alternative visions of America to those presented by scientists and travelers from the Old World. On the other hand, he also targets American readers, particularly in the poem's concluding lines (Appendix 102–12).

65. At the same time, Landívar's positioning within the Society of Jesus continues to overdetermine the discourse of the poem, to the extent that it is unlikely that he was able to accept or acknowledge fully the implications of the epistemological position his philosophical and scientific investigations lead him to assume.

Chapter One
Framing the *Criollo* Archive

1. Eguiara y Eguren lists the individual authors included in the text according to their first names, not their surnames, as is normal practice in modern bibliographies. On this topic see Torre Villar (ccli).

2. In addition to the sections mentioned, the manuscript of what would have been the volumes covering the names between D and J is also available, and is part of the Latin American collection of the University of Texas, Austin.

3. The letter was first published in Madrid in a volume of Martí's letters (1735). Eguiara y Eguren appears to have known the text through another edition of his collected letters, titled *Ecclesiae Alonensis Decani, Epistolarum libri duodecim* (1738).

4. The history of this dispute is exhaustively documented by Gerbi. See, in particular, his discussion of *criollo* responses to eighteenth-century European writings about America (183–209).

5. In similar fashion, Mignolo also inserts Eguiara y Eguren into a seamless narrative of Mexican nationalism (*The Darker Side* 163–69). All translations from Spanish into English are my own, unless otherwise noted.

6. The work of Beristáin is discussed by Torre Villar, insofar as it relates to the *Bibliotheca Mexicana* (ccxcviii–cccix). Beristáin himself was very critical of Eguiara y Eguren's work, as it was published, finding fault with him for compiling it in Latin, noting the counterproductive consequence of not writing it in a language that a wider audience would understand; for writing in an unnecessarily convoluted, Baroque style; for failing to include certain important figures in the history of New Spain; and for alphabetizing individuals according to their first names, not their surnames, as was becoming prevalent with the increasing rationalization of social organization (quoted in Torre Villar cccvii–cccviii; cccxxv–xxvii).

7. In addition, he served in a variety of other capacities, the importance of which I will discuss in the following pages. For a detailed analysis of the different posts that Eguiara y Eguren occupied, see Torre Villar (cvii–cl).

8. On this matter, see Beverley (*Del "Lazarillo"* 89–90). González Stephan has proposed a different line of analysis, attempting to place Eguiara y Eguren's work within the process of the emergence of a discourse of literary historiography (*La historiografía* 60–82).

9. On the role of the catalogue and the encyclopedia in the accumulation and presentation of knowledge in the early modern period, see Hodgen (7–9; 115–44) and Rabasa (125–79).

10. The thesis of Eguiara y Eguren's protonationalism is also reiterated in Heredia Correa's recent short study of the *Bibliotheca Mexicana* (107–24).

11. On this, see Torre Villar (cxlv–cxlvii).

12. For more information on this aspect of the policies of the Spanish Crown in the sixteenth century, see Maravall (*Carlos V* 97–118).

13. An interesting example of these strategies is to be found in the career of the Peruvian José Baquíjano during the second half of the eighteenth century. The practice of simultaneously pursuing activities in both education and administration is analyzed by Burkholder (82–97).

14. Of particular significance here is the emphasis that humanist scholarship places upon the formation of subjects with a high level of oral eloquence, as is outlined by Grafton and Jardine (xiv; 1–4). My exploration of the use of the notion of the *locus amoenus* develops out of Beverley's discussion of that topos (*Del "Lazarillo"* 70–75).

15. This antinomy receives perhaps its most famous treatment in Derrida's analysis of its role in the thought of Rousseau (96–164).

16. For a discussion of the treatment of this theme in Fray Luis de León's "La vida retirada," see Durán (56–63). It is also central, although with certain philosophical differences, in Góngora's *Soledades*. On the theme and concept of solitude within Spanish poetry, see Poggioli (166–93) and Beverley (*Aspects* 70–79).

17. López's *Aprilis Dialogus* appears in volume 3 of the 1986–90 edition of Eguiara y Eguren's *Bibliotheca Mexicana* prepared by Fernández Valenzuela and Torre Villar, but is paginated using Arabic numerals, starting from the number 1, in the same fashion as the text of Eguiara y Eguren's catalogue. In order to avoid confusion, I will quote from the original Latin text of Vargas Alquicira's 1987 bilingual edition of López's dialogue.

18. Torre Villar asserts that López himself is represented in the character of the Belgian humanist (ccxix). For more on the role of the pastoral topos as a space conducive to the elaboration of thought, see Poggioli (1–17).

19. All translations of López's dialogue from the original Latin into English are my own.

20. The text is preceded by a note marking the viceroy's granting of approval for the book to be published on April 28, 1755 (Eguiara y Eguren, *Bibliotheca* 3: c).

21. He states that he will not argue with the Belgian on account of the fact that he is not well-versed "ni en los embrollos de Mercurio ni en cuestiones del foro" (López 2; "neither in the imbroglios of Mercury nor in the questions of the court").

22. In López's dialogue, as in the work of Eguiara y Eguren, the word *Hispanus* prevents an easy distinction between Spaniards and *criollos.* The possibility of the appearance of negativity toward Spain itself is mediated, and forestalled, by, among other things, the Italian character's rebuttal of criticisms of Spaniards as being disdainful and neglectful of the study of the humanist disciplines (López 21–24).

23. One thinks not only of eighteenth-century figures such as Martí and Cornelius de Pauw, but also of the chronicles of the period of exploration and conquest. On the topic of negative European representations of American nature and its inhabitants, see Gerbi (52–74). It is important to note also that López's ideal space is situated within the realm of the bucolic, the dominant mode of the pastoral in early modern Hispanic thought and writing. On this, see Curtius (183–202) and Poggioli (1–17). As I will argue later, Landívar's version of the pastoral, which is written in the Georgic mode, constitutes a significant break with earlier versions of the bucolic, and the principles that inform it. Although the images portrayed in poems composed in accordance with the principles of the Georgic mode are no less utopian, they do demonstrate a more analytical concern for the practices and techniques of agriculture (Lilly 1–18; 19–50).

24. This kind of rearticulation of the image of American agricultural and natural environments is expressed with more force and with greater frequency in the nineteenth century. Such a conception is developed in Andrés Bello's *A la agricultura de la zona tórrida* (1826).

25. For a thorough discussion of this aspect of the education system in New Spain, see Gonzalbo Aizpuru (*Historia de la educación en la época colonial. La educación* 46–48; 95–121).

26. On this, see Braudel (vol. 3).

27. For an analysis of different forms of resistance effected during the colonial period, see Lienhard.

Chapter Two
Supplementing Authority: The Prologues to the *Bibliotheca Mexicana*

1. My discussion here is informed by Derrida's use of the concept of the *supplement* (*supplément*) to denote elements or signifiers seemingly excluded from the central core of a text, but upon which the text's signifying structure is, nevertheless, dependent. See Derrida's deployment of the concept in his analysis of the relation of the notion of "writing" to that of "speech" in Rousseau's *Essay on the Origin of Languages* (Derrida 165–94). Norris offers an illuminating exposition of the workings of the *supplément* in Derrida's thought (34–37). For an articulation of the concept of supplementarity with respect to postcolonial situations, see Spivak ("A Literary Representation of the Subaltern" 241, 250).

2. The prologues appear in volume 3 of the 1986–90 edition of the *Bibliotheca Mexicana,* but, like the text of the catalogue itself, are paginated using Arabic numerals starting with the number 7. In order to avoid confusion, I will quote from Millares Carlo's 1944 bilingual edition of the prologues, which is the text most widely used by scholars. All translations from the original Latin into English are my own.

3. I do not mean to portray Eguiara y Eguren as an individual who initiates this mode of cultural presentation, but, rather, prefer to see it as a discursive formation that is intermittently taken up, and rearticulated by *criollos* of many time periods. One significant instance of this is found in the disjunction between Sigüenza y Góngora's inclusion of the figures of indigenous emperors and leaders in the text he dedicates to the viceroy Marqués de la Laguna, *Teatro de virtudes políticas* (1680), and the contempt and antipathy he demonstrates toward the indigenous and *mestizo* inhabitants of Mexico City in his *Alboroto y motín de los indios* (1692). Cogdell offers an excellent analysis of this contradictory attitude in Sigüenza's work. Among the most significant discussions of native archivism are those of Adorno (*Guaman Poma*) and Lienhard (55–72; 133–44).

4. As will be seen, Eguiara y Eguren largely reproduces the terms of the arguments about the status of Amerindians made by the principal contributors to the debates about natural slavery and the "just war" in Spain during the sixteenth century, particularly around the issue of whether the pre-Hispanic peoples had possessed symbolic systems adequate for the recording of their history. On the trajectory of these polemics, especially in the writings of Vitoria, Sepúlveda, Las Casas, and Acosta, see Pagden (64–99; 109–18; 123–45; 158–92). However, he was, no doubt, also seeking to respond to the doubts cast as to the intellectual capacity of all America's inhabitants by European thinkers like Martí, and articulated through recourse to arguments about climatic and environmental determinism by natural historians such as Buffon and Cornelius de Pauw (Gerbi 4–13; 32–33; 53–55; 74–75).

5. Trabulse has produced a useful survey of Sigüenza's investigations in this field, most of the texts of which are now lost.

6. It is likely that Eguiara y Eguren is referring to native scholars such as Alva Ixtlilxóchitl and Fernando Alvarado Tezozomoc. For a discussion of their works, see Lienhard (55–72; 133–44).

7. Mignolo offers an extensive and illuminating discussion of the workings and effects of the hegemony of alphabetic writing in the cultural and legal dynamics of colonial society (*The Darker Side* 29–67).

8. What might be regarded as the two dominant contemporary critical readings of the development of these poetic modes in the Hispanic colonial world are those of Beverley (*Del "Lazarillo"* 77–97) and González Echevarría (*Celestina's Brood* 1–6).

9. On the importance of this concept in the poetry of Góngora, see Beverley (*Aspects* 7–8; 59–63). For a discussion of the development of the three classical styles of language in early modern Hispanic poetry, see Darst (52–53) and Porqueras Mayo (33).

10. The most systematic theorization of this mode of discourse is Gracián's treatise *Agudeza y arte de ingenio* (1649). Porqueras Mayo provides a useful overview of the debates around poetic style in the Hispanic world during the sixteenth and seventeenth centuries (19–72).

11. On this question, see Grafton and Jardine (xii–xiv).

12. Derrida offers an interesting discussion of the position occupied by Egyptian hieroglyphics within European theoretical writings about language in the seventeenth centuries (74–93).

13. The Neapolitan's work was published in 1708. Eguiara y Eguren notes that Gemelli Careri reports having participated in exams and academic exercises at the Real y Pontificia Universidad de México (*Prólogos* 84).

14. Grafton and Jardine have produced a broad image of the kind of education fostered by the various branches and schools of early modern European humanism. They describe the skills that humanist educators worked to instill in their students, seeking to emulate the example of Rome, in the following terms: "There, according to the humanist, 'culture' in the broad sense of a preparedness to deal wisely with the civilised communal existence went hand in hand with a programme for passing on the skills of eloquence which had come down almost intact to the modern world. Revive the latter, the humanist argument went, and 'new men' on the Roman model would inevitably follow" (4).

15. Eguiara y Eguren is referring to Feijóo's essay "Españoles americanos" (Feijóo 155–60).

16. On the history of the printing press in colonial Spanish America, see Johnson (1–7) and Medina's *La imprenta en México (1539–1821).*

17. Largely for the purpose of more efficient governing, the Spanish established institutions for the education of the children of the upper echelons of various Mexican indigenous societies (Gonzalbo Aizpuru, *Historia de la educación en la época colonial. El mundo indígena;* Osorio Romero, *La enseñanza*).

18. On the work of this institution, see Gruzinski (58–59).

Chapter Three
The Fragmentary Archive: The Catalogue of the
Bibliotheca Mexicana

1. In using the alphabet as the ordering framework for his catalogue, Eguiara y Eguren maintains the terms of the hierarchy of representational systems established during the sixteenth century in the aftermath of the various military conquests in the New World. The process of the expansion and consolidation of the Spanish empire was facilitated, in part, through the unfolding of a regime in which alphabetic writing assumed a position of privilege over and above the status of Amerindian symbolic systems, both oral and pictographic, particularly in matters of law and learning (Mignolo, "La lengua" 142–43; 152–53; *The Darker Side* 97–110; 121).

2. I place importance on this aspect of Eguiara y Eguren's work not just within the overall framework of the *Bibliotheca,* but as an indication of the loci of most *criollo* and *mestizo* scholars and writers during the seventeenth and eighteenth centuries. Such figures write from a locus heavily overdetermined by institutionality and are able to produce significant scholarly interventions or literary works as a function of their positioning within viceregal bureaucracy, universities, colleges, or the ecclesiastical hierarchy. I view this as a necessary caveat to modern scholars who seek to reconstruct certain writers of the colonial period as precursors of the model of the autonomous twentieth-century author maintained by some strands of idealist liberal criticism. Strong examples of this mode of thinking are González Echevarría's reconstructions of Balboa (*Celestina's Brood* 128–48) and Espinosa Medrano (149–69).

3. As I argued in the previous chapter, the *criollo* subject can with equal facility articulate positions of identification with elements of native cultures and history. Useful accounts of *criollo* recuperations of the *conquistadores* as founders of an order of which seventeenth-century *criollos* regard themselves as heirs are to be found in Cogdell and Ross ("*Alboroto y motín de México*").

4. Cervantes de Salazar is notable as the author of an important chronicle of scholarly culture in Mexico City at the middle of the sixteenth century. For a discussion of this scholar's role as a disseminator of humanistic learning in New Spain, see Abbott (43–44).

5. I quote from Torre Villar and Fernández Valenzuela's facsimile edition. In order to facilitate continuity, I have standardized the spelling of the quotations to make them conform to the norms used in the modern editions from which the Latin quotations in chapters 1, 2, 4, 5, and 6 are derived. I have removed all diacritics, substituted "ae" for the ligature "æ," "et" for the ampersand "&," "ii" for "ij," and the standard "s" for "ſ." All translations from the original Latin are my own.

6. Eguiara y Eguren accords a shorter entry (*Bibliotheca* 3: 438–40) to Bernal Díaz del Castillo, author of the famous account of the conquest of Mexico that contests and revises Cortés's version on several key points (1632).

7. It is not unreasonable to assume that the frustrations experienced by Columbus in his efforts to extract from the Crown the rewards he felt he deserved in return for his discoveries would have held poignant resonances for eighteenth-century *criollos* in their ongoing struggles for influence and power with the Bourbon monarchs (Eguiara y Eguren, *Bibliotheca* 3: 497–98).

8. The expression provides the title for José Martí's most famous collection of essays (1891).

9. For an important account of Sigüenza y Góngora's role as one of the initiators of a discourse of *criollo* historiography, see Ross (*The Baroque Narrative* 40–47; 77–79).

10. The act of naming and renaming places forms an important part of the earlier dynamics of conquest and colonization. For a discussion of this, see Mignolo ("La lengua" 153–54).

Chapter Four
Subject, Archive, Landscape

1. Gaos uses this terminology in particular to describe the pedagogic practices and thought of the Jesuits in the eighteenth century (22–25; 51–53). See also Navarro (140–45).

2. Vidal has highlighted the disparity between the dense, highly ornate, and artificial configurations produced through the endless play of the syllogism in scholarly texts and the material realities of the colonial world (111–13).

3. My understanding of these aspects of modernity is derived, here, from the ideas of Weber (*From Max Weber* 302–22; *Economy and Society* 1: 69–74; 2: 753–75; 3: 956–63).

4. For more information on this, see Coatsworth ("The Limits" 34–36).

5. On the process and extent of the Mexican Jesuits' accumulation of farm lands, see Riley (36–74).

6. One finds here an instance of the systematic organization in the workings of the medieval monasteries that led Weber to discern, in such institutions, earlier manifestations of the forms of rationalization he held to be central to modernity (*Economy and Society* 3: 1158–73).

7. For more information on the contents of these courses, see Navarro (21–23; 31–40; 111–32).

8. Osorio Romero offers an interesting reassessment of the importance of Greek and Latin scholarship in New Spain (*Conquistar el eco* 9–49; 73–133). Most notable among such scholars is Francisco Javier Alegre, who produced such important works as an annotated translation of Boileau's *Art poétique* (1–132).

9. This enterprise is undertaken most notably in Clavijero's *Historia antigua de México* (1780). Clavijero published this text first in Italian, intending it to be read by inhabitants of the country in which he, like most of the members of his generation of Mexican Jesuits, lived after the events of 1767.

10. For the purpose of my analysis, I will quote from the Chamorro González edition, which contains the text of 1782.

11. This kind of observation continues in Chamorro González (xxxii; xxxviii) and Osorio Romero (*Conquistar el eco* 37), although these critics regard it as one element among many others.

12. Nemes writes: "In spite of quandaries which reveal a conflict between the old ideas and the new, the most noticeable trait of *Rusticatio Mexicana* is its scientifically oriented approach, providing precise explanations of industrial and agricultural processes, of natural and human phenomena, and of natural and human resources" (304). Regarding the political implications of Landívar's approach to modern ideas, she notes: "Landívar represents the intellectual man who was breaking away from colonial tradition. He was not a reformer, much less a revolutionary, but as a member of the Jesuit order, a major cultural, economic, and political force in the colonial Spanish world, he was slowly moving toward a new spirit characterized by a rational approach to learning and a concern for economic development and progress" (304).

13. González Echevarría constructs such an image of the seventeenth-century Peruvian writer (*Celestina's Brood* 161–64; 168–69).

14. Lacouture notes the presence of this duality both in the figure of Ignatius of Loyola (1: 10) and in the history of the Society of Jesus (1: 364–65; 438–39).

15. I am referring here to the kind of critic who practices and writes a form of general ethical humanism, avoiding specialization, such as is described by Eagleton for the case of eighteenth-century England (18–23).

16. Landívar was born in 1731. For more information on his family origins, see Chamorro González (xiii–xxxvi).

17. All translations from the original Latin into English are my own. For a rendering of the entire text into English, see Regenos.

18. One thinks, especially, of the images evoked in Balbuena's *Grandeza mexicana* (1604).

19. See, for example, Luzán (178–94).

20. On the role of the element of belatedness in *criollo* literary discourse, see Cornejo Polar (99) and Moraña (*Relecturas* 39–44).

21. A lucid discussion of this issue is offered by Monk (29–42; 63–76).

22. On this, and the shift from poetics to aesthetics, see Lyotard (203–11).

23. On the initial dissemination of the text in the early modern period, see Hertz (1–2).

24. Monk provides a useful account of Boileau's role in the dissemination of *On Sublimity* (29–36).

25. The history of the articulation of this hierarchy of styles in the sixteenth- and seventeenth-centuries is well documented by Porqueras Mayo and Darst.

26. An important counter-reading to that of Boileau can be found in Hertz's influential exegesis of *On Sublimity* (1–20).

27. For more detailed descriptions of this first stage, see Monk (1–42) and Ashfield and de Bolla (1–11; 18–21).

28. On this, see Monk (iii; 30–36).

29. Monk discusses this in the English context (2–3; 56–57).

30. The most important sections of Addison's essays dealing with these issues can be found in the anthology by Ashfield and de Bolla (62–71).

31. On this, see Monk (7–9; 15–17. Over time the debate would add a third concept, that of the picturesque (Hipple 185–213; 308–20; Addison and de Bolla 14–16; 264–67).

32. Hertz develops a deconstructive reading of this conception of the sublime (14–20).

33. For a more detailed account of the development of this thinking on the grounds of, and dynamics pertaining to, the elaboration of knowledge, see Cassirer (xi; 3–5), Hazard (279–80), and Guyer (22–23).

34. I am thinking, in particular, of the poem "Niágara" (1824).

35. Most notable, in this respect, are McVay's essay on Heredia (35–38), Pérez's discussion of avant-garde literature ("El efecto"), and Walsh's investigation into the trajectory of the sublime in eighteenth-century Spain.

36. An interesting exception to the rule can be found in Pérez Valderrabano's Spanish translation of the treatise attributed to Longinus (1770).

37. This paradigm is established primarily by scholars such as Hatzfeld through his application of the scheme of art history to Spanish literature outlined in Wölfflin's *Principles of Art History.*

38. Among the most significant interventions on this issue are those of Schwarz and Dussel.

39. The most serious attempt to theorize the discussion of such issues is that undertaken by Godzich and Spadaccini (ix–xv). The problem of Spain's position within the overall framework of eighteenth-century European literature is raised, in passing, by Curtius (266–69). The concept of Spanish American Romanticism is problematized most famously by Losada (137–39).

40. At the same time, Alegre is also notable for his defense of many of the major writers of the Spanish Baroque (19–25; 65).

41. I regard this as a dynamic that unfolds in a series of different texts over the course of the eighteenth century, receiving its most systematic theorization in Kant's "Analytic of the Sublime" (*Critique of Judgement* 90–203). In an important passage, he offers the following formulation of the problematic: "Sublimity, therefore, does not reside in any of the things of nature, but only in our own mind, in so far as we may become conscious of our superiority over nature within, and thus also over nature without us (as exerting influence upon us). Everything that provokes this feeling in us, including the *might* of nature which challenges our strength, is then, though improperly, called sublime, and it is only under presupposition of this idea within us, and in relation to it, that we are capable of attaining to the idea of the sublimity of that Being which inspires deep respect in us, not by the mere display of its might in nature, but more by the faculty which is planted in us of estimating that might without fear, and of regarding our estate as exalted above it" (114). For more comprehensive treatments of the trajectory of the concept of the sublime within eighteenth-century aesthetics, see Monk (1–9), de Bolla (32–58; 61–72), and Ashfield and de Bolla (1–16). Most notably, Hertz analyzes the poetic encounter with the sublime as it is staged in Wordsworth's *Prelude* (54–60).

42. In his discussion of Kant's "mathematical sublime," Hertz offers the following illuminating description of the concept: "Kant describes a painful pause—'a momentary checking of the vital powers'—followed by a compensatory positive movement, the mind's exultation in its own rational faculties, in its ability to think a totality that cannot be taken in through the senses" (40).

43. These processes can also be discerned in a variety of other texts written over the course of the eighteenth century, a selection of which can be found in Ashfield and de Bolla. The ways in which the sublime is mobilized in English Romanticism have been analyzed in the light of Freudian psychoanalysis by Weiskel, who views the staging of this drama as a pretext for the establishment of the supremacy of reason among the faculties (22–33; 37–50; 107–64). Hertz subjects such an account to a deconstructive reading in his discussions of Longinus and Wordsworth (1–21; 40–60). Makkreel offers a useful account of Kant's theorization (48–58; 67–87).

44. Differentiated from its Cartesian predecessor, the Kantian subject is theorized as an abstract function of logic, disassociated from any sense of substance. For discussions of the contradictions that characterize the modern concept of the subject, see Cascardi (*The Subject of Modernity* 179–80; 214–16).

45. This characteristic of modernity is articulated most famously by Berman.

46. Pindus is the mountain range that separates Thessaly from Epirus in Greece.

47. One thinks again here of Heredia's poems "En el teocalli de Cholula" (1826; 1832) and "Niágara" (1824). On the role of the trope of the sublime within Anglo-American poetic projections of the nation, and the differences between Enlightenment and Romantic versions of the sublime, Wilson writes: "If the Enlightenment sublime had represented the unrepresentable, confronted privatization, and pushed language to the limits of imagining the vastness of nature and stellar infinitude as the subject's innermost ground, the Americanization of this sublime rhetoric represented, in effect, the interiorization of national claims as this Americanized self's inalienable ground. The Protestant bliss of conversion and the liberal conviction of exalted subjectivity conspired to produce a widely disseminated landscape, and language, confirming and eventuating in the American sublime of Emerson's era—decades after the sublime had seemed a moribund aesthetic in England. The genre of the sublime helped to consolidate an American identity founded in representing a landscape of immensity and wildness ("power") open to multiple identifications ("use")" (4–5).

48. Buffon depicts America as an unusually humid environment that is not conducive to the healthy growth and development of humans, mammals, and plants (1: 279; 18: 74–75; 20: 316–23; 423–26).

49. Central to Landívar's poem as a whole is the concern to subject not only natural objects, but also things made at least in part through human artifice, to a scrutiny that brings forth the material conditions of their production (see chapter 5 below, in particular). The poem's exposition of the hidden dynamics of the elaboration of commodities, works of art, and social practices sharply contrasts with much of the canon of most colonial Mexican poetry, which tends to mystify these key components of the viceregal order, as Vidal has noted (101–37).

50. Landívar adds authority to his evocation of this extraordinary work by reference, in a footnote, to the accounts of the Spaniard Father Acosta and the Italian traveler Gemelli Careri (18–19n3).

51. The depiction of the multicolored, exotic birds of the New World as ciphers for *criollo* experience can be found repeatedly in the writing of the colonial period. On the development of this theme in Espinosa Medrano's *Apologético en favor de Don Luis de Góngora,* see González Echevarría (*Celestina's Brood* 153–54).

52. For more information on Abad, see Maneiro and Fabri (165–90).

53. As noted above, Alegre is most notable for his annotated translation of Boileau's *Art poétique,* a translation of the *Iliad,* and a history of the Society of Jesus's activities in Mexico. His most important works were published by García Icazbalceta in a single volume (1889).

54. Ruiz de Alarcón is the author of such famous *comedias* as *La verdad sospechosa* (1618–20).

55. Sor Juana is the most famous of all *criollo* poets. Together with Sigüenza y Góngora, she is also one of the two most notable precursors of Landívar and his contemporaries in the development of scientific thought in New Spain. She demonstrates her incursions into empirical and experimental investigation in her *Carta en respuesta* (1691).

56. It is significant that Landívar uses this Latin term, which is more or less equivalent to the Spanish *ingenio,* a word commonly used to denote the intelligence, or wit, of highly educated minds. For a more detailed discussion of the concept, see Beverley (*Against Literature* 47–65).

57. For a discussion of this, see Burke (83–114). Monk offers a useful summary of this aspect of neoclassical thought (1–7).

58. Landívar's comments here closely echo typical conceptions of the ambivalent feelings of pleasure and pain associated with the experience of the sublime. See, for example, Burke (119–25). Also important in this context is Burke's assignation of a socializing power to the beautiful and an individuating effect to the sublime (35–42). Kant also maintains such a distinction (128–30).

59. Although Mexican agriculture in the viceregal period seems to have been an often precarious business—see Van Young (65–82) and Riley (64–71; 306–13)—the images depicted here might be taken as representations of the situation of relative economic prosperity achieved in the first half of the eighteenth century (Florescano and Gil Sánchez 473–86).

60. On the topic of *criollos'* defense of their rights on these terms, see Ross (*"Alboroto y motín de México"* 183–89) and Cogdell (249–51). Nutini has produced a monumental account of the history of the Mexican colonial aristocracy. As Brading has noted ("Government and Elite" 392–98), the perennial economic problems of the American landowning class reduced the level of its political influence over the course of the seventeenth and eighteenth centuries.

61. On this topic, see Burkholder (83–135) and Brading ("Government and Elite" 400–05).

62. Kerson has analyzed Landívar's depiction of this episode in terms of the poet's use of the "miniature epic" mode ("The Heroic Mode" 151–56).

63. I use the metaphor of the grid to convey the systematizing order imposed by the rational subject on its objects of knowledge, following the description offered by Foucault in *The Order of Things* (11–14; 137–76). The configuration of such a structure for the discipline of natural history is theorized by Buffon in the discourse "De la manière d'étudier et de traiter l'Histoire Naturelle" (1: 24–25).

64. The role of the missionary experience in introducing pragmatic elements into Jesuit ideology is discussed by Lacouture (1: 401–36). On the irruption of material realities into ecclesiastical ideology and practice in the New World, see Cesareo (*Cruzados* 186–92).

65. *Anxiety* is the term used by Kant to describe the subject's state of mind during the experience of sublimity (106–09).

66. The overflowing, shifting character of the sublime has been explored most strikingly by de Bolla (27–58; 59–102).

67. My reading of Landívar's mobilization of the drama of sublimity diverges clearly here from the thought of Burke and Kant, both of whom attribute to the experience of the sublime the production of an effect of individuation in the observing subject (Burke 35–37; Kant 128–30).

68. As thinking on aesthetics develops over the course of the 1700s, one finds increasing instances of slippage and overflow between the concepts of the beautiful, sublime, and picturesque, the last of which comes more fully into discussions in the second half of the century. The interplay of the three concepts in the most important English, Irish, and Scottish treatises of the time has been analyzed by Ashfield and de Bolla (14–16; 264–67). Hipple offers the most detailed account of conceptions of the picturesque (3–10; 185–213).

69. Of significance for the discussion of the sublime here is the semantic range of the word *portentum,* which also includes the sense of something monstrous or vast.

70. It is probably most accurate to read in the poem's development here an approach similar to that effected by Boileau, that is, an attempt to maintain sublimity as a supplement to beauty, as an element that cannot yet destabilize neoclassical poetics to the point of rupture. One might also interpret the description of the Guatemalan citizens' collective awe at the spectacle of the gorge as a restatement of the terms of the shared notion of the taste and refinement of a gentlemanly elite such as one finds in much of eighteenth-century aesthetic theory (Monk 10–41). Alternatively, a more radical reading might find here the bare sketchings of an effort to theorize a conception of aesthetic appreciation that would allow for the participation of a wider segment of society, one founded on the less stable and ordered dynamics of the sublime. Such a reading would place Landívar's thinking closer to that of Kant, who articulates, at least theoretically, a more universalist understanding of aesthetic judgment, tied to the notion of the latter's communicability (Kant 82–84; 226–27; Cohen and Guyer 5–6).

Chapter Five
After the Sublime: The Rationalization of Colonial Space

1. In order to limit the length of this part of my analysis, I have chosen to focus on these topics as being representative of this section of the poem and have not discussed the cantos devoted to the production of indigo dye and sugar (cantos 5 and 9).

2. My discussion is informed here by Engström's discussion of the problems involved in the trajectory of the concept of the sublime in relation to the Enlightenment and the theorization of postmodernism. Of particular importance is his attempt to recuperate it from the apocalyptic formulation of Lyotard, and reinsert it into a framework of a more pragmatic politics of representation (204).

3. Kerson provides a detailed analysis of the relations between this segment and classical models ("The Heroic Mode" 157–62).

4. On the labor-intensive character of many areas of the colonial Mexican economy during the seventeenth and eighteenth centuries, and the consequent stagnant levels of productivity, see Riley (306–58) and Van Young (65; 69–71).

5. Landívar appears to be referring to the Nicoya peninsula, an area of the Pacific coast of what today is Costa Rica.

6. In a footnote, Landívar delimits the immense geographical expanse over which the species lives, remarking that he has records of some having been killed in California and others having been seen in New Mexico (80n2).

7. This aspect of the work has been placed by Kerson within the paradigm of humanist utopias ("El concepto" 374–79).

8. I refer here to Beer's description of the defining features of mercantilism, which are also, by necessity the conditions required for the coterminous and interrelated emergence of national bourgeoisies and statism. Beer outlines the following elements as being central to mercantilism: "(i) Conception of money (coin and bullion or treasure) as the essence of wealth. (This conception prevailed from the end of the Middle Ages up to the end of the seventeenth century.) (ii) Regulating foreign trade with a view to bringing in money by the balance of trade. (iii) Making the balance of trade the criterion of national prosperity or decline. (iv) Promotion of manufacture by supplying it with cheap raw materials and cheap labour. (v) Protective customs duties on, or prohibition of, import of manufactured commodities. (vi) The view that the economic interests of nations are mutually antagonistic" (13).

9. On the topic of the Spanish state's limited efficiency in the gathering of tax revenues, see Coatsworth ("The Limits" 26–28; 30–34).

10. Such a mode of thought is, I would contend, already active in Jesuit practices in New Spain from the time of the establishment of the order's presence there. On the subject of the Jesuits' economic pragmatism in New Spain, see Riley (1–35).

11. Landívar refers here to the practice of the "partido," whereby mining laborers supplemented their pay with a part of their daily haul. On eighteenth-century efforts to eliminate this activity and the labor unrest they helped cause, see Brading (*Miners*), Ladd (29–35; 36–44; 46–84), and Hamnett (74–76).

12. Landívar's description of the cowherds' skills stands as a precursor of the *gauchesca* literature of the nineteenth century, most notably, of Hernández's *Martín Fierro* (1.181–251).

13. It is safe to assume that Landívar would have garnered such knowledge merely by observing the haciendas that belonged to the Jesuits in New Spain. Riley relates that on those belonging to the Colegio Máximo de San Pedro y San Pablo, the members of the order and their workers produced crops—particularly beans, maize, sugar, wheat—and raised livestock—cows, goats, pigs, sheep (75–88).

14. The relatively high degree of development manifested in the use of the technique of transhumance in New Spain allowed Mexican farmers to maintain larger flocks than their Peruvian counterparts, and also helped foster a greater specialization of tasks within the agriculture of the northern viceroyalty (N. Jacobsen 122–23).

Chapter Six
Framing American Heterogeneity

1. The appendix is one of the sections added to the Bologna edition of 1782.

2. For fuller accounts of the concept of the beautiful, and its relationship to the sublime, in eighteenth-century aesthetics, see Monk (1–6), Hipple (3–10), and Ferguson (44–53).

3. Buffon articulates this notion in a 1749 treatise on the methodology of natural history, in which he observes that the student should apply the following procedure in observing plants and animals: "he will study them in proportion to the use he can extract from them, he will consider them as they are presented as being most familiar to him, and he will arrange them in his head in relation to this order of his knowledge, since it is, in effect, the order according to which he has gathered them, and according to which it concerns him to preserve them" (1: 40; my translation).

4. Jacques Vanière (1664–1739) wrote extensively in Latin, the most important of his works being his *Praedium Rusticum.*

5. Buffon notes that the depiction of animals should encompass details of each species' reproductive process, the rearing of its young, their methods of education, instincts, dwellings, food, customs, hunting practices, and the uses and commodities that can be derived from them (1: 36–37).

6. Interestingly, Landívar compares the peacock's dazed reaction to the stupefied silence of young peasants, who have never been to large towns or cities, when they see sumptuous houses (13.80–84).

7. Buffon theorizes the procedure of classification in the following terms: "it seems to me that the only way to produce an instructive and natural method is to place those things which resemble one another together, and to separate those which differ from each other. If the individuals have a perfect resemblance, or some differences which are so small that one can only notice them with difficulty, these individuals will be of the same species; if the differences start to be noticeable and, at the same time, there is still much more resemblance than difference, the individuals will be of another species, but of the same genus as the first; and if these differences are even more marked, still without surpassing the resemblances, then the individuals will not only be of another species, but even of genus other than those of the first or second ones, and, however, will still be of the same class, because they will resemble each other more than they differ; but if, on the contrary, the number of differences exceeds that of the resemblances, then the individuals will not be of the same class" (1: 24–25; my translation). Buffon offers here a conventional statement of the principles of knowledge associated with the classical episteme (Foucault, *Order* 67–77; 128–38).

8. One sees here the historical shift in paradigms of representation discussed by Foucault in *The Order of Things,* in accordance with which the Renaissance episteme, based on the principle of resemblance, is gradually displaced by an Enlightenment episteme, oriented around relational systems of differences between objects and signs (*Order* 17–25; 128–50). For a discussion of the workings of the Renaissance episteme in the writings pertaining to Columbus's first voyage to the New World, in which difference has to be transformed into similitude through the use of the rhetorical trope of the marvelous, see Greenblatt (19–25; 70–85).

9. Landívar assiduously refers the reader back to his earlier study of the *cenzontle,* which is found in book 1.216–31.

10. This kind of matrix has been analyzed by scholars within the framework of Baroque aesthetics and modalities of social organization. Most notable in this respect are the descriptions of seventeenth-century Spain and colonial Mexico undertaken by Maravall (*La cultura*) and Leonard, respectively.

11. On the polysemic quality that the word *monstra* comes to possess in early modern Spanish writing, see González Echevarría (*Celestina's Brood* 81–113).

12. An interesting articulation of such concepts is produced by the seventeenth-century Peruvian writer Juan de Espinosa Medrano in his *Apologético en favor de Don Luis de Góngora* (1662). González Echevarría offers a provocative analysis of how in his treatise Espinosa Medrano simultaneously exploits the image of the unusual birthmark on his face and the freakish image that Europeans have of the inhabitants of the New World (*Celestina's Brood* 156–67; 164–66).

13. The role of spectacle and the mask, both as physical object and metaphor, is central to the dynamics of viceregal society, in which *criollos, mestizos,* and indigenous subjects had to assume different guises and roles in order to survive or advance. The classic study of this element of colonial life is offered in chapter 8 of Leonard's study of the Mexican Baroque. More recently, Moraña has discerned, in this play of identities, the emergence of forms of Latin American subjectivity: "Beligerante, irónico, reivindicativo, el discurso virreinal utiliza el juego de espejos y máscaras barrocas: es el caleidoscopio en que se compone y recompone la imagen propia, como reflejo y fragmentación de la del Otro. Alteridad e identidad son por lo tanto cara y contracara de una misma experiencia colectiva y de un mismo proyecto: el que pugna por materializar la utopía del ser americano en tanto sujeto social diferenciado" ("Belligerent, ironic, vindicatory, viceregal discourse uses the Baroque play of mirrors and masks: it is the kaleidoscope in which self-image is composed and recomposed, as the reflection and fragmentation of the Other. Alterity and identity are, therefore, the face and counterface of the same collective experience and the same project: that which struggles to realize the utopia of the American being as a differentiated social subject" (*Relecturas* v; my translation).

14. Noriega Robles offers an interesting account of the numerous Jesuit writings dealing with this natural sign.

Conclusion

1. For critiques of such a vision, see Florescano and Gil Sánchez (473–87) and Pérez Herrero (109–11).

2. I refer, in particular to the thesis articulated by Roggiano ("Para una teoría" 1–4 and 9–11). I also discern a continuation, albeit in more nuanced form, of this thinking in the work of Moraña (*Viaje al silencio* 34–59; 259–78).

Bibliography

Abbot, Don Paul. *Rhetoric in the New World: Rhetorical Theory and Practice in Colonial Spanish America.* Columbia: U of South Carolina P, 1996.

Adorno, Rolena. *Guaman Poma: Writing and Resistance in Colonial Peru.* Austin: U of Texas P, 1986.

———. "Reconsidering Colonial Discourse for Sixteenth- and Seventeenth-Century Spanish America." *Latin American Research Review* 28.3 (1993): 135–45.

———. "El sujeto colonial y la construcción de la alteridad." *Revista de crítica literaria latinoamericana* 28 (1988): 55–68.

Ahmad, Aijaz. *In Theory: Classes, Nations, Literatures.* London: Verso, 1994.

Aldridge, A. Owen, ed. *The Ibero-American Enlightenment.* Urbana: U of Illinois P, 1971.

Alegre, Francisco Javier. *Opúsculos inéditos del padre Francisco Javier Alegre.* Ed. Joaquín García Icazbalceta. Mexico City: Imprenta de Francisco Díaz de León, 1889.

Althusser, Louis. *For Marx.* Trans. Ben Brewster. London: Verso, 1990.

Anderson, Benedict. *Imagined Communities: Reflections on the Origins and Spread of Nationalism.* London: Verso, 1983.

Arenal, Electa, and Stacey Schlau, eds. *Untold Sisters: Hispanic Nuns in Their Own Works.* Albuquerque: U of New Mexico P, 1989.

Arrom, José Juan. *Certidumbre de América.* Madrid: Gredos, 1971.

Ashfield, Andrew, and Peter de Bolla, eds. *The Sublime: A Reader in British Eighteenth-Century Aesthetic Theory.* Cambridge: Cambridge UP, 1996.

Batllori, Miguel. *La cultura hispano-italiana de los jesuitas expulsos: españoles, hispanoamericanos, filipinos, 1767–1814.* Madrid: Gredos, 1966.

———. *Del Descubrimiento a la Independencia: estudios sobre Iberoamérica y Filipinas.* Caracas: Universidad Católica Andrés Bello, 1979.

———. *Gracián y el Barroco.* Rome: Edizioni di Storia e Letteratura, 1958.

Beer, Max. *An Inquiry into Physiocracy.* New York: Russell, 1986.

Bello, Andrés. *Obra literaria.* Caracas: Biblioteca Ayacucho, 1979.

Beristáin y Souza, José Mariano. *Biblioteca hispano americana septentrional.* 3 vols. Mexico City: UNAM, 1980.

Berman, Marshall. *All That Is Solid Melts into Air.* New York: Simon, 1982.

Beverley, John. *Against Literature.* Minneapolis: U of Minnesota P, 1993.

———. *Aspects of Góngora's "Soledades."* Purdue University Monographs in Romance Languages 1. Amsterdam: John Benjamins, 1980.

———. *Del "Lazarillo" al sandinismo: estudios sobre la función ideológica de la literatura española e hispanoamericana.* Minneapolis: Prisma Institute, 1987.

Bhabha, Homi. *The Location of Culture.* London: Routledge, 1992.

Boileau, Nicolas. *Œuvres complètes.* 4 vols. Paris: Société Les Belles Lettres, 1966.

Brading, David. *The First America: The Spanish Monarchy, Creole Patriots, and the Liberal State 1492–1867.* Cambridge: Cambridge UP, 1991.

———. "Government and Elite in Late Colonial Mexico." *Hispanic American Historical Review* 53.3 (1973): 389–414.

———. *Miners and Merchants in Bourbon Mexico 1763–1810.* Cambridge: Cambridge UP, 1971.

Braudel, Fernand. *Civilization and Capitalism, 15th–18th Century.* Trans. Siân Reynolds. 3 vols. Berkeley and Los Angeles: U of California P, 1992.

Browning, John. "Rafael Landívar's *Rusticatio Mexicana:* Natural History and Political Subversion." *Ideologies and Literature* 1.3 (1985): 9–30.

Buffon, Georges Louis Leclerc. *Histoire naturelle, générale et particulière.* 127 vols. Paris: Dufart, 1808.

Burke, Edmund. *A Philosophical Enquiry into the Origin of Our Ideas of the Sublime and the Beautiful.* Ed. Adam Phillips. Oxford: Oxford UP, 1990.

Burkholder, Mark A. *Politics of a Colonial Career: José Baquíjano and the Audiencia of Lima.* Wilmington: Scholarly Resources, 1990.

Burkholder, Mark A., and D. S. Chandler. *From Impotence to Authority: The Spanish Crown and the American Audiencias, 1687–1808.* Columbia: U of Missouri P, 1977.

Carilla, Emilio. *La literatura barroca en Hispanoamérica.* Buenos Aires: Anaya, 1973.

Cascardi, Anthony. "The Subject of Control." *Culture and Control in Counter-Reformation Spain.* Ed. Anne J. Cruz and Mary Elizabeth Perry. Minneapolis: U of Minnesota P, 1992. 231–54.

————. *The Subject of Modernity*. Cambridge: Cambridge UP, 1992.

Cassirer, Ernst. *The Philosophy of the Enlightenment*. Trans. Fritz C. A. Koelln and James P. Pettegrove. Princeton: Princeton UP, 1968.

Cesareo, Mario. *Cruzados, mártires y beatos: emplazamientos del cuerpo colonial*. Purdue Studies in Romance Literatures 9. West Lafayette, IN: Purdue UP, 1995.

————. "Menú y emplazamientos de la corporalidad colonial." Moraña, *Relecturas* 185–221.

Chamorro González, Faustino. Introducción. Landívar, *Rusticatio Mexicana* xiii–lxiv.

Chatterjee, Partha. *Nationalist Thought and the Colonial World: A Derivative Discourse*. Minneapolis: U of Minnesota P, 1993.

Chevalier, François, ed. *Instrucciones a los hermanos jesuitas administradores de haciendas (Manuscrito mexicano del siglo XVIII)*. Mexico City: UNAM, 1950.

————. *Land and Society in Colonial Mexico: The Great Haciendas*. Trans. Alvin Eustis. Berkeley and Los Angeles: U of California P, 1970.

Chiaramonte, José Carlos, ed. Prólogo. *Pensamiento de la ilustración*. Caracas: Biblioteca Ayacucho, 1979. Ix–xxxix.

Clavijero, Francisco Javier. *Historia antigua de México*. Mexico City: Porrúa, 1958.

Coatsworth, John. "The Limits of Colonial Absolutism: The State in Eighteenth-Century Mexico." *Essays in the Political, Economic and Social History of Colonial Latin America*. Ed. Karen Spalding. Newark: U of Delaware, 1982. 25–51.

————. "The Mexican Mining Industry in the Eighteenth Century." Jacobsen and Puhle 26–43.

Cogdell, Sam. "Criollos, gachupines, y 'plebe tan en extremo plebe': retórica e ideología criollas en *Alboroto y motín de México* de Sigüenza y Góngora." Moraña, *Relecturas* 245–79.

Cohen, Jean L. , and Andrew Arato. *Civil Society and Political Theory*. Cambridge: MIT P, 1992.

Cohen, Ted, and Paul Guyer, eds. *Essays in Kant's Aesthetics*. Chicago: U of Chicago P, 1982.

Colás, Santiago. "Of Creole Symptoms, Cuban Fantasies, and Other Latin American Postcolonial Ideologies." *PMLA* 110.3 (1995): 382–96.

Concha, Jaime. "La literatura colonial hispano-americana: problemas e hipótesis." *Neohelicon* 4.1–2 (1976): 31–50.

Cornejo Polar, Antonio, ed. *Discurso en loor de la poesía.* Lima: Universidad Mayor de San Marcos, 1964.

Curtius, Ernst. *European Literature and the Latin Middle Ages.* Trans. Willard R. Trask. Princeton: Princeton UP, 1990.

Darst, David. *Imitatio (Polémicas sobre la imitación en el Siglo de Oro).* Madrid: Orígenes, 1985.

de Bolla, Peter. *The Discourse of the Sublime: Readings in History, Aesthetics and the Subject.* Oxford: Blackwell, 1989.

de Man, Paul. *Allegories of Reading.* New Haven: Yale UP, 1979.

———. *The Resistance to Theory.* Minneapolis: U of Minnesota P, 1986.

Derrida, Jacques. *Of Grammatology.* Trans. Gayatri Chakravorty Spivak. Baltimore: Johns Hopkins UP, 1976.

Dews, Peter. *Logics of Disintegration.* London: Verso, 1987.

Di Camillo, Ottavio. "Humanism in Spain." *Renaissance Humanism.* Ed. Albert Rabil, Jr. Vol. 2. Philadelphia: U of Philadelphia P, 1988. 55–108. 3 vols.

Durán, Miguel. *Luis de León.* Twayne's World Authors Ser. 136. New York: Twayne, 1971.

Durand, José. "En torno a la prosa del Inca Garcilaso: a propósito de un artículo de Roberto González Echevarría." *Nuevo texto crítico* 1.2 (1988): 209–27.

Dussel, Enrique. *1492: el encubrimiento del otro (Hacia el origen del "mito de la modernidad").* Santafé de Bogotá: Antropos, 1992.

Eagleton, Terry. *The Function of Criticism.* London: Verso, 1991.

Eguiara y Eguren, Juan José de. *Bibliotheca Mexicana.* Facsimile ed. Prologue and Spanish trans. Benjamín Fernández Valenzuela. Introduction, notes, appendices, and general ed. Ernesto de la Torre Villar with Ramiro Navarro de Anda. 5 vols. Mexico City: UNAM, 1986–90.

———. *Prólogos a la "Biblioteca mexicana."* Bilingual ed. Ed. and Spanish trans. Agustín Millares Carlo. Mexico City: Fondo de Cultura Económica, 1944.

Engström, Timothy H. "The Postmodern Sublime?: Philosophical Rehabilitations and Pragmatic Evasions." *Boundary 2* 20.2 (1993): 190–204.

Feijóo y Montenegro, Fray Benito Jerónimo. *Obras escogidas.* Ed. Vicente de la Fuente. Biblioteca de Autores Españoles 56. Madrid: Sucesores de Hernando, 1924.

Ferguson, Frances. *Solitude and the Sublime: Romanticism and the Aesthetics of Individuation.* London: Routledge, 1992.

Fernández Retamar, Roberto. *Para una teoría de la literatura latinoamericana.* Havana: Casa de las Américas, 1975.

Florescano, Enrique, and Isabel Gil Sánchez. "La época de las reformas borbónicas y el crecimiento económico, 1750–1808." *Historia general de México.* Vol. 2. Mexico City: El Colegio de México, 1976. 471–589.

Flynn, Thomas. "Foucault's Mapping of History." *The Cambridge Companion to Foucault.* Ed. Gary Gutting. Cambridge: Cambridge UP, 1994. 28–46.

Foucault, Michel. *The Archaeology of Knowledge.* Trans. A. Sheridan. New York: Pantheon, 1972.

———. *Discipline and Punish.* Trans. A. Sheridan. New York: Pantheon, 1979.

———. *The Order of Things.* Trans. A. Sheridan. New York: Random, 1973.

———. "What Is an Author?" Trans. Donald Bouchard. *Language, Counter-Memory, Practice: Selected Essays and Interviews.* Ed. Donald Bouchard and Sherry Simon. Ithaca: Cornell UP, 1977. 113–38.

Gaos, José. *En torno a la filosofía moderna.* Mexico City: Alianza Editorial Mexicana, 1980.

García Canclini, Néstor. *Las culturas populares en el capitalismo.* Havana: Casa de las Américas, 1982.

García Icazbalceta, Joaquín. *Bibliografía mexicana del siglo XVI: catálogo razonado de libros impresos en México de 1539 a 1600 con biografía de autores y otras ilustraciones. Precedido de una noticia acerca de la introducción de la imprenta en México.* Ed. Agustín Millares Carlo. Mexico City: Fondo de Cultura Económica, 1954.

Gerbi, Antonello. *The Dispute of the New World.* Trans. Jeremy Moyle. Pittsburgh: U of Pittsburgh P, 1973.

Godzich, Wlad, and Nicholas Spadaccini, eds. *Literature among the Discourses.* Minneapolis: U of Minnesota P, 1986.

Gómez de Orozco, Federico. Prólogo. *Prólogos a la "Biblioteca mexicana."* By Juan José de Eguiara y Eguren. Mexico City: Fondo de Cultura Económica, 1944. 9–13.

Góngora y Argote, Luis de. *Soledades.* Ed. John Beverley. Madrid: Cátedra, 1987.

Gonzalbo Aizpuru, Pilar. *Historia de la educación en la época colonial. La educación de los criollos y la vida urbana.* Mexico City: El Colegio de México, 1990.

———. *Historia de la educación en la época colonial. El mundo indígena.* Mexico City: El Colegio de México, 1990.

González Echevarría, Roberto. *Celestina's Brood: Continuities of the Baroque in Spanish and Latin American Literature.* Durham: Duke UP, 1993.

———. *Myth and Archive: A Theory of Latin American Narrative.* Cambridge: Cambridge UP, 1990.

González Stephan, Beatriz. *La historiografía literaria del liberalismo hispanoamericano del siglo XIX.* Havana: Casa de las Américas, 1987.

———. "Narrativa de la 'estabilización' colonial." *Ideologies and Literature* 2.1 (1987): 7–52.

Grafton, Anthony, and Lisa Jardine. *From Humanism to the Humanities: Education and the Liberal Arts in Fifteenth- and Sixteenth-Century Europe.* London: Duckworth, 1986.

Greenblatt, Stephen. *Marvelous Possessions: The Wonder of the New World.* Chicago: U of Chicago P, 1991.

Gruzinski, Serge. *The Conquest of Mexico.* Trans. Eileen Corrigan. Cambridge: Polity, 1993.

Guyer, Paul. Introduction. *The Cambridge Companion to Kant.* Ed. Guyer. Cambridge: Cambridge UP, 1992. 1–25.

Habermas, Jürgen. *The Structural Transformation of the Public Sphere.* Trans. Thomas Burger. Cambridge: MIT P, 1991.

Hamnett, Brian. "Absolutismo ilustrado y crisis multidimensional en el período colonial tardío, 1760–1808." Vázquez 67–108.

Harland, Richard. *Superstructuralism: The Philosophy of Structuralism and Post-Structuralism.* London: Routledge, 1991.

Hatzfeld, Helmut. *Estudios sobre el barroco.* Madrid: Gredos, 1964.

Hazard, Paul. *European Thought in the Eighteenth Century: From Montesquieu to Lessing.* Trans. J. Lewis May. New Haven: Yale UP, 1954.

Henríquez Ureña, Pedro. *Obras completas.* 10 vols. Santo Domingo: Universidad Nacional Pedro Henríquez Ureña, 1979.

Heredia, José María. *Poesías completas.* Mexico City: Porrúa, 1985.

Heredia Correa, Roberto. *Albores de nuestra identidad nacional.* Mexico City: UNAM, 1991.

Hernández, José. *Martín Fierro*. Ed. Ángel J. Battistessa. Madrid: Castalia, 1994.

Hertz, Neil. *The End of the Line: Essays on Psychoanalysis and the Sublime*. New York: Columbia UP, 1985.

Hipple, Walter John, Jr. *The Beautiful, the Sublime, and the Picturesque in Eighteenth-Century British Aesthetic Theory*. Carbondale: Southern Illinois UP, 1957.

Hobsbawm, Eric. *The Age of Empire 1875–1914*. London: Weidenfield, 1987.

Hodgen, Margaret. *Early Anthropology in the Sixteenth and Seventeenth Centuries*. Philadelphia: U of Pennsylvania P, 1964.

Holton, Robert J. "Classical Social Theory." *The Blackwell Companion to Social Theory*. Ed. Bryan S. Turner. Oxford: Blackwell, 1996. 25–52.

Horkheimer, Max, and Theodor Adorno. *Dialectic of Enlightenment*. Trans. John Cumming. New York: Continuum, 1990.

Jacobsen, Jerome V. *Educational Foundations of the Jesuits in Sixteenth-Century New Spain*. Berkeley: U of California P, 1938.

Jacobsen, Nils. "Livestock Complexes in Late Colonial Peru and New Spain: An Attempt at Comparison." Jacobsen and Puhle 113–35.

Jacobsen, Nils, and H. J. Puhle, eds. *The Economies of Mexico and Peru during the Late Colonial Period*. Berlin: Colloquium, 1986.

Jameson, Fredric. *Postmodernism, or, The Cultural Logic of Late Capitalism*. Durham: Duke UP, 1992.

Johnson, Julie Greer. *The Book in the Americas: The Role of Books and Printing in the Development of Culture and Society in Colonial Latin America*. Providence: John Carter Brown Library, 1988.

Jones, Oakah L., Jr. *Guatemala in the Spanish Colonial Period*. Norman: U of Oklahoma P, 1994.

Kant, Immanuel. *The Critique of Judgement*. Trans. James Creed Meredith. Oxford: Oxford UP, 1952.

Kerson, Arnold. "El concepto de Utopía de Rafael Landívar en la *Rusticatio Mexicana*." *Revista iberoamericana* 96–97 (1976): 363–79.

———. "The Heroic Mode in Rafael Landívar's *Rusticatio Mexicana*." *Dieciocho* 13.1–2 (1990): 149–64.

———. *Rafael Landívar and the Latin Literary Currents of New Spain in the Eighteenth Century*. Diss. Yale, 1963. Ann Arbor: UMI, 1968.

Kristeller, Paul Oskar. *Renaissance Thought and Its Sources.* New York: Columbia UP, 1979.

Lacan, Jacques. *Écrits.* New York: Norton, 1977.

Lacouture, Jean. *Jésuites: Une multibiografie.* 2 vols. Paris: Seuil, 1991.

Ladd, Doris M. *The Making of a Strike: Mexican Silver Workers' Struggles in Real del Monte, 1766–75.* Nebraska: U of Nebraska P, 1988.

Landívar, Rafael. *Rusticatio Mexicana.* Bilingual ed. Ed. and Spanish trans. Faustino Chamorro González. San José, CR: Asociación Libro Libre, 1987.

Lanning, John Tate. *The Eighteenth-Century Enlightenment in the University of San Carlos de Guatemala.* Ithaca: Cornell UP, 1956.

———. *The University in the Kingdom of Guatemala.* Ithaca: Cornell UP, 1955.

Larsen, Neil. "DetermiNation: Postcolonialism, Poststructuralism and the Problem of Ideology." *Dispositio* 47 (1995): 1–16.

Lawrance, Jeremy. "Humanism in the Iberian Peninsula." *The Impact of Humanism on Western Europe.* Ed. Anthony Goodman and Angus Mackay. London: Longman, 1990. 220–58.

Lemaire, Annika. *Jacques Lacan.* Trans. David Macey. London: Routledge, 1994.

Leonard, Irving. *Baroque Times in Old Mexico.* Ann Arbor: U of Michigan P, 1959.

Lienhard, Martin. *La voz y su huella: escritura y conflicto étnico-social en América Latina (1492–1988).* Havana: Casa de las Américas, 1989.

Lilly, Marie Loretto. *The Georgic: A Contribution to the Study of the Vergilian Type of Didactic Poetry.* Baltimore: Johns Hopkins P, 1919.

Longinus, Dionysius. "On Sublimity." Russell and Winterbottom 143–87.

López, Vicente. *Aprilis Dialogus.* Bilingual ed. Ed. and Spanish trans. Silvia Vargas Alquicira. Mexico City: UNAM, 1987.

Losada, Alejandro. "Los modos de producción cultural de los estratos medios urbanos en América Latina: las culturas dependientes (1780–1920) y las culturas autónomas (1840–1970)." *La literatura en la sociedad de América Latina.* Århus, Den.: Romansk Institut, Århus Universitat, 1981. 134–63.

Luzán, Ignacio de. *La poética.* Ed. Isabel M. Cid de Sirgado. Madrid: Cátedra, 1974.

Lyotard, Jean-François. "The Sublime and the Avant-Garde." *The Lyotard Reader*. Ed. Andrew Benjamin. Oxford: Blackwell, 1992. 196–211.

Makkreel, Rodolf A. *Imagination and Interpretation in Kant: The Hermeneutical Import of the "Critique of Judgement."* Chicago: U of Chicago P, 1990.

Maneiro, Juan Luis, and Manuel Fabri. *Vidas de mexicanos ilustres del siglo XVIII*. Mexico City: UNAM, 1989.

Manrique, Jorge Alberto. "Del barroco a la ilustración." *Historia general de México*. Vol. 2. Mexico City: El Colegio de México, 1976. 357–446.

Maravall, José Antonio. *Carlos V y el pensamiento político del renacimiento*. Madrid: Instituto de Estudios Políticos, 1960.

———. *La cultura del Barroco*. Barcelona: Ariel, 1975.

———. *Estudios de la historia del pensamiento español (siglo XVIII)*. Madrid: Biblioteca Mondadori, 1991.

Mariscal, George. *Contradictory Subjects*. Ithaca: Cornell UP, 1991.

Martí, Manuel. *Ecclesiae Alonensis Decani, Epistolarum libri duodecim. Accedit auctoris nondum defuncti vita a Gregorio Majansio conscripta.* 2 vols. Amsterdam: J. Wetstenium & G. Smith, 1738.

Martínez Peláez, Severo. *La patria del criollo*. Guatemala City: Universitaria, 1973.

McVay, Ted E., Jr. "The Sublime Aesthetic in the Poetry of José María Heredia." *Dieciocho* 17.1 (1994): 33–41.

Medina, José Toribio. *La imprenta en México (1539–1821)*. Facsimile ed. 8 vols. Mexico City: UNAM, Coordinación de Humanidades, 1989.

Méndez Plancarte, Gabriel. *Horacio en México*. Mexico City: Ediciones de la Universidad Nacional, 1937.

———. *Humanismo mexicano del siglo XVI*. Mexico City: UNAM, 1946.

———. *Humanistas del siglo XVIII*. Mexico City: UNAM, 1941.

Mignolo, Walter. "Afterword: From Colonial Discourse to Colonial Semiosis." *Dispositio* 36–38 (1989): 333–37.

———. *The Darker Side of the Renaissance*. Ann Arbor: U of Michigan P, 1995.

———. "La lengua, la letra, el territorio (o la crisis de los estudios literarios coloniales)." *Dispositio* 28–29 (1986): 135–57.

———. "El metatexto historiográfico y la historiografía indiana." *Modern Language Notes* 96.2 (1981): 358–402.

Bibliography

Millares Carlo, Agustín. "Noticia biográfica de don Juan José de Eguiara y Eguren." *Prólogos a la "Biblioteca mexicana."* Mexico City: Fondo de Cultura Económica, 1944. 25–37.

Monk, Samuel H. *The Sublime: A Study of Critical Theories in XVIII-Century England.* Ann Arbor: U of Michigan P, 1960.

Moraña, Mabel. "Barroco y conciencia criolla en Hispanoamérica." *Revista de crítica literaria latinoamericana* 28 (1988): 229–51.

———. "Máscara autobiográfica y conciencia criolla en *Infortunios de Alonso Ramírez.*" *Dispositio* 40 (1990): 107–17.

———. "Para una relectura del barroco hispanoamericano: problemas críticos e historiográficos." *Revista de crítica literaria latinoamericana* 29 (1989): 219–31.

———, ed. *Relecturas del Barroco de Indias.* Hanover, NH: Ediciones del Norte, 1994.

———. *Viaje al silencio: exploraciones del discurso barroco.* Mexico City: Facultad de Filosofía y Letras, UNAM, 1998.

Navarro, Bernabé. *Cultura mexicana moderna del siglo XVIII.* Mexico City: UNAM, 1964.

Nemes, Graciela. "Rafael Landívar and Poetic Echoes of the Enlightenment." Aldridge, *Ibero-American Enlightenment* 298–306.

Noriega Robles, Eugenio. "Los jesuitas y la cruz de Tepic." Pérez Alonso 327–34.

Norris, Christopher. *Deconstruction: Theory and Practice.* London: Methuen, 1982.

Nutini, Hugo. *The Wages of Conquest: The Mexican Aristocracy in the Context of Western Aristocracies.* Ann Arbor: U of Michigan P, 1995.

Osorio Romero, Ignacio. *Conquistar el eco: la paradoja de la conciencia criolla.* Mexico City: UNAM, 1989.

———. *La enseñanza del latín a los indios.* Mexico City: UNAM, 1990.

Pagden, Anthony. *The Fall of Natural Man: The American Indian and the Origins of Comparative Ethnology.* Cambridge: Cambridge UP, 1982.

Pastor, Beatriz. "Lope de Aguirre el loco: la voz de la soledad." *Revista de crítica literaria latinoamericana* 28 (1988): 159–73.

Pauw, Cornelius de. *Recherches philosophiques sur les Américains.* 2 vols. Paris: Chez J. G. Baerstecher, 1772.

Pérez, Alberto Julián. "El efecto estético vanguardista." *Hispanófila* 108 (1993): 15–23.

Pérez Alonso, Manuel Ignacio, ed. *La Compañía de Jesús en México: cuatro siglos de labor cultural (1572–1972).* Mexico City: Editorial Jus, 1975.

Pérez Herrero, Pedro. "El México borbónico: ¿un 'éxito' fracasado?" Vázquez 109–51.

Pérez Valderrabano, Manuel. *Del sublime.* By Dionysius Longinus. Madrid: Palau y Dulcet, 1770.

Picón Salas, Mariano. *De la conquista a la independencia.* Mexico City: Fondo de Cultura Económica, 1944.

Pietschmann, Horst. "Protoliberalismo, reformas borbónicas y revolución: la Nueva España en el último tercio del siglo XVIII." Vázquez 27–65.

Poggioli, Renato. *The Oaten Flute: Essays on Pastoral Poetry and the Pastoral Ideal.* Cambridge: Harvard UP, 1975.

Porqueras Mayo, Alberto, ed. *La teoría poética en el renacimiento y el manierismo españoles.* Barcelona: Puvill, 1986.

Prasad, Madhava. "On the Question of a Theory of (Third World) Literature." *Social Text* 31/32 (1992): 57–83.

Pratt, Mary Louise. *Imperial Eyes.* London: Routledge, 1992.

Quesada, Vicente G. *La vida intelectual en la América española durante los siglos XVI, XVII, XVIII.* Buenos Aires: La Cultura Argentina, 1917.

Rabasa, José. *Inventing A-m-e-r-i-c-a: Spanish Historiography and the Formation of Eurocentrism.* Norman: U of Oklahoma P, 1993.

Ragland-Sullivan, Ellie. *Jacques Lacan and the Philosophy of Psychoanalysis.* Urbana: U of Illinois P, 1986.

Rama, Ángel. *La ciudad letrada.* Hanover, NH: Ediciones del Norte, 1984.

Raynal, Abbé. *Histoire philosophique et politique des etablissemens et du commerce des européens dans les deux Indes.* 7 vols. Paris: Lacombe, 1778.

Regenos, Graydon W., trans. *Rafael Landívar's "Rusticatio Mexicana."* By Rafael Landívar. Philological and Documentary Studies, I, 5. New Orleans: Middle American Research Institute, Tulane U, 1948. 155–312.

Rico, Francisco. *El sueño del humanismo (de Petrarca a Erasmo).* Madrid: Alianza, 1993.

Riley, Charles Denson. *The Management of the Estates of the Jesuit Colegio Máximo de San Pedro y San Pablo of Mexico City in the Eighteenth Century.* Diss. Tulane U, 1972. Ann Arbor: UMI, 1980.

Robertson, William. *History of America.* 2 vols. London: Printed for W. Strahan; Edinburgh: Balfour, 1778.

Roggiano, Alfredo. "Acerca de dos barrocos: el de España y el de América." *El barroco en América.* Madrid: Centro Ibero-americano de Cooperación, 1978. 39–45.

———. "Para una teoría de un Barroco hispanoamericano." Moraña, *Relecturas* 1–15.

Ross, Kathleen. "*Alboroto y motín de México:* una noche triste criolla." *Hispanic Review* 55 (1988): 181–90.

———. *The Baroque Narrative of Carlos de Sigüenza y Góngora: A New World Paradise.* Cambridge: Cambridge UP, 1993.

Russell, D. A., and M. Winterbottom, eds. *Classical Literary Criticism.* Oxford: Oxford UP, 1989.

Ryan, Michael. *Marxism and Deconstruction.* Baltimore: Johns Hopkins UP, 1982.

Sabat-Rivers, Georgina. *Estudios de literatura hispanoamericana.* Barcelona: PPU, 1992.

Said, Edward. *Orientalism.* New York: Random, 1978.

Sarrailh, Jean. *L'Espagne éclairée de la seconde moitié du XVIIe siècle.* Paris: Klincksieck, 1964.

Schwarz, Roberto. "As idéias fora do lugar." *Ao vencedor as Batatas.* São Paolo: Livraria Duas Cidades, 1977. 13–28.

Seed, Patricia. "Colonial and Postcolonial Discourse." *Latin American Research Review* 26.3 (1991): 181–200.

Sigüenza y Góngora, Carlos de. *Teatro de virtudes políticas. Alboroto y motín de los indios de México.* Mexico City: UNAM/Miguel Ángel Porrúa, 1986.

Smith, Paul. *Discerning the Subject.* Minneapolis: U of Minnesota P, 1988.

Spivak, Gayatri Chakravorty. "Can the Subaltern Speak?" *Marxism and the Interpretation of Cultures.* Ed. Cary Nelson and Lawrence Grossberg. Urbana: U of Illinois P, 1987. 277–313.

———. "A Literary Representation of the Subaltern: A Woman's Text from the Third World." *In Other Worlds: Essays in Cultural Politics.* New York: Routledge, 1987. 241–68.

Stolley, Karen. "The Eighteenth Century: Narrative Forms, Scholarship, and Learning." *The Cambridge History of Latin American Literature.* Ed. Roberto González Echevarría and Enrique Pupo Walker. Vol. 1. Cambridge: Cambridge UP, 1996. 336–74.

Torre Villar, Ernesto de la. Estudio Preliminar. *Bibliotheca Mexicana.* Juan José de Eguiara y Eguren. Vol. 1. Mexico City: UNAM, 1986. Xlix–ccclvii.

Trabulse, Elías. *Los manuscritos perdidos de Sigüenza y Góngora.* Mexico City: El Colegio de México, 1988.

Valenzuela Rodarte, Alberto. "La educación jesuítica en Nueva España." Pérez Alonso 577–602.

Vanière, Jacques. *Praedium rusticum.* Paris: Barbou, 1774.

Van Young, Eric. "The Age of Paradox: Mexican Agriculture at the End of the Colonial Period, 1750–1810." Jacobsen and Puhle 64–82.

Vázquez, Josefina Zoraida, coordinadora. *Interpretaciones del siglo XVIII mexicano: el impacto de las reformas borbónicas.* Mexico City: Nueva Imagen, 1992.

Vidal, Hernán. *Socio-historia de la literatura colonial hispanoamericana: tres lecturas orgánicas.* Minneapolis: Institute for the Study of Ideologies and Literature, 1985.

Virgil. *Georgica.* Ed. Richard F. Thomas. 2 vols. Cambridge: Cambridge UP, 1988.

Walsh, Catherine Henry. *The Sublime in Spain.* Diss. U of California, Los Angeles, 1992. Ann Arbor: UMI, 1993.

Weber, Max. *Economy and Society: An Outline of Interpretive Sociology.* Ed. Guenther Roth and Claus Wittich. Trans. Ephraim Fischoff et al. 3 vols. New York: Bedminster, 1968.

———. *From Max Weber: Essays in Sociology.* Ed. and trans. H. H. Gerth and C. Wright Mills. New York: Oxford UP, 1958.

Weiskel, Thomas. *The Romantic Sublime: Studies in the Structure and Psychology of Transcendence.* Baltimore: Johns Hopkins UP, 1976.

Whitaker, Arthur P. *Latin America and the Enlightenment: Essays.* Ithaca: Cornell UP, 1961.

Williams, Patrick, and Laura Chrisman. "Colonial Discourse and Post-Colonial Theory: An Introduction." *Colonial Discourse and Post-Colonial Theory: A Reader.* Ed. Patrick Williams and Laura Chrisman. New York: Columbia UP, 1994. 1–20.

Williams, Raymond. *Marxism and Literature.* Oxford: Oxford UP, 1977.

Wilson, Rob. *American Sublime. The Genealogy of a Poetic Genre.* Madison: U of Wisconsin P, 1991.

Wölfflin, Heinrich. *Principles of Art History.* Trans. M. Hottinger. New York: Dover, 1962.

Žižek, Slavoj. *The Sublime Object of Ideology.* London: Verso, 1989.

Index